My Manor

CHARLIE RICHARDSON

WITH BOB LONG

My Manor

PAN BOOKS

First published in 1991 by Sidgwick & Jackson

This edition published 1992 by Pan Books
an imprint of Pan Macmillan Ltd
Pan Macmillan, 20 New Wharf Road, London N1 9RR
Basingstoke and Oxford
Associated companies throughout the world
www.panmacmillan.com

ISBN 0 330 32400 4

19 18 17 16 15

A CIP catalogue record for this book is available from
the British Library.

Typeset by Hewer Text Composition Services, Edinburgh
Printed and bound in Great Britain by
Mackays of Chatham PLC, Chatham, Kent

To Lord Justice Lawton O.B.E. who in his infinite wisdom sentenced me to twenty-five years.

To my brother, Eddie, who has just been sentenced to twenty-five years.

To my mother and kids and all the people who did not believe all the shit that was written about me.

To my wife Veronica who is a brilliant brain on beautiful legs.

To Bob Long who helped me write my own story.

CONTENTS

CHAPTER ONE
The Key

I stood in the Old Bailey, Court Number One, having been escorted each day by a motorcade that would have flattered the president of a dodgy country. The jury were hand-picked by Special Branch and had been given hotline telephones at home in case we tried to nobble them. The Briefs for the Crown were straining at the leash at the smell of a kill. From his high chair dominating centre court the judge was ready to umpire a vicious game where daily excitement and drama were a certainty.

Justice Lawton was the son of a hated prison governor who, it was rumoured amongst ex-inmates of Wandsworth Prison, was notorious for gloating at men on the way to the gallows. He was known as a hard judge and an ex-supporter of Oswald Mosley's Fascist Blackshirts before the war. At the tender age of twenty-five he was a young eager beaver barrister and Blackshirt candidate for Hammersmith North.

Sad, sad little people sitting in the courtroom. Some had queued for hours outside in the grey London morning. What were they expecting? Crowds who turn up to a car race claiming to be auto enthusiasts often secretly hope to see a dramatic and gory pile-up. In what could this morbid bunch pretend such interest as they fought their way into the public gallery of the trial every morning? They could hardly claim to be fascinated by the English legal process. In courts all over London on the same day poor beggars were explaining to empty courtrooms why they had peed in the street or how some goods from Woolworths had found their way into their own pockets.

No, this lot had as much chance of pretence as a man shuffling around a porn shop claiming to be interested in contemporary literature. Sad little grey people with sad little grey lives. They were hoping for something in the courtroom to bring a spark to their dull existence, to feel the blood racing around their bodies for a few seconds. They were hoping finally for an execution which would justify the insignificant lives they spent waiting for death. We, the accused, had stepped outside the rules and patterns of that living death, we had gorged ourselves on life. We must be punished as a lesson that no one except those born into the élite have the right to escape lives of misery. So the sad little people came, bringing with them the musty smell of their houses. They came to see the 'Torture Gang Boss'.

Incidentally, it was 1966 and I was on trial for five counts of G.B.H. (Grievous Bodily Harm) together with the four others in my 'Torture Gang' – my brother Eddie, Tommy Clark, Frankie Fraser and Roy Hall. I say incidentally because those charges were a minor detail in the spectacle that was being created. The trial was a cancer growing fiercely from a tiny lump to a raging monstrous tumour of tales of the unexpected. All of the lead actors onstage had adapted their roles to suit the hungry desires of a public desperate for drama. It was more like a B-film that I was watching before me, except that I was auditioning as Boris Karloff in the leading role of a horror story. Sometimes I found myself listening to the evidence with the same open-mouthed wonder as those in the public gallery. Occasionally when a witness was telling a story I would be sitting on the edge of my seat wanting to know what happened next. What evil deed did Charlie Richardson do next – was there no limit to his cruelty . . . ?

It was a very cheap thriller. I was a little surprised by the legal profession. They were educated boys from the best schools and universities. I thought they might be bored by the lesser intellects of the police force. Not a bit of it. They loved it too. Like the lord who likes to bang a tart up against the wall of a toilet, they seemed fascinated by the grubbiness of it all. They were the real spectators, privileged to be able to peep into what was for them the seedy, frightening world of south-east London. Some of it was clearly very confusing to them. They were pleased when references from that other

world like 'scampi and chips' were understandable to them –
how quaint!

The case rolled on day after day, a lurid fairy story. The judge
and audience had problems keeping up with it all. They sometimes had to listen for hours through complicated business
transactions just to get to the really juicy bits. On the sixteenth
day of the trial they were rewarded with another horror
story. James Taggart had just been describing his business
connections with me when he started to tell of a time when I
was supposed to have dragged him into a car and back to my
office. The prosecution counsel was a Mr Sebag-Shaw. How do
they get names like that? In the witness box Taggart was posing
as a respectable textiles salesman. The crowded courtroom was
hushed as the tale emerged. Sebag-Shaw paused for effect and
then asked Taggart, 'Can you remember any particular parts
of your body which were struck in the course of being dragged
into the office?'

Taggart answered quietly, a little boy who has fallen over
and is looking for sympathy.

'Yes. I was struck on the head, sir.'

'And what happened inside the office?'

'Well, I was beaten again. My clothes were taken from
me.'

This mention of nakedness sent an electric current through
the courtroom. The press scribbled madly and the court artists
sketched with quick sweeps of the pencil, trying to capture the
moment when somebody talked about clothes coming off. The
Old Seabag relished the instant and tried to squeeze whatever
advantage he could from it.

'Just stop there again. Where were you in this office? You
have mentioned three men. Charles Richardson, Francis Fraser
and Tom Clark.'

'Yes, sir.'

'Were all three of them there at this time?'

'Yes, sir.'

'Anybody else apart from you?'

'No, sir.'

'And was anything said before your clothes were taken off or did they just proceed to do that without anybody giving a direction?'

'Not to my recollection, sir.'

'Can you remember anything about the office that you were in?'

Taggart, with help from Sebag-Shaw, painted a picture of my office in Camberwell. This was to establish that he knew the office but more than that, it set the scene for the silent courtroom to imagine in all the sick and sordid detail the story that was to follow. A naked man standing in front of three monsters in a scrapyard office. It was a scene delicately described with perverse accuracy and the damp, smelly minds of the public in the gallery could imagine the tableau before them. To everyone's relief he got back to the story.

'You have told us your clothes were taken off. Which of your clothes?'

'All of my clothes.'

'Right down to your underwear?'

'No, my underwear was taken off as well.'

'Well, including your underwear, I meant.'

'Yes.'

'What about your socks?'

'I cannot recollect, sir.'

'In that condition what were you doing? Were you standing up or sitting down or what?'

'I was crouched on a box in the corner of the office.'

A naked, frightened man in a dark office, crouching on top of a box in the corner of the room. It sent a shiver up my spine and I was supposed to have been there. The whole courtroom was dumbstruck apart from a few barely audible whispers of 'Fucking Hell' and 'Jesus Christ' from some members of the public.

Old Seabag could see he was making progress. He faced his witness, the star of the show for now at least.

'Tell me, was anything said at this stage of the proceedings?'

4

'Yes. Mr Richardson made a telephone call.'

What the hell was this *Mr* Richardson business from some-body who knew me only as Charlie or even affectionately as Charlie Boy? The 'Mr' was for dramatic effect. Like Count Dracula or Doctor Jekyll, Pete Dracula or Tim Jekyll just do not have the same ring to them.

Playing his role to the hilt, and pleased with the course his rehearsed questioning was taking, Sebag-Shaw looked at his witness with all the sympathy of a ham actor.

'And did you gather from the conversation what the call was about?'

'Yes, he was asking for some type of apparatus.'

'How did he describe it, what did he call it?'

'Well, it was apparatus. I heard the word "apparatus" or "box". He was obviously trying to trace something.'

Oh no. Not this one again. 'The Black Box'. This was the pride of the prosecution, the delight of the press, and the invention of an ambitious policeman. The Black Box (it would have to be black, wouldn't it) was supposed to be a generator we had apparently used to torture people with. The Court had already heard several days before how we had connected the wires to somebody's testicles and wound the handles to give him a shock. The soggy grey people had sparked to life and the bright young vultures in the press benches had almost jumped out of their seats. The prosecution had looked at the defence in triumph while some of those present in Court secretly envied the man with the electrodes on his testicles. The story went on that we had shoved one up his arse. I am sure that I caught a lawyer blushing. It was probably the sort of thing he got up to at public school. The cleverness of this story was in the sharp evil it portrayed. If we had just proceeded to beat somebody about the head with a lump of wood it would have been violent, but not so evil, not so sexy. When you bring out a black box with a handle and wires and you connect it up to somebody's testicles there's a ritual involved, and the British love ritual. The inventor of this story had a thorough grasp of the British psychology. He should have been in advertising.

Old Seabag wanted to pursue the box for all it was worth:

'Could you gather from the part of the conversation you were able to hear whether the box was available or not?'

Taggart wanted to get as much as he could from this too. We were all dying to know if the box was produced.

'It appeared that the box was not available.'

Now who talks like that? This pathetic toerag was trying to speak courtroom language, trying to be accepted as part of the game that was being played by his betters. I had tried that once . . . I had spent my childhood with a very healthy contempt for my 'betters' but when I got into business as a young man I tried hard to join their club. I had swallowed pride, suspended intelligence and even sometimes a little dignity to listen to their shit for years. I tried to ingratiate myself – not to be like them, but as a good business move.

I realized that they had taken centuries to develop an incredible and intricate system of control and authority. I wanted to be on their side of the line, to understand and play by their rules. But the thousands of rules in their game are so ancient and complex that the players have to understand them instinctively. It was in the blood that flowed through their spoilt inbred veins. I realized my mistake. If you are not a blood brother then you just cannot join. The most you can do is grovel low at their feet and kiss their soft fat arses and they just might grant you a superficial tolerance for your money. I was not prepared to do that. I played outside the rules and without their cloak of respectability and protection.

But by 1966 the establishment Mafia of power recognized me as a dangerous rival from an unfamiliar source. The police could not stop burglary in south London but I did. If anyone broke into a house on our territory, our manor, they would get a clip round the ear, take the stuff back and be directed to the West End to thieve from those who could afford it. Meanwhile the police would be filing incident reports. Power is a delicate thing. I understood at an early age that power is also the most exciting sensation a person can enjoy.

I was born in 1937 in Twickenham but we soon moved to Wyndham Road in Camberwell. My mother and my little brother Eddie lived with our grandparents above their sweet shop. My dad was a merchant seaman and a scallywag. So we did not see him very often. I got no stars for attendance at school. It was a musty old dungeon where you sat with your hands behind your head and recited your times tables. I was too interested in learning about *real* things to waste much time there.

But I did learn one vital lesson of life at school. We were sitting at a big table at dinner, a large group of boys. One boy much bigger and older than me kicked me with incredible ferocity under the table. A massive bump started to grow over the bone of my shin and blood dribbled out of the broken bruised skin. The other boys at the table stared with agitated anticipation. I was known to be a little hard-case and despite the odds they expected me to throw myself over the table and tackle him. Without thinking twice I did not wince. Instead I looked him in the eye, then smiled and leaned forward.

'You missed, you twat. You've just kicked the bloody table leg.'

'Bloody' was pretty strong language in those days. My eyes twinkled at him. It was my dad's twinkle. He was famous for it. It can be warm and funny but the same twinkle can scare the shit out of you with its ice-cold cruelty.

The other boys had stopped breathing. My gaze did not falter for a second while his eyes filled with tears and he ran away. I looked around the table, smiling and twinkling, and returned to my dinner. The other boys stared at each other, oblivious to the fact that I had a throbbing lump on my leg, and yet I wanted to jump up and dance around with joy. My ecstasy was not from beating him. I was jubilant because one of life's great secrets had just been revealed to me. Some people spend their whole lives not knowing how the world works. I knew at eight years old. It was as if I could take a motorbike to bits and put it back together again so that I was the master of the bike and not a victim of its mysteries. Knowledge is power, yes, but knowledge of power and how to control it became my hobby, almost my obsession.

Also in that dingy old school I learned that I do not really feel pain. Since that day I cannot think of a time that I was upset at all by it. Not physical pain anyway. I have howled with grief and anguish and screamed with frustration, but punch me in the face and I will smile and twinkle at you, and you will tremble at that twinkle. I am not a religious freak or a masochist. I have never gone out looking for pain. I simply learned at an early age that the pleasure of controlling pain overcomes its physical impact. Power over pain is stronger than pain itself.

Twenty-four years later as I stood in the dock I realized that I had probably pushed the experiments with power too far. For so many years I had juggled people, institutions, businesses and all the established centres of power. All the skittles came crashing around me in 1966 and now here I was listening to tales of visualized torture with a black box. But with Taggart it appears we could not get hold of the box. I almost felt sorry for the press who had been yapping around my feet for weeks. I wanted to say to Taggart, 'Go on . . . give them the box.' I almost felt sorry for him, too. He must have been terrified to give this evidence. If I was such a monster with a gang that held south-east London to ransom it was remarkable that Taggart was more frightened of the Establishment than of me. This black box story was straight out of the sewer and aimed at the gutter press. But it did worry me because with a story like that I realized they were not going for a bent businessman who gave some petty villains the odd smack in the face. They were not looking for a few years' porridge for me and my friends. They were creating a monster to be locked away for ever.

So they managed to find a few dubious scars on the unsavoury bodies of some small-time crooks who were paraded before a hungry public. And then all the flea-ridden hacks from the tabloid press would run around with savage glee. The 'quality' papers were just as bad. Only they pretended to be one step up on the pavement by using a different language. They started taking nips out of my heels and as the sordid tales of torture grew they took big bites out of my legs. I kept my hands over my balls, just in case. Sebag kept the drama bubbling.

'In what fashion were you beaten; with fists, legs, feet, or what?'

Taggart had an incredibly detailed instant recall considering what had apparently happened to him.

'Yes . . . Richardson and Clark were using their fists and then Fraser picked up a wooden pole . . . he was striking me with it.'

'What sort of pole was it? Tell us in relation to a familiar object like a broom handle. Was it shorter, longer, as long?'

'Well, it would possibly resemble a broom handle. I think it was slightly thicker; it must have been long because it broke but he was still able to use it subsequently, what was left of it.'

'Broke in the process of what?'

'Hitting me on the head with it.'

'And having broken it in that way, you say Fraser kept on using the remaining part still in his hand.'

'Yes.'

The whole courtroom shared a collective orgasm. The press could hardly contain their excitement. The jury was wide-awake and glad not to be at work that day. I could imagine the soggy grey people in the public gallery talking on the bus – '. . . and then after he broke it over the man's head he kept on hitting him with the fucking stump.'

Meanwhile our defence briefs shrank in their seats probably wishing they had not been so foolish as to take on the case. Perhaps they had bitten off more than they could chew. You had to feel sorry for them, their careers might be on the line. But then again, it was our lives that were at stake.

The case was not all drama and lurid tales of horror and suspense. Sometimes the prosecution unearthed mountains of documentary evidence. They needed a solid base for their story which they built by amassing quantity rather than being too concerned with quality. It's an old trick. If you are worried about the strength of your evidence you walk into court with a wheelbarrow full of documents and photographs. It is as if by weighing it all down with boring and laborious detail you will divert people from the weakness of your case. Never mind the quality, feel the width. During those dull moments my mind would sometimes wander to the brighter things in the past. I have a great memory for the most intricate details of past experiences. I could remember the smell and taste of a room and the exact words in conversations. I was only thirty-two but there was a lot to remember. I had achieved so much because all my life I had had an incredible energy-force racing through my veins. All my life I could not sit still. Life had too many opportunities for me to cope with. I often wished that there were two of me and that I did not ever have to sleep. If by some miracle I had been able to walk out of that courtroom I would not have gone to a pub to celebrate. I would have raced to the nearest telephone box. Within minutes I would have been buzzing deals all over the world. Power and energy. I loved it. I wanted to fly and they were determined to clip my wings.

Sometimes I would look around the courtroom. The living death on the public benches would avoid my eyes for fear of turning into a pillar of salt. (Although being a pillar of salt would have upgraded their intelligence and vivacity.) As soon as my glance passed them they would continue to stare from the safety of the herd. If I had met them on their own in the street they would have grovelled, wringing their hands in fear and homage. They would have rushed home, relieved, to tell their families casually over bread and margarine how they had bumped into Charlie Richardson. The Torture Gang Boss. The Monster From The Deep who ate children for his breakfast, or electrocuted them at least.

Amongst all the dandruff, pot bellies and spotty fat arses on the press benches sat a beautiful young woman reporter. She was a constant distraction and she realized I was looking at her. Every now and then she would unconsciously throw me a little treat by crossing and uncrossing her legs. Sometimes she would stretch her back after leaning forward to make notes. Her breasts would be pushed forward under her blouse beneath her open jacket. She was dressed very properly, but she would not have been more enticing if she had been naked. She displayed so little but I have a big imagination and like most people in the world I worship shapes. I had studied art in prison. Even at the tender age of thirty-two I had done a few spells inside. In fact, I had even done a stretch before I started shaving. I always made sure I spent as much time as possible in the prison education department. It was a lot better than work and a good investment for the future. I love learning, and one of the things that I learned for myself in the art class was that art is all about enjoying shapes. Shapes on a canvas or in clay or bronze – even music is just shapes made by sound and poems are the shapes of language. When I realized this I knew it was another secret key to understanding life around me. It meant that everybody actually loves art because we all enjoy shapes. A man of great power and dignity can be turned into a shivering moron by the shape of a woman's leg or the curve of a breast glimpsed under a sweater. The shape of a face *can* launch a thousand ships. If we all love shapes then we're all art critics. Until I understood that I had thought as most of us do that art was not for the likes of me but the likes of *them*.

All they, the nobs, ever did was convince the likes of us that their kind of appreciation of shapes was more sophisticated and important than ours. If we take a liking to something of theirs it becomes popular and falls from the ranks of Art down to the level of our living room walls. They also make sure that the things they fancy are bloody expensive and take a lot of time to enjoy. When you do get a few quid together to try and enjoy some of their pleasures you cannot believe anybody in their senses could want to do them. They breed pheasants all year round so that they can blast them out of the sky at a drunken fancy dress orgy on the heather of Scotland. Then they hang the poor dead birds up until they are rotting and worms are crawling out of their eyes. Then they eat it! They call it 'high' because it stinks, but also 'high' for High Society – who else would eat decayed flesh and seafood that smells of unwashed genitals, finished off by a sweaty socks cheese? But we *all* appreciate things, and people will die for a shape whether it's a swastika or the smile on a lover's face.

My Manor

My earliest memory was of a beautiful shape that excited and inspired me to dream of it and dream of owning it. When I was five I fell in love with the shape of a toy wooden speed-boat. It sat in a pool of dim light amid the smelly clothes and furniture of a big pawnshop around the corner from the Lyons tea-shop where my mother worked. Nearly every day I would go to the Lyons where my mother would sneak me a sticky cake and a cup of tea as she rushed around between the tables. It was such a big café, always warm and steamy with a dense cloud of cigarette smoke hanging permanently under the ceiling. I loved it there. Everybody knew everybody else and they all knew me because of my mother.

After tea I would take my little brother Eddie home. On our way we passed the pawnshop. It was a magic place for me, full of such a variety of worn and much-loved things. I was strangely excited by the idea that you could make money out of junk.

I would like to be able to say that at such a tender age I was conscious of and embittered by the sight of poor people, our friends and neighbours, sneaking in to pawn their coats in the middle of winter so that their kids could eat on the day before payday. Although that was true, I was blinded by the ingenuity of the whole process. You borrowed money – if you could not manage to repay it then you lost your coat. Fair enough! Of course the money you borrowed was much less than the value of the coat. It was a lending process with a strong incentive scheme and when I understood it I envied the pawnbroker. I would also like to have been able to say that he was a cuddly fat old man with both a heart and teeth of gold. In fact he was middle-aged, thin and miserable. He must have worn clothes that were brought in to pawn because the collars of his frayed shirts were much too big for his skinny neck.

The boat was in the shop for weeks. Each day as we walked home me and Eddie would stand outside the shop steaming up the window panes as I stared longingly at the object of my dreams. Eddie would say how great it was, but he was only pretending to keep up with his elder brother. The boat was lovingly hand-carved by some dad for his son. It must have taken months to make in such intricate detail and then paint with such skill. Somewhere in Camberwell was a father and son with broken hearts. That did not particularly bother me; I was more concerned with whether it would float or not. It looked like it would and I hoped it would, but I knew deep down that even if it sank I loved it and wanted it.

Each day I held my breath as we approached the window and each day I asked my mum if I could have it; each day she said we could not afford it. One day as we neared the pawnshop I knew before I looked that it had gone. I was completely broken when I saw the empty space where it had been. Eddie asked where the speed-boat had gone and I told him that somebody had bought it and it was no good anyway.

When I got home my father was sitting at the kitchen table smoking a cigarette. He smiled and his eyes twinkled as we came into the room. We were always pleased to see him because he was not around much. At that age I had no idea what he did with his time, but later I found out that he spent much of it with other women. His rare visits home were always a treat. He was so full of life and energy, and fun. He grinned at the two of us as we came running. Next to him on the kitchen table was the speed-boat from the pawnshop. I was overjoyed.

The next day I found a deep puddle in a muddy bit of wasteland and discovered that it was not only beautiful – it floated! I carried it everywhere with me for weeks. At night I had it by my bed as I slept and when I woke up in the mornings the boat was the first thing that I saw. Sometimes I would wake a little earlier than usual in a general state of excitement. It would take me a minute or two to realize what I was excited about.

One Sunday my father rolled up early outside the house in a car. I have no idea where he got it from – he probably borrowed it. (Probably.) He ran into the house and danced grinning from room to room announcing that we were all going to Westcliffe-on-Sea for the day. It was the 'on-Sea' bit that excited me almost to trembling. Like anybody, a visit to the seaside was a big treat for me but on top of that this was my chance to put the boat through its paces. As I got into the car clutching my pride and joy, my dad looked around and saw the boat under my arm, and told me to take it back into the house. I was heartbroken and pleaded with him. My mother gently persuaded him to let me take it in the end.

A car ride in those days was an event in itself but after an hour or so Eddie and I were bored, and settled back in our seats. My dad, in his element, was singing out loud and shouting to people in the streets. Eddie asked if he could hold the boat. He often asked and I usually grudgingly allowed him to hold it and play with it while I watched possessively. But this was different, a special day, a big event and there was no chance that I would part with it. Eddie became persistent and made a lunge for it. He was so much smaller and younger than me that he did not stand a chance. We pulled and tugged and screamed at each other. My father stopped singing, turned around and shouted at us. While he was still driving he tried to take the boat from me, but I would not let go. Again, my mother came in to pacify the situation and my father turned suddenly to steer away from the pavement. He looked around at me with his famous twinkle and gave me a strange grin.

At Westcliffe-on-Sea we did the usual stuff, we ate toffee apples and had a half-pint of tea with some winkles. At last we settled in our own space among the crowds of day trippers. In those days of low expectations a trip to any muddy bit of seashore was a huge treat for all the family. It might have been just my age, but the day seemed a long adventure, full of possibilities. All we did was sit by the sea, eat our sandwiches and mess around with muddy wet sand while my dad ogled, whistled and flirted publicly with every woman who passed. My mother ignored all that, kept an eye on us and just appreciated the chance to do nothing for a few hours.

I immediately took off my socks and shoes and paddled up to my knees in the gentle grey sea.

My speed-boat floated perfectly. It had probably been carved by someone who spent his working life carrying boxes of fruit on his head in Covent Garden. What a waste of talent. He should have been a naval architect.

In no time I became the envy of a large group of kids who formed a circle to admire the boat. I was a very proud owner and a very nervous one as older and bigger boys passed by. Luckily I had no problems and spent a happy day with my toy. Eddie moaned that I was not playing with him and my father cursed a few times about that 'ruddy boat' – he would not say 'bloody' in front of my mother.

As the sun got low and my mother started to pack up all our things, my dad came and stood by the shoreline and watched me for a few minutes. Then he had a brilliant idea. Why not push the boat out to sea so it could travel on its own back to London. We could then drive back and by the time we got there the boat would have arrived and we could pick it up on the Thames near London Bridge.

It sounded like a good idea but I was a bit suspicious about the boat finding the right way. Dad explained that because of the currents it could only go back to London and would be back about the same time as us. I was a bit concerned that I might miss the company of the boat on the way back but I was pleased that my dad was taking such an interest in it. I pushed it out to sea and looked around for approval. My dad winked and grinned. When I looked back the boat had drifted back to shore. It did this every time I pushed it out to sea. My father was not to be deterred from his plan. He explained to me about tides and told me if I was to bury the boat in the sand near the waterline the tide would keep on coming in, cover the boat and then when the tide changed whisk it out to sea and carry it round to London Bridge.

This, he said, was even better because it would delay the progress of the boat. Now we would definitely be back there before the boat so nobody would be able to steal it when it arrived.

This was an ingenious plan but I was still a little suspicious as I buried my toy in the sand. All the way back in the car I worried about my beloved boat but said nothing. As we hit the streets of London I fell asleep. I was horrified when I

15

woke up at home and not at London Bridge. It was dark, we would have to go tomorrow, but tomorrow never came. London Bridge might as well have been the other side of the planet to me then. I was too young to go there alone. After a few days, a long few days for me, I realized what had happened and gave up waiting for my boat to return.

The sociologist or psychologist might imagine that this little tale of childhood woe may perhaps in part account for the sociopathic make-up of the 'Torture Gang Boss'. 'No wonder he is so bloody twisted,' the laymen might say, 'with a father like that.' It must have led to a life of insecurity, a constant fear of rejection, a suspicious mentality and an inability to trust anybody. Rubbish! I grew up in a social group which has as its foundation absolute trust. If you operate outside the protection of the rules and morality of the established society you are potentially more vulnerable. Trust takes on a massive importance within this group. That is why the greatest sin you could commit in the morality of my group was to 'grass' on a fellow member. You could beat somebody over the head with a bit of wood and when the wood broke carry on beating with the blood-sodden stump. That is forgivable. If he then reports you to somebody – the police for example – on the other side of the line that divides us, that is completely unforgivable. Beating him just makes a mess of his face, but grassing undermines the fabric that holds our society together. Civilization as we know and *choose* it to be is threatened.

It took several years before the real lesson from the day at Westcliffe-on-Sea dawned on me. It could be that my dad had intended that I learn that lesson but I do not think so. He was very sharp, and known for it, but he was not that clever. I was still a little boy and already I understood another exciting secret about the workings of people in the world. Of course we should all be careful on choosing who and when to trust. Up until that moment I had trusted my father absolutely. He represented a total unquestioned authority, and what I learned that day was not to question my father in particular but to question authority. I understood from then on that authority or, as it becomes, 'the authorities' do not know everything and they may not have my best interests at heart. I therefore began to develop my own powers of judgement and my own ideas of right and wrong. Even more exciting was the realization of how power can be exercised by gaining trust. If my dad could persuade me to part with the one thing I loved most in the world because I trusted him, then what an incredible amount can be gained simply through trust. If people trust you they will part with things dear to them, even their lives if necessary.

Somebody told me a story once from the upper bunk of a prison cell. It was about some Roman general or emperor or somebody big in Roman times who ordered thousands of men to walk into the sea. They did, and many of them drowned. That was explained to me as blind loyalty and obedience almost as if all those Roman soldiers in their little skirts were stupid.

To me that story is about trust. They did what they were told not because of unquestioning loyalty but unquestioning trust. Maybe the story is a load of shit, maybe it did not happen at all. It does not matter really. What matters is that I understood that the more somebody trusts you the more they will do for you. If they trust you completely your power is so great that you own them.

The real monster in the Old Bailey was in such a powerful position and commanded such trust in that courtroom that nobody thought it strange that he should dress up like a woman.

Justice Lawton sat in his powdered wig and flowing robes and as judge it was his privilege to steal centre stage from the other actors whenever it took his fancy. He interrupted all the time to get his facts straight and at the same time made sure that the witnesses repeated all the quotable bits.

Sometimes I looked at him and wondered if men like him had ever been little boys who could not understand why their cocks got hard. Was he ever frightened by the boy down the road who liked to kick his arse and did he ever lose sleep because his best pal would not talk to him? I doubted it. All I could imagine was a small version of the judge; I wish I

17

had known him at school; I could have painstakingly won his trust and controlled him. Now he sat at the altar of this cathedral of British justice. He had the public, the press and my whole world in his hands. He played the scene like the experienced conductor of an orchestra. Sometimes the band was playing so well by itself he was happy to sit back and watch.

Taggart was describing greater depths of ritualized depravity to a hushed room while Sebag helped him paint a grotesque canvas that would make a Francis Bacon look like the naïve work of a schoolgirl. (Oh yes; uneducated degenerates like me can occasionally drop the names of famous artists.)

Sebag-Shaw for the Crown asked his friend, Taggart, in the witness box, 'What was the result so far as your body was concerned?'

'Well, my body was a mess.' (Perfect understatement just begging a more detailed description and Sebag and Taggart both knew it.)

'What sort of a mess?'

'Well, there was a lot of blood streaming from my head and most of my body was covered in blood.'

'And was the blood only covering your body and head or did it find its way elsewhere?'

Taggart having been nicely prompted had no difficulty in remembering his lines.

'No, it splashed over the walls of the office and on the floor.'

Now here we have a naked man covered in blood having been beaten to a pulp and Sebag seemed to be more concerned about stains on the carpet. I had little idea of what was coming next, only a suspicion, but like the rest of the court I was dying to know. Sebag did not want to let go of the messy blood.

'Was it allowed to remain there as it came from you?'

I should hope not! It was bad enough being accused of the most barbaric brutality and sadistic torture, but I hope nobody was going to charge me with not leaving a room as I found it. Taggart thankfully defended me on this one.

'No, I was forced to clean the blood up.'

'Using what to mop it with?'

'My pants.'

Here we go again. Just the mention of underwear got the courtroom agitated. This was a very English story. I took time off for a second to catch the woman reporter cross her legs. All this talk of underwear was getting to me too.

Sebag-Shaw took time off too. The audience needed a short break to catch their breath, so he took a little time to remind everybody who was in the room with Taggart and then he made sure we were all sitting comfortably before he resumed the story.

'Now, you got to the point of being made to mop up the blood, from where?'

'From the walls and the floor.'

'And when you finished that chore what is the next thing you remember happening?'

'The arrival of Alfred Berman.'

Just when the story is starting to get a little boring, we have a new actor to liven things up. What part will he play in this drama of mystery and suspense? Over to Sebag.

'Did he bring anything with him?'

Oh no, not the black box with its little handle and wire electrodes to attach to this poor man's testicles or stick up his arse.

Taggart surprised us all with his reply. I nearly fell off my seat.

'Yes. He brought beer and sandwiches.'

What a scene! We were obviously a little hungry. Beating a man to a pulp builds up an appetite.

'And when Mr Berman arrived with the sandwiches and the beer what was done with these refreshments?'

'The beer was drunk and the sandwiches were eaten.'

'Well, who shared in that repast?'

'Charles Richardson, Fraser and Clark.'

'Were you offered any?'

'Not at that stage.'

Sebag looked around the courtroom slowly before returning to Taggart.

'There you were, sitting without any clothes on in the corner?'

'Yes, sir.'

So now we have a naked man covered in blood in the corner of the room. He has just cleared us of being untidy by admitting that he cleaned up the mess only to accuse us of not letting him join us for dinner. But seriously, this scene worried me because it was too clever. The almost irrelevant detail of it somehow gave the story a credibility it would not have had if they had stuck to the bare brutality. It also had an ingenious way of increasing the general picture of us as the most callous maniacs. A naked bloody man is sitting next to us and we stop for a picnic. The audience could imagine us passing the sandwiches around and peering between the slices of bread to see what was in them while Taggart shivered a few feet away. I felt a twist in my stomach and I wanted to scream at Taggart for co-operating in such depth with the frustrated novelist of Scotland Yard who should have been writing for Alfred Hitchcock. They were going to lock me up and throw away the key . . .

Keys have always fascinated me. Now there is a system, ageless and universal, that depends on shapes. A small piece of metal with a precise shape can open the door to a council house or a country mansion . . . It can open a safe containing millions and as such a key can be worth more than its weight in diamonds. I once had a key that opened a small box in a foreign bank that contained a fortune. I used to look at that little shiny shape of metal and wonder at its value – and fear its loss. The loss of that key would mean the loss of the fortune. Such was the discretion of the foreign bank.

'Discretion' is one of those lovely words that shroud so many dodgy deals in a respectable world that does not even think of itself as naughty, never mind downright illegal. Somehow if you have or make a lot of money it is almost expected of you to steal more. It is made respectable with words and ideas like 'tax haven'. The words conjure up the image of an exotic island paradise full of unfortunate rich people suffering their exile to avoid a punitive and vicious taxman. Bollocks! A tax haven is a country that announces to the rich all over the world, 'Come to us and we will help you steal from your own country. Just spend some of your loot here.' Walk out of Marks and Spencer with a jumper that you haven't paid for and you might spend three months inside; steal millions of pounds from the inland revenue and bask in both the sun and respectability of an island fringed with palm trees.

I found a beautiful key when I was a little boy. I could not say what age I was, old enough to walk, talk and think, and to go out all day without my mother. The rusty key I found one day in the smelly remains of a derelict old warehouse looked important and the events that followed its discovery will be ingrained in my memory to my grave. However old I was, I was not old enough to realize that keys are all different shapes. This one was big and official. It looked like the kind of key that opened the door to a deep dungeon rather than a little house. At that time my dad was locked up in a dungeon at Wandsworth. I do not know to this day why he was there that particular time but I did understand the basic idea of prisons. I knew he did not want to be there and I understood that my mother found life without him hard. I also understood that he was locked behind big doors and that keys were the way that you opened big doors.

There were years of my childhood when I cannot properly make sense of what my father did. To us he was a big tall exciting man who would just occasionally be there in bed with our mother when we woke up. He would stay a few days and disappear again. Sometimes he went to sea for months at a time, returning with a twinkle in his eye and exotic presents in his overcoat pockets. Sometimes he was around for months but never much at home. One of the times he was out he did something to end up in Wandsworth prison. When we asked our mother why he could not come home she said he was locked up and couldn't get out. I kept the key I had found to give to my father when we went to visit him. I thought it might open the doors to let him out.

It was my first visit to a prison, but certainly not my last.

Eddie was left behind in the care of a neighbour while I was dressed up in my smartest clothes and off we went to the railway station on a cold, wet London day. That is not just a trick of memory. I am sure it was a bleak day but it is true that so many of my memories at that time were of cold wet days wrapped up in scarves and balaclavas. That whole period of my life seemed to have dirty weather just as my teenage years were full of long summer days with excitement in the air and beautiful cool evenings. I suppose a psychiatrist would tell me those early childhood days were times of hardship and oppression while adolescence was a period full of the dawning of sexual change and growing maturity. But what do they know, they are just nutcases who sit in the chair listening to the messy lives of lesser loonies on the couch.

The train ride was a big adventure even though it was just across a small part of London. It stopped every few minutes while people wrapped up and breathing steamily got in and out. At one station a mother and a boy got on. He was about my age, perhaps a little older, but we had nothing in common. He was dressed in a cub's uniform with neatly-pressed shorts and long socks with pink and blue knees between the two. His hair was recently cut and it looked like the barber had cut around the boy's cub cap and left what looked like a pink potato. The skin around his yellow scarf and leather toggle was also pink and scrubbed as if it had been boiled along with his shirt. He sat upright next to his mother, with unconscious poise and what I took at the time for well-bred dignity. He gave no hint of embarrassment at wearing the uniform of a baby fascist on a Sunday when nobody would be dib-dib-dibbing anywhere in London. His mother looked like she had just stepped out of British Home Stores. She was smart, neat, tastefully made up and definitely too good to be sitting anywhere near the likes of us. She made my poor old mum look shabby and worn, although the two women must have been about the same age. I realized then that there were other worlds within the greater world. All I had known were the few streets around our home in south-east London. Even day trips away were among those same type of people. All the boys I knew dressed like me and all their mothers looked like my mother and all the little girls smelled like digestive biscuits.

As I sat across from him in the train I felt grubby and conscious of my dirty fingernails, and I wondered if any snot was dribbling from my nose. The scrubbed boy and his prim mother probably did not even notice us as we blended in with the surroundings but they aroused a strange tension in me. I started to hate the little bastard and the snooty cow beside him and I immediately felt better. I hated his lack of interest in his surroundings. How could he, at his age, not be restless and fascinated by the adventure of a day out and a train ride? How could those little piggy eyes set in pink shiny cheeks not look around and reflect curiosity? What was reflected there instead was the dull glaze of discipline and proper behaviour. He was trained and confident. He was taught to deal with this situation unemotionally and any playful childlike wonder was buried deep down and held there. He had inherited the most precious asset that his kind passes from generation to generation like a congenital disorder; from birth he had been taught by an unconscious process of instructions and firm examples that he was to be one of the righteous class. He would grow up to believe he was a respectable pillar of society, that he had some control of his own destiny, but in fact he would just do what he was told for the rest of his life by the real ruling class, who had us all by the balls.

They were the delicate green moss enjoying the rays of the sunshine on top of the great compost heap of the rest of humanity beneath them. Every minute of every day they knew it as fact – like a heartbeat, it was a force so natural it was rarely thought about.

We fool ourselves into believing that their money is their only power – if we only had that start in life we would be on top. But take away their riches and the bastards will still leap ahead in the race. They run in front of us fuelled only by the belief that they are where they belong and we plod behind doffing our caps because we think that is where we belong.

I looked at the little pink baby pig opposite and I knew

I could kick his head in and enjoy the bubbling tears. He would look at me and be frightened for now but he would know that he was born superior and that one day I would wipe his arse. He would have been wrong. I knew more than the streetwise, salt-of-the-earth humility of my father, who despite his strength and position in the community was still silenced by the presence of a posh accent and an expensive suit. He was a dignified man, well-respected locally, but he was the leader of a pack of dogs, grateful for a pat on the head from his masters.

At that early age my only response to the scrubbed cub was a blind, uneducated hatred. Years later I was to learn of his confidence and of my greater strength. He had received his belief in himself and in his place in the world by soaking it in from his parents and surroundings. He had been given his confidence. My belief in my right to a good place in life was learned through observation and experimentation. I fought for my confidence so when I got it I protected it fiercely.

We stopped at a station and the prim lady took the hand of the boiled boy and left. My mother realized in a fluster that it was our station also, grabbed her shopping bag, wrapped my scarf around me and we jumped onto the platform. As we walked to the prison, we passed our fellow travellers waiting at the bus stop in the drizzle under an umbrella that matched the woman's clothes. Little dib-dib-dib looked cold without a coat. I gave him the best threatening, kick-your-face-in look that I could manage but he didn't even notice me.

At the prison we waited in a queue inside a large, grey room. The walls were bare and the smell was that of boiled food, polished floors, fetid human stench that underlies all prisons, hospitals and schools. People were searched and my mother's shopping bag was emptied onto the table. She was upset because they confiscated the cigarettes and food she had brought him – he was a convicted prisoner and could not have any privileges.

We sat on a bench among people waiting to see their brothers or fathers or husbands. They were a sad sight, women with kids all around them and nobody talking to anybody. It was like a doctor's waiting room without magazines. Eventually we filed through to a long thin room with half-cut cubicles and large glass windows behind each of which sat a man. It was the homo sapiens house at Wandsworth zoo and one of the exhibits, in unnatural habitat, was my dad. If he had been an animal in a zoo people would have campaigned about the harshness of his conditions. As it was, he was only a man who had sinned and who deserved his punishment.

He was very cheerful and pleased to see us. His eyes sparkled behind the glass of his aquarium and he joked with me about nothing in particular. My mum reported back all the little bits of gossip from our street and he laughed and teased her, making her blush sometimes with his ribald comments. It was a happy time for us. He was kind and attentive to my mother and we knew for once he was not going to disappear suddenly for months.

During a break in the conversation I took the key, warm from my pocket, and showed it to him. He exploded with good-natured laughter when I explained it could help him escape and come home. My mother laughed and although I could not see the joke, I laughed too.

Suddenly my father's face changed and the sparkle of fun in his eyes became menacing and vicious. His relaxed position immediately tensed as if he were ready to leap at the throat of an attacker. My mother noticed and fell silent, confused and worried. I had no idea what had happened. Then I heard a stranger's voice behind me, full of the authority of a policeman and tinged with contempt.

'What have you got there, son?'

I turned, and at the level of my face there was the nicotine-stained hand of a huge overfed prison officer in dark blue.

My dad, with a hint of compromise, spoke to him.

'Leave him alone – it's only a joke. He brought me a key 'cos he thought it would let me out.'

The prison officer held out his hand and asked to see the key.

This time my dad, despite his helpless situation behind the glass, spoke with warning in his voice.

'Leave it alone, for God's sake. It's only an old key: let the boy alone.'

But the bored prison officer wanted to play prefect and confiscate my toy.

'Come on son, give it to me.'

I did not know what to do so I waited. My father pushed back his chair and stood up.

'Leave him alone – it's only a rusty old key. Let him have it!'

The whole scene was now a battle between men for respect and authority. The prison officer was in a land where he was king but my father was defending his family and was now being watched by other prisoners and their families. The officer pointed at my dad and almost shouted as he reached down to take the key off me:

'You! Sit down. NOW!'

My dad lunged forward and banged his fist massively against the window. The whole glass shuddered and he screamed, 'Leave him alone, screw! Leave him alone, you fucking fat pig!'

Within seconds, two, three then four officers leapt on him and dragged him away fighting and shouting. The officer on our side of the cabinet took the key from me and my mother burst out crying. I was confused. I had seen my father angry a hundred times and I knew and feared the strength of his temper, but I had never seen him overpowered before. Until that day it had never even occurred to me that he could be beaten in anything by anybody. I learned later, when I was old enough to understand, that my dad earned himself a spell in solitary and a loss of remission for his outburst. He also earned the respect of the other inmates. It was an introduction to the world of authority. Until then, authority to me was mostly my mother. It was an authority you could navigate around and manipulate because she cared and wanted us to be happy. When he was around my father commanded respect with a little fear thrown in. His authority was unquestionable and non-negotiable. It was unnerving for a stranger to have automatic authority over me and my family.

I began to realize that there was a whole web of authority that did nothing to earn respect but had power given to it. They could be recognized visually by their uniforms; policemen, judges, screws and even teachers. I began to suspect at a very early age the motives of people who take on jobs where they can boss others around. They all seemed like park wardens who strutted around the playground making sure kids did not enjoy themselves. Their pleasure comes from telling people what not to do and feeling powerful at work because they are often pathetic outside the uniform. Later I learned to manipulate them by letting them feel they have exercised power.

When the war started we moved into a flat above my grand-parents' sweet-shop. With my mother round at the Lyons tea-shop and my dad either at sea, inside or gallivanting off somewhere, we were looked after by our grandparents. They were strict and very proper people, but easy to manipulate as long as I said the right things and gave them the right impression. My grandfather worked at home putting gold lettering on leather-bound books, and my grandmother looked after the shop. They were my mother's parents and very respectable. When my father was courting my mother the grandparents sent her to Brighton to try to shake him off. He was from a family of villains and they wanted her to do better than that. But he followed her, they got married and the grandparents had to accept it. We were a happy family living above the shop in a street of similar shops. I would serve behind the counter selling Woodbines to favoured customers and the Turkish shit to unknowns. Those were the days of food coupons and rationing and making do; everybody helping everybody else out. Perhaps it takes a war for the British to be good to each other.

With my mother at the Lyons and my grandparents in the shop we were well-known, respected and liked. People probably felt sorry for Eddie and me because of my dad and his adventures but I did not feel any kind of hardship. Life was full of excitement, even without the bombs and fires of the Blitz.

Somehow you imagine that during the war only intense, warlike things happen. But for a lot of people, life just went on as usual. People bought and sold businesses in our street, got married, had kids, got into debt and went to the seaside. They died too, and death was something you grew up with during the war, around you constantly. One day you would pass a house which had a family sitting round the radio eating rissoles and drinking Ovaltine just like the adverts; the next, the house would be a pile of rubble and the Ovaltinees were no longer sitting round the fire. But other deaths happened too.

Outside the shop was a knife grinder who sat all day sharpening people's kitchen knives and tools. He did a healthy trade in the days when a knife might last half a lifetime. He did a good job which was lucky for him because he had few other qualities. He grunted as he worked and talked to nobody, but sometimes his presence outside the shop would bring customers in so he was happily tolerated by my gran. She had a big heart and I think she felt sorry for him, mainly on account that he made the Elephant Man look attractive. We kids would often take the piss and then run past him before he could clout us. Sometimes adults, especially young men, would make fun of him. Soldiers home on leave would tell him he was the secret weapon the allies needed to scare off the Germans. He took it all in and said nothing, bent over his grinding-wheel, grunting away to himself.

One day a young man was visiting a girl in the street and they had a few drinks in the local pub called the Windmill. Emerging full of drunken high spirits with his girl on his arm, he walked down the street and stopped outside the shop. He taunted the knife grinder about his ugliness and asked him his name. The poor sod ignored him and carried on sharpening his knives. The drunk was not going to give in so easily. He poked the grinder in the arm and said, 'I know you're the Hunchback of Notre Dame – but what do your friends call you?'

That was the last time anybody mentioned the grinder's appearance. There was a small commotion and a scream from the woman. The young man who had been full of the joys of spring a few moments before now had a knife in his throat.

My grandmother grabbed me and Eddie and took us into the back room where she told us urgently that if anybody asked, then we had seen and heard nothing. The police came round and my gran swore blind that she knew nothing, but it hardly took Sherlock Holmes to look at the grinding-stone, a set of knives with one missing and the remaining knife in the victim's throat to work out who had done it. The grinder was hanged and the executioner was pleased to put his black hood over such an ugly face. So while soldiers were killing each other in their thousands all over the world, it did not stop the killing also going on at home.

I had learned a few more lessons in life after that incident. I understood from my grandmother's immediate response that if you see a crime – then you deny it. More importantly than that, I learned that you do not take the piss out of a knife grinder when he is at work.

When people died we were not allowed to have the radio on which was no real hardship, because there was so much to do outside. It took a really miserable rainy day and stern instructions from my gran to keep me and little Eddie indoors. There were a lot of people dying as the bombs dropped but I kept myself busy collecting from the remains of flattened houses, and I gathered shrapnel like other kids collected stamps. When the bombs came at night we would all huddle under the big oak table in the kitchen together with Mr and Mrs Styles who had a shoe repair shop next door. One night after a really noisy bout, I crept out from under the table and ran into the street. Half of Wyndham Road was destroyed and the whole sky was blazing red with the inferno that had been our street. I was stunned and excited. People were running around in a panic of activity trying to control the blaze. Women were screaming and men were scrambling amongst the rubble with bare and bleeding hands desperately digging for people and possessions. My grandfather saw me. He ran over and knelt down to talk to me. He held my shoulders and spoke softly. 'Don't look, Charlie. Everything's going to be all right, don't worry, son. Now just you go inside and look after Eddie.'

I was not in the least bit worried. As I turned to go inside, I thought disappointedly of the fun I would have had searching amongst the rubble, and the things I would probably find the next day. It was all such a dramatic and exciting adventure. Even then I had a very low boredom threshold. I have always had energy and have used it in an unceasing battle against boredom and banality. There was nothing boring about the war for a little boy. But the great adventure, and the warmth and happiness of life in the sweet-shop with my mum and grandparents were soon to end. It was to make way for a new adventure that turned into a real nightmare more terrifying than anything German bombs could produce. I was sent to Dorset.

We were to be evacuated to the country like lots of other London kids were during the war. At first I could hardly wait. I was a street kid, but like all kids the idea of living on a farm with pigs and chickens and cows was exciting. My mum had a tear in her eye as she hugged us before we boarded the bus at Camberwell town hall with a load of other local kids. I was just embarrassed and impatient for the new world I was going to. Lots of stories had come back to us and for most kids it might have been a good time. They grew up, and some still talk affectionately of their time in the country and the second parents they gained. It was not like that for us. Eddie and I were sent to a huge house owned by an old couple who did not like kids, especially Londoners. We were crammed into a dormitory full of other boys who quickly put us straight about the old bastards who ran the place and made a nice little income from having us there. They kept chickens who were better fed and cared for than we were.

I became friends with a boy called Roy who came from Peckham. He was my age and was not too keen on Eddie following us around all the time, but Eddie soon showed that he could keep up with us. The discipline was strict. After a day at the village school we came home, ate shit for tea and were sent to bed early. My mother sent food parcels full of treats but in those days of rationing they were too much of a temptation for our guardians and we never got them. When mum visited us, we told her what was going on but she could do nothing. We begged her to take us home, telling stories of how we were beaten by the old man on any excuse. I was too young then to realize that the dirty old bugger probably got a thrill out of seeing little boys' bottoms glow red from the lashes of his belt.

We did manage to have some good times somehow. There were farms around us and we were fascinated by the animals. I had no idea how big pigs could become, nor how ferocious. All the farm animals in the kids' books were so friendly that it took us time to realize that little Porky Pig was in fact a big evil bastard, and Goosy Goosy Gander had a vicious temper. We would wander into farmyards and most of the farmers were friendly, but we found our way into a yard one day and ran out screaming and giggling as we were chased by a flock of very territorial geese. After that we started to dare each other how far we could get into the farm before running hell for leather back behind the gate. After a good half-hour of running around Roy turned to me and said with a mischievous smile, 'Watch this. I'll show you somethin' . . .' He climbed over the gate and walked into the yard. We only had to wait a few seconds before the geese came racing towards him screaming. As they came close, he stood absolutely still. The geese stopped a few feet away and surrounded him, pecking at the air and making a terrible racket. Roy clenched his fists and leaned over them and shouted: 'Piss off! Goo oorn, gerroutofit!' He waved his hands and carried on shouting and screeching. The geese turned as one and ran, making a racket as he chased them into the yard. We all ran after him shouting and chasing the geese. When I caught up with him he laughed and told me, 'You mustn't show them you're frightened. If they smell fear on you, then they've got you licked.' A thousand times since then I've stood in front of men that could have scared the shit out of me, but I've stood my ground and hid my fear and a thousand times they've backed down. I could smell their anxiety like stale sweat wafting from their bodies.

The house we stayed in was a wreck. In the corner of our

dormitory there was a hole in the wall where a small bird of some kind had built a nest. I convinced Roy that if we nicked a chicken's egg and put it in the nest, it would hatch and then we could have a chick as a pet. The stolen egg was discovered by the old bugger in the house, and when he failed to discover who the culprit was because nobody would talk, he decided that it was Roy anyway. While we lay in our beds shaking with fear and helplessness, Roy was stripped and beaten with a belt. The old pervert continued his sadistic pleasures by forcing Roy into a cold bath and holding his head under the water. As he ranted and raved about brats from London and how it was time that we all learned some proper behaviour, he held Roy's head under. I lay in my bed trembling and as I heard the splash of his head going under water again I too held my breath. Just as I was about to explode I would hear him come up for air and I could breathe too. After about six bouts of this I held my breath until I turned purple and finally had to breathe. Roy was still under and the man was in a trance of foaming anger. I jumped out of my bed and into the bathroom. I grabbed the largest scrubbing-brush I could find and hit him with all my might. Before he had time to respond I grabbed his short hair and pulled as hard as I could. He jumped up with a bellow of rage and I clung onto his neck and tried to punch him on the face. As he shouted and threw himself around to shake me off Roy surfaced and desperately sucked in some air. Within seconds he also launched himself at the man and was punching wildly. The woman came running in and held Roy down while the man banged me up against the wall and finally got control of me. While she held Roy I was bent over the bath with my hair touching the water while in a fury the man belted my arse until it was bruised black and blue and criss-crossed with red weals. We were led by our ears back into bed.

The next morning we decided to escape. Without food, money or clothes, Roy, Eddie and me set off during playtime at school down the road in what we thought was the vague direction of London. We didn't have a clue where we were or how far we had to go. We hid all day from adults who would have turned us in. We were in enemy territory, and any grown-up was a certain collaborator. As darkness fell we trudged down the road, starving and cold until a village bobby travelling without lights in the blackout almost ran us down with his bike. He was a friendly old idiot. We did not protest too much when he took us to the police station and fed us sandwiches and tea. I told him what had happened, and although he listened patiently I could tell he was sceptical. So I turned around and pulled down my trousers to show him the marks of the previous night's orgy of violence. He was a bit taken aback and embarrassed. We waited in a room while the old pervert was sent for. A while later he arrived and we could hear them talking in the next room. To our horror we heard great gusts of laughter coming from the copper. He eventually came back into the room and said something about a house martin not being too comfortable sitting on a hen's egg, wiping the tears of laughter from his face. The old sadist, our guardian, paid by the state to save us from bombs, spoke kindly to us. 'Now come on, Charlie, Roy, Eddie. Enough of this nonsense. You're going to have to take your punishment like men.' He turned and winked at the policeman, who smiled at us. As we trudged out of the police station, he chuckled, 'Now wait until your mothers hear what you've been up to.'

Not surprisingly, he did not tell our mothers, but I told mine when she next came to visit us. She believed my story, and also that we had not been getting our food parcels. I had scabies then and it was the final straw. She was embarrassed by it all but she stuck to her guns and walked out with one of us holding onto each hand. Eddie was taken home but I was left in a local hospital surrounded by sick and dying men. A few miserable days later as I lay in bed, my dad stomped into the ward. Without a word to the protesting nurses he ignored them all, strode up to my bed, gave me a sly wink and threw me over his shoulder like a sack of potatoes.

All those years later as I stood in the Old Bailey, I should have liked my old dad to have pushed past everybody, thrown me over his shoulder and taken me home. The poor bugger would have collapsed under the weight of thirty-two years of good living. Now *I* was the evil pervert who had tortured people and the 'children' that I had abused were ugly villains in business suits who were paraded in front of the world to tell their tales of woe. This time they were believed and nobody was going to believe us. Whatever the evidence, the court desperately wanted to believe the drama that the prosecution was creating. It's like settling down to a Sunday afternoon film on the telly and then suddenly up come the words 'This is a true story'. It makes the film much more interesting and solid. If at the end words were to come up saying that in fact it was not true, it was all a pack of lies, then you would have a very pissed-off audience. It would have broken the hearts of our audience if suddenly the prosecution had turned around and said, 'Sorry, only joking. None of this actually happened. We just got a bunch of small-time crooks to squeal for us.' With a court so intent on creating a public monster to enter the mythology of British crime history, our defence lawyers did not stand a chance. It was Goliath in the shape of the whole legal machinery together with the foaming, hungry public against little Davids in the shape of public schoolboys with no sling shots and not enough balls.

We put on a brave face in the dock. We did not show this snapping gaggle of geese that we were frightened. But if we shouted they would not back off, either. On the way to the court each day we sang in our motorcade. We shouted to each other and kept our morale high. In court we would wave to friends with a smile. But down below in the loneliness of the cells there was the lingering smell of boiled food, bringing memories of prison. I was worried. It was going to be a long time before I once more ate food I could not pronounce in the best West End hotels and paid for it with a roll of dosh in my pocket. My own five kids were going to grow up visiting their dad in prison. We had a few tricks left up our collective sleeve but the opposition had narrowed the field of play.

CHAPTER TWO
Great Escapes

The jury was made up of twelve people sitting in their burnished wooden stall, feeling very self-important and conspicuous. They were stars in a legal epic. For the first time ever in history, the jury had been vetted by Special Branch. They were in the headlines. Justice Lawton had ruled that they were to have special hotline telephones at home in case they were nobbled. Plain clothes detectives were assigned to watch their houses in case we tried to get to them. At that time villains and coppers grew up together and went their separate ways in adulthood to do battle for the rest of their lives. We played an elaborate game and we all understood the rules. Nobbling juries was one of our tactics to outwit them just as they were about to bang us up for a couple of years. It was an easy process. If you had a friend in court you sat in the public gallery and tried to spy a likely candidate amongst the jury. At the end of the day you followed them home and offered them money, more money than they had ever seen, to see your side of things. Sometimes stupid villains would threaten violence but that would often backfire. Almost everybody was happy to pocket the money and return a reasonable verdict. You nobbled a few more and then you could be sure of success. But there was no chance with this little lot. Some of our friends had tried but they could not get near them.

It's hard to know what to do with a jury. They have your life in their hands, but you have to talk to them through public school interpreters who wear women's clothes and dusty white wigs. I wanted to take them to one side and say, 'Look, I'm not such a bad bloke really. So I have smashed a few people in the mouth because they owed me a few quid, but I've given a fortune to charity, I love my mum and I've got five kids. All I ever wanted was to have a good life. You know what it's like if you wear the wrong clothes and speak

like I do, they won't give you a fucking chance. Tell you what
. . . why don't we all run round to the Savoy for a nice chicken
dinner and I can put it all straight. Don't believe all this shit
they're telling you, they made it all up to further their various
careers. I'm like you and we should stick together.'

But I was not like them. The biggest excitement that they
had ever had in their lives was the odd case of piles from
sitting in draughty offices and reading the *Daily Express*. I
had dared to stray from the path of righteousness and living
death. I had the cheek to want to feel life in my veins and I
had to pay the price of my transgression. I wanted at least to
look at them and smile to show that I was not such a monster,
but they would have interpreted it as the evil smile of Satan.
So I ignored them. They were too enthralled by the pathetic
creatures in the witness box to take much notice of me, except
for the odd stolen glance at the serpent from the deep that
could eat sandwiches in front of a naked man sitting in a pool
of blood.

Now we had another man in the room, Alfred Berman,
who had arrived with the sandwiches which we had not
had the decency to offer round. It seems Fred tried to talk
us out of our bloody orgy and let Taggart go. This was a bit
worrying because it probably meant that Fred was going to
give evidence against us, otherwise the prosecution would
not have laboured the point.

Sebag reminded everybody of the scene although it was only
minutes since he had so graphically portrayed it. He turned to
the jury but spoke to the pathetic excuse for humanity in the
witness box. 'There you were, sitting without any clothes on
in the corner?'

'Yes.'

'Did you hear anything from Mr Berman after that?'

'Yes.'

'What was it? First of all, who said it?'

'Berman appeared quite shocked when he walked in. He
asked on several occasions whether I could be let go, let
out.'

'At that stage, although you had done what you could to

clean the blood off the walls and the floor, had the blood been cleaned off you?'

'No, sir.'

'Well, what was the reaction of the others present to what Mr Berman was saying?'

'Totally indifferent to what he had to say.'

'How did they show that?'

'They attacked me again.'

'That is, the three men apart from Mr Berman?'

'Yes. Not Mr Berman.'

So Fred Berman was obviously in the clear and co-operating with the prosecution. It was a clever plot. We were so brutal, the scene so horrific that even one of our associates, a friend who took care of the catering on this occasion, was horrified. Somebody who was used to the rough and tumble of a villain's life on our manor was shocked by this scene. He was so moved by the victim's treatment he went out on a limb to persuade us to stop. It all had to be true – I just wish that I could remember it because he said that I was there at the time!

Having portrayed Freddy Berman as a concerned soul with the milk of human kindness flowing through his veins, Sebag, ever aware of an audience with its tongue hanging out, asked Taggart, 'What form did the attack take on this occasion?'

'The same as before except that Fraser hit me over the head with a pair of pliers.'

'How long did this go on for?'

'I cannot say, sir. It seemed like a long time . . .'

'And how about the blood – were you still bleeding?'

'Yes, there was more blood.'

'Where did that go?'

This really was labouring the point but it was working. How could anybody erase this scene from their mind? How could the jury, after weeks and weeks of evidence, think of anything else? What did it matter where the blood went to unless of course they were going to produce it as an exhibit? 'My lord, I respectfully submit exhibit A, one pool of O positive.'

Taggart remembered very well what had happened to his

blood, though. 'It was spattered very much over the walls. I was bleeding quite a lot from the head then.'

'And again, was it partly, at any rate, cleaned up?'

Sebag-Shaw was a bugger for tidiness – so were we, it seems.

'I had to clean it up again, sir.'

'Using the same mop as before?'

'Yes.'

'Namely, part of your underwear?'

'Yes.'

'How did things go on?'

'I was tied up by Clark.'

Sebag then reintroduced the juicy bit for the benefit of the jury.

'Were you still naked?'

'Yes.'

'Tied up with what – how?'

'A rope, tied around my neck, body and legs.'

'Like a sort of cocoon around your body, do you mean?'

'Something like that, sir.'

Standing in the court listening to this litany of horror, I might as well have been bound naked in a cocoon of ropes. There were police and screws everywhere. I had looked at my chances of escape, and if I could have got out of the courtroom I would have taken my chances in the street. I had escaped countless times in the past from all sorts of institutions and had learned not to underestimate the spontaneous dash for freedom. Sometimes escapes had to be planned in detail and worked on for months but now and again a quick dash for the door was the best way.

And to prove this point, a few years before the trial I had had dealings with the New York Mafia. They were nice people, interesting and adventurous and very polite. I had a deal with them which fell flat. It was not my fault but they were convinced that I had cheated them. They did not bother with tying me up, beating the shit out of me and making me wipe the mess up with my underpants. They just sent round a very polite man in a business suit to blow my head off, with a beautifully maintained and seasoned revolver.

He walked into my office on Park Lane, asked me politely if I was Mr Charles Richardson. If it hadn't been for his dignified stance and impeccable dress sense I would have thought he was from the Fraud Squad. Unusually I was on my own. When I admitted my identity with a little caution he pulled out his gun and without the bat of an eyelid he started loading the chamber. What was I to do? Bargain with him? Beg him for mercy? Try and explain that there had been a misunderstanding? Without a fraction of a second of thought I leaped for the door and ran through a corridor and out the back door. I have no idea what happened to him but I never saw him again. I returned to the office that afternoon and continued business as usual.

I developed the fine art of fast evasion as a small boy. After the war the streets around my home were like a huge adventure playground for an eleven-year-old. Near us there was a massive gutted building that used to be the Haycock Press building. Part of it overlooked a bus stop. A gang of us would throw stones at the people in the bus queue until eventually somebody was so pissed off they would chase us through the labyrinth of doors and half rotten roofs which we knew like the back of our hands. Sometimes they would lose us and we would taunt them by jumping out near them and running off. It was like a game of tag but the stakes were higher. If you got caught you were not just 'it', you got a good thumping. If any of us were caught the rest of us would set about the man who had caught us. If it was a copper then so much the better, they were just bumbling adults with uniforms. Policemen were just part of the fun and we lost our special fear of them as they sweated and puffed around, chasing us through the wreckage of post-war London. Like all kids, we adapted continuously to our surroundings and played with whatever was available. Our adventure playground was not constricted by the local council with frightened aspiring social workers running it. Our territory came with the compliments of the Luftwaffe and it was rich with pickings. Bombed-out buildings were full of booty in the shape of scrap metal and even old fireplaces. Our biggest problem was our age. We had trouble in transplanting the things we found and had to enlist the help of adults who would take a big cut of the rewards. Scrapyards would not deal with us so we had to find fences who would. There were plenty of Fagins around, but they took more than half the money for themselves. I realized that adults would often try to con kids, thinking that they were stupid. When I did a paper round for my gran for two shillings a week, the people I delivered to had me working for nothing by arguing about how much they owed. I started keeping a book with their payments recorded properly and neatly, and from this I learned the power of documentation. On my own, with my word against theirs I could never win, but armed with a neat row of figures, and a conviction that I was right, they would not dispute their debt. Then I discovered the interesting art of creative accounting, so that I more than doubled my two bob by persuading people with my neat, doctored figures that they sometimes owed more than they really did. Who was going to question the polite, efficient little boy with his ever-present notebook? I would be sensitive to any hint of suspicion or mistrust and make sure that the figures were spot on for a few weeks, and then they would relax their guard.

The war had left more than bombsites for us to play in. Rationing was very strict for some time, and where there are shortages there is always somebody operating a black market. We were too young to take proper advantage of some of the career opportunities that the black market opened up for likely lads. Instead, we found our own corner of the market by nicking off the spivs who sold sugar, chocolate and cigarettes whilst keeping a watchful eye on the police. I was amazed that the coppers didn't just arrest them on sight, because when everyone else was walking round in demob suits and hand-me-downs, the spivs stood on street corners dressed like pimps selling their wares. They tempted passers-by with pork chops as if they had dirty books hidden under their coats. At fairgrounds they sold toffee-apples and kept lookouts posted to warn of approaching coppers.

We watched them and noticed that when a policeman was sighted they would hide their tray of goodies under a table or one of the fairground rides. It was easy for us to crawl under while the spiv whistled innocently as the copper passed by, and then we could sneak away with a great tray of toffee-apples. With planning we became more sophisticated. Instead of hanging around waiting for a chance copper to walk by we would make sure the law paid a visit. One of the younger boys would run up to a policeman and tell him he had lost his mum. PC Dobbins would take the lad by the hand and ask him where he had last seen her. They would make for the spiv who would hide his toffee-apples which we would nick, and then little-boy-lost would disappear, leaving a worried PC, a thoroughly pissed-off black marketeer, and we would all go off and get sick on too many toffee-apples.

Always keen to keep abreast with new technology, we quickly worked out a new area of activity with the introduction of pressure pads and automatic traffic lights. At first we were amazed to see how cars and trucks arriving at the lights would pass over the pads which controlled the flow of traffic. It did not take much savvy to work out the system and we soon learned to enjoy controlling the traffic ourselves by jumping up and down on the pads. After a few days of this harmless mischief we developed a system, whereby one of us would deliberately stop likely trucks while the others jumped on the back. We'd ride the trucks and steal from them, get off at another set of lights and get a ride home the same way. Jumping on the bandwagon or what? But we did get caught once, and I was put on probation for stealing a book. It was about the only contact I had with books at that time.

I found out when I was older that the world is a fascinating place and the way it works will never cease to interest me. Unfortunately at school the world is split into Maths, English, History, Geography and Science. These subjects were all taught by tired and underpaid social failures who took their solace in the dubious pleasures of discipline and control. How they managed to make something like Geography so boring I will never know. Later in life I was feverish in my hunger for knowledge especially in Economics and Geography. I cursed the system that sours the rich delicious fountain of human knowledge into a lumpy gruel of boredom. I did not bother to attend school too often. It was simple to write an excusing letter from my mum and to pay other kids to do my homework for me. It was a pity I took no interest, because I was keen to learn about everything; it was also a pity because when I was a curious adolescent school was about the only place I had any contact with girls. To me and my friends in our *Boy's Own* world of boxing and thieving, girls were almost like a church roof you stole the lead from. They were primarily there to provide a source of boasting and mischief. There were always older boys who made such great claims to voyages of discovery inside the blouse or knickers of some poor girl. Most of it was wishful thinking, but the stories led you to believe that even compared with the most frightening ride at the fairground, love – or rather, sex – was a very special thrill. Smoking cigarettes and being able to inhale up to a quarter of an inch of nicotine was one thing, but the real, best adult experience was to be found between a girl's legs. One boy claimed that he had 'Done It' with a girl who lived down our street but that he had 'gorn up the wrong bleedin' 'ole'. At the time we all laughed and he was famous for five minutes but it only showed how ignorant we really were of the ins and outs of anatomy.

I was concerned to keep up with the rest of the lads and like them, made up stories about local girls who were actually completely virgo intacta and innocent. A girl could get a reputation without ever setting foot outside her own doorstep. In the end I did get to be very curious about the unique thrill you get just from seeing bits of girls, let alone touching them or Doing It. I decided to investigate further.

One day, at the start of the dinner break when some kids ran home and some opened little packets of sandwiches, I took a deep breath and walked up to Rita Bartlett who, for the first time in weeks, was all on her own. I had no real problem talking to girls when my motives were otherwise, but now I had to go into the uncharted waters of seduction. It made me shy, which made her suspicious. I said a nervous hello, and she looked at me cautiously and replied, 'I haven't got any sandwiches left, Charlie, and I haven't got any money and anyway Mr Patterson's on duty today.' This all came out in a rush. The latter part of her speech was supposed to frighten me off since Patterson was an evil pig whose main pleasure in life was beating little children. Her suspicion of me grew when I said I just wanted to talk to her. But I had a reputation at school, despite – or perhaps because of – the fact that I was hardly ever there and she was, against her will, curious. I found it very difficult to talk to her, though, beyond telling her that I saw her mum at the Oval last week. 'I think she was at the butcher's.' So what? But it kept the conversation going, just about, and threw Rita off the scent for a bit.

The scent was, in fact, Rita's tits. She was not very good-looking compared with some of the girls in her class, but she was way ahead of them in the old breast development stakes. Where other girls were as flat-chested as me, Rita definitely had two burgeoning mounds. It made her a target for all sorts of the usual abuse from boys but it also made her an object of desire. What was more, whereas the other girls had gained completely unearned reputations for being 'goers', Rita had entered local adolescent mythology for being the impossible 'tight-arsed cunt', who never gave in despite all concerted attempts to rub her chest. Any boy who could get the others to believe that he had handled Rita's not-so-little Golden Delicious was destined to be written into local history. Lots had tried, many much smoother than me. She had been flattered by their attention but her blouse remained unopened, and, despite idle boasts to the contrary by the teenage studs, was still intact. All sorts of methods including force had been tried, but Rita was strong and would fight as if her life depended on it. I had a much

43

more sophisticated method in mind and I put my proposal to her that day. She took a step back, startled by my suggestion.

'What? You'll give me half a crown to see inside my knickers?'

'Yeah – for thirty seconds, half a crown.'

'Charlie Richardson! You must have seen it all before – what's so special about mine?'

The answer to that was nothing really, but it was a decoy to win her trust. I knew she would be surprised. Her chest was what she was known for – why should I be after something that all the girls had? I confessed to her that the boys just boasted and lied, that most of us had never seen 'it' before. She laughed, and just for authenticity I said that if she told anybody I would give her a punch in the mouth. We went behind a wall in the school grounds, and she took a week's paper round money from me to reveal what looked suspiciously like Kirk Douglas's chin after a few days' growth. I thanked her and while she went back to school I had an important date with some lead on a roof.

A week or so later I sought her out again and asked her if I could have a repeat performance for a shilling. It was a reduced rate because it was not the first time. She liked what was rapidly becoming a new source of income. We went behind the wall and as she knelt, she pulled up her skirt and pulled down her knickers. I looked while she counted one thousand, two thousand, three thousand. At thirty thousand she pulled up her knickers and let her skirt fall back into place.

I did this for four weeks running and Rita was getting richer and richer. It became a routine that I think she almost enjoyed. On the fifth week after twenty-nine thousand, thirty, I took a chance, a deep breath, and asked, 'Rita, can I have a look under your blouse? I'll give you three shillings for twenty seconds?'

She whipped down her skirt and was ready to jump up and run away. I promised her that it was our secret, nobody knew what we were doing. She was very reluctant and obviously found her breasts an embarrassment. I promised her that I would not touch or tell or anything, just look. Three bob was a fortune and she had become used to the extra money. Without a word she unbuttoned her cardigan and her blouse, and pulled them aside. I held my breath. She looked to one side while I stared intently at the source of so much fantasy and speculation, frustration and teenage dreams. I stared harder and harder at the growths with their little pink ends, hoping that something would suddenly happen to me. I knew I was supposed to be excited by those twin molehills of pale pointy flesh with their blue veins and thin skin, but nothing happened. By the time we got to twelve thousand I was bored, and reached out a hand to see how they felt. For a few seconds she did not seem to notice but then by about eighteen thousand she opened her eyes and realized that I had a hand over each of her breasts. She gave a scream, jumped away and started shouting at me. In for a penny, in for three shillings. I wanted my money's worth and I held on, determined to learn what all the fuss was all about. I was never to know. As we tussled on the ground, a huge roar went up behind me.

'Richardson!' It was Mr Patterson, the Geography monster who hated all kids, especially me. He was beside himself with rage. While Rita burst into tears and ran off before stopping and remembering to ask for her three shillings, Patterson dragged me by the hair into the building. He was screaming and spitting, totally out of control. Lots of the kids stopped to watch, and plenty had seen Rita run off, unbuttoned. My achievement was at least registered.

Patterson dragged me into the nearest classroom, still holding onto my hair and pulling me close to him. I gagged on the smell of chalk and boiled cabbage that clung to his faded, frayed checked jacket. He threw me into the room and grabbed his cane. His rage had the edge of a perverted, frustrated old man who watched us change after games on the pretext that he had to make sure we washed properly. All of that pent-up frustration was unleashed on me as he grabbed my hand and held it out. He put all his strength into six whacks on my right hand. I did not flinch or even register each stroke, but stared at him, enjoying the power of overcoming the pain. He hit harder each time and was driven to complete madness by my lack of reaction. He grabbed my hair, threw me over the teacher's desk at the front of the classroom and still shouting at me, like a man possessed, he started to whack my arse with whatever adrenalin he could muster. I turned my face to see a whole gang of kids fighting for a view at the door and faces pressed against the windows from the playground. I was humiliated by my position and maddened by his ridiculous reaction to a harmless and expensive grope behind a wall. On the sixth stroke I could sense he was about to break the rules and give me more. He was out of control. He had been ranting on that I was about to turn out like my dad, a useless good-for-nothing jailbird and disgusting womaniser. I was a filthy, filthy molester like him. That was enough. Before he could lay another stroke on me I jumped up and the cane fell out of his hand. I grabbed it and held it ready to strike him. He was astonished and seeing the look on my face he suddenly got control of himself and his voice returned almost to normal. He held out his hand and tried to negotiate.

'Right then, Richardson, you've had enough. Give me the cane, lad, don't be silly.' He added, 'Come on now – you've caused enough trouble – come on, let's have it!' Everybody waited a few seconds, watching to see what I would do. I looked at the man in front of me, twice my size, and thought of something witty and clever to say. Then I said it. 'Fuck off, you old fucking cunt,' and I laid into him with a shower from the cane. He crouched and raised his arms to protect himself. I shouted out the strokes and aimed for whatever part of him I could hit, mostly the back of his hands and his head. When I had counted to eleven, I threw the cane at him and walked out of the room. The awestruck crowd parted silently as I made my way out of school. It had been a fruitful afternoon which had earned me two entries into the local history books. I had gazed upon Rita's hidden assets, and had given old Patterson a taste of his own medicine.

'Bring back the birch, it's all they understand.' Definitely! Give me a few whacks on the arse any day rather than one whiff of an approved school, remand centre or prison. I would rather limp for a few days while the wounds healed than shit in a bucket, eat cold porridge or share a cell with other men.

I had an early start in the courtroom drama gameshow which had its advantages. You learn very quickly when you are young, especially new languages. I was in court for the book theft job when I got probation. That almost worked because it upset my mum and grandparents so much that I tried really hard to be a good little boy from then onwards. I helped my grandfather with his gold-leaf book covers job but I soon got bored. I helped my grandmother in the shop but after a while I really wanted a bit of excitement.

I had developed a real fascination for scrap and metals generally. I loved keeping up with the changing prices for the various types of scrap. Lead was always very good and so easy to nick; you could tear it off a roof like soft thin toffee. The problem was its weight. Transporting it was difficult because of my age. Usually I would borrow a horse and cart from a Fagin fence who bought the lead from me at a fraction of the price he got from the scrapyards. I used to feel very exposed going down the street with an open wagon loaded with stolen lead and covered only by an old blanket that really looked as if something dodgy lay beneath it. Sometimes it was during the week, when I should have been at school.

One day I discovered tons of lead on the roof of the post office at Camberwell Green. I kept the find to myself and working through the night, stripped the lot of it and hid it in a disused cellar. A few days later I arranged to borrow a horse and cart to get the load to the fence I dealt with. On my way to see him I bumped into another boy who was a couple of years older than me; Pete Buckley was a bit of a lad and a well-known local lead thief. Because he was older than me I boasted to try and impress him about my lead load. Pete told me about another fence, Mr Allen, who gave kids a better deal on lead but what seemed even more important was that he had a van. I decided to go to Mr Allen with the idea that we load up the lead in his van.

An hour later Allen and I were working up a sweat outside the cellar. He was excited by the amount of lead I had found and congratulated me as if I had written an excellent essay at school. A minute or two later a police car drew up and four coppers jumped out. They ran towards us and caught Allen immediately, but I ran across the post office roof and got away. When I returned home, the police were waiting and my mother was in a state. I promised her and them that it was not me but they seemed very confident that it was. An hour later at the police station I found out why. Pete Buckley had written a statement saying I had done it. The little bastard had made a deal with the police. They stuck to their end of the bargain. In court they said he was a poor lad taken in and influenced by me. A Catholic priest and his doting parents were paraded in front of the court who said how wonderful he was, such a good Christian and a real help at home. The little toerag had been nicking lead before I even had hair on my balls. He was given a conditional discharge and I was remanded to a shithole in Shepherd's Bush while reports were made. I was put on probation. I remember looking at Pete in court in disbelief. I really couldn't understand how he could save his own skin by grassing me up. There was nothing unusual about my attitude. Loyalty to a group is not confined to criminals. In wartime if you give information to the enemy you are a traitor and will hang for it. Doctors and teachers stick together like a herd of gazelle being chased by a lion. Free-masons do not grass on each other and neither do criminals. Loyalty was the bedrock of our community. The police and authorities represented the enemy. No matter what was going on you only joined forces with the other side at your peril.

' Later in life when we were running a number of businesses in south-east London we were attacked one afternoon by a rival organization led by the future Great Train Robber, Charlie Wilson, who wanted to sort us out. They came with shotguns and were firing all over the place. We never had guns so we were busy hiding around the yard while they tried to kill us. Eventually with all the racket going on the police sirens could be heard screaming through the streets, heading for the scrapyard. Everything stopped, we opened the gates and hid the mob with their shotguns and all. The police were puzzled to discover business as usual. When they claimed shots had been reported we just laughed and said we were trying to fix up an old wreck of a car that kept backfiring. They had a sniff around and went away, uneasy but unable to do anything. I opened a bottle of whisky and the whole lot of us had a good laugh. We may have been rivals but we had a common enemy and when it surfaced, our loyalty to each other was greater than anything. Is that so unusual? During wartime Tory and Labour MPs unite, minor rivalries are forgotten while a crisis exists. But small-time crooks will sell their grandmother, their children and their wives for a reduced jail sentence and we had some of those selling their pathetic worthless souls to an ex-fascist judge and a bunch of career coppers for a shorter time inside. The longer our sentence, the shorter theirs would be. What use is a bag of minnows and sprats compared with a bloody great thrashing salmon? And like the fishermen's tales, the fish were getting bigger and bigger with every detail of the story.

It seems we agreed to let Taggart go on a majority verdict providing he paid us the princely sum of £1200 he was supposed to be worth. Taggart told the court that he was then allowed to get dressed. The scene was changing and the audience was going to get bored with a fully-clothed victim. Just as the press were thinking it was time to get round to the pub for a lunchtime pint, Sebag-Shaw pulled another rabbit out of the hat. It was the same as before but it worked anyway. He interrupted Taggart.

'Just pause there for a minute. What about your underwear?'

Heads turned back to Taggart. Yes, what *did* happen to his underwear? Surely he was not going to put on those now-historic blood-soaked undies, which had been used mercilessly to wipe the wall and floor clean of his own blood? Taggart, as if he had forgotten his lines, was grateful to be prompted and solved this little mystery for us. He answered Sebag:

'No, not my underwear. First of all Clark helped me outside. There were either buckets or bowls of cold water poured over my head. Apparently there is a tap outside the office.'

'So you were allowed to wash off and dry?'

'Yes, sir.'

'And then did you put on your trousers and jacket?'

'Yes, sir – also, sir, I think I mentioned earlier as to whether or not my socks were on or off. I had no socks because I left with just shoes on my bare feet, if I can make that point.'

'So when you say you were naked, you were absolutely naked?'

'Yes, sir.'

This was all very vital. Up until then, we had of course imagined a gruesome scene where a man was not fully naked. He had his socks on and being an Englishman, this was terribly important. It meant that he had been allowed to retain some small shred of dignity. His little pink willy was exposed but At Least He Had His Socks On. Now, heaven forbid, what did we learn but that this brutality took place without his socks. I nearly laughed out loud, but then something even funnier happened. It seems that after brutally assaulting this poor, pathetic sockless creature for several hours and threatening to kill him, he asked us if he could give us a post-dated cheque! And being reasonable people, despite all evidence to the contrary, we accepted! It was turning into a farce. While chuckling away at this revelation, we were startled to learn that Taggart was then escorted to his car and he drove all the way home to Hampstead. After all that, repeated beatings and pools of blood, he apparently just . . . drove home. I looked around the courtroom thinking that at last they would all realize that they had just heard a fairy story, but they sat in open-mouthed wonder. They wanted to believe Taggart. If he had been lying it would have been just another disappointment in lives already full of daily letdowns and sinking hearts. It was madness, and I wanted to run away from it all like I had done so many times before when I found myself surrounded by lunatics. Madmen do not think that they are mad, and the crazy people who inhabit courtrooms are perverted weirdos who think they are the last corner of sanity in a decaying world.

By the time I was fourteen, I had a basic understanding of how the courts operated. I also had a good idea how cars worked and sometimes involvement with one would bring me to the other. I loved driving and in those days cars were very easy to unlock and start without proper keys. When we went out for a night on the town to meet girls we would just take a car for the night and park it round the corner when we came home. We got to be fussy about which type of car we 'borrowed', and it was while a friend and I were looking over a car near East Street market that a copper came running up to us and we scarpered. Ten minutes later we were sitting in a café having a cup of tea and the copper came in to nick us both. There was a bunch of car keys in my pocket which was fairly damning evidence. They gave us a good smack at the police station, and sent for our parents. When my friend's dad came there was a bit of a commotion but as we sat on a bench in the courtroom I could sense that there was something funny going on.

In the court I soon found out what had happened. Another deal had been struck. I was apparently trying to steal the car and the other boy was some distance away. It looked once again like I was going to take the full rap but the magistrate asked me if I had any questions. To everyone's surprise I said that I wanted to ask the policeman some questions. I knew the local geography so well that I was able to run rings round the copper and in the end he had to admit that he could not possibly have seen my friend at all if he was thirty yards from me, and that he had not actually seen me get into or even try to get into the car. He also had to admit that he did not know if any of the keys I had in my possession actually fitted the car's locks. I explained to the magistrate that I collected keys, that I was only looking at the car admiringly, because it was smart, and that we only ran off because a lumbering great copper came tearing towards us. We got off completely. My friend's dad was very impressed, and walked up to me with a big smile and his hand out to congratulate me. I looked at his hand and then into his eyes and said, 'Fuck off, bastard – you were ready to drop me in it.' His smile disappeared. He was a hard man, but he was a bit shamefaced that he had been so ready to drop me in it in order to save his son.

There are two ways that you can learn to swim. You can have an instructor at school teach you properly, a bit at a time, exercise by exercise, until you swim efficiently and happily. The other way is to jump in the deep end, splutter away and learn from watching other people until you are swimming better than they are. With everything in life I jumped in at the deep end. Caution and security stop people from really living. Work hard all week, get pissed on a Saturday night, two weeks in Butlins or Benidorm, pay the electric and wait to die. Always frightened, full of ideas but no nerve to try them. Never bite off more than you can chew so nibble away until you're freezing in the one room of your council flat, a few days away from death – but still worried about the electricity bill. Not for me. I've always thought that you should bite off more than you can chew, then chew it – you'll be surprised to find out how easy to digest it really is.

I learned to drive cars by stealing them. In fact, I knew how to steal a car *before* I could drive one. It was a sensible progression because the first few cars ended up smashed into other ones. Eventually I got the hang of it and I loved driving. I was about thirteen or fourteen so there was no question of owning a car. Stealing was so simple that I would plan a trip and then just before I went out, pick a car to take me there. Sometimes I had dates with girls and would turn up in a car I had nicked only a few minutes ago. They would be amazed because even though I told them all I was eighteen they didn't believe me. I knew I did not look anything like that age, and anyway, who had a car that young in those days? But like everyone else, they believed what they wanted to believe.

It was good to have something to impress the girls with, because I don't know if I had much else. I had money from scrap and all sorts of small burglaries so I could afford good clothes and fashionable gear. But even in the latest and best Teddy Boy gear, complete with quiff, I somehow always felt I didn't look quite right. There was nothing I could do about it but it always made me feel a little shy and self-conscious with girls, especially at dance halls.

But it was a different matter at the end of the evening when they were all worried about catching the last bus home or having to walk, and I would offer them a lift. They would be very suspicious but it was too good a chance to miss. I would walk out of the dance hall with a girl, triumphant and making sure my friends would be taking note. We would walk round the corner and I would suggest she got us a bag of chips while I got the car. A few minutes later I would roll up in a beautiful, recently acquired motor with big plush bench seats and drive a stunned and speechless girl home. By the end of the evening she was seeing me in a very different light. Although I usually used a different car to get me there and get me home, I did make the mistake once of using the same car to get me and a friend to Brixton roller-skating rink and take us home again. I had met a girl at the rink and offered her a lift to Lewisham, and so the three of us set off. I was showing off a bit and being a bit nippy on the road. She was squealing with pleasure every time I cut in front of another car and screaming when I took corners almost on two wheels. I dropped her off at her home and the two of us were having a great time until suddenly a police car was racing beside us on the Old Kent Road with the bells ringing and the copper in the front shouting and waving to us to pull over. No bloody chance! I had a choice; pull over, get my head kicked in and be charged with nicking the car – or, carry on, get caught anyway and have my head kicked in and be charged. It was an easy decision. At least this way I might even get away. The sinking dread I felt when the copper appeared was replaced immediately by excitement as my foot hit the accelerator and the car shot forward. It made their day too. Where would they be without the likes of me to make their jobs exciting? Where would all the American films get their stories from if people like me did not give a good car chase? It was not my car and so I couldn't give a shit what happened to it or anything else that got in the way. I jumped the car onto the pavement, screeched over into the oncoming traffic, missing trams by a fraction of a second, and hit a road-sign with the wing. My mate was loving it. He had his head out of the window, yelling back at the police. I dodged around, my foot always on the floor, as if the car was a bumper ride at the fairground. I laughed at the abuse my friend was giving the coppers as I tore round a bend and smashed straight into a wall. The car was a write-off and my passenger and I were pretty dazed but before the police could get their doors open and adjust their fat arses to running gear, we were off down the street and dodging through people's backyards. I am sure they all went for me because as I came round a corner, I was tackled and brought to the ground by a massive copper who did his best to control my kicking and punching until another three arrived and they took me to the station where, of course, they put me in a cell and kicked the shit out of me.

A few days later I was up again in Lambeth juvenile court. The four coppers who had seen me home that night had washed my blood off their boots and were waiting for the case. They paced up and down impatiently. No wonder there are so few bobbies on the beat to help old ladies cross the road – they're all inside courts, waiting for some case or other.

After a while one of them approached me and asked me how I was planning to plead. I looked up at him, a beaten boy, anxious to please. 'Guilty, sir, what else can I say? You caught me red-handed and there's four of your lot and nobody to speak for me . . .' He smiled and walked back to his colleagues. They had a chat and realized that there was not much point in all of them hanging around. It was, as they say, an open and shut case. So three of them took off to cause more trouble on the streets, leaving the one who talked to me to give his evidence.

When I got into the dock I pleaded 'Not Guilty'. I had met a girl at the skating rink and escorted her home on the bus. I held out a ticket stub and quoted the price. I was walking all the way home from Lewisham because I had no money, when these three policemen jumped out at me and arrested me for stealing a car when I couldn't even drive! The copper was astonished. He was left on his own and one of the magistrates asked where the other witnesses were. They were suspicious of the police sometimes, and I thought I might be going to get off. But they decided to remand me on my mother's bail to give me time to produce the girl. That was going to be a serious problem. I knew her address because I had driven her home, but she had no idea that the car was stolen; she could not be counted on to lie for me. What was worse, if she attended the court she would find out my real age. That would have been embarrassing and despite my original Irish heritage there was enough Englishness in me to risk jail rather than lose face with a girl.

I carefully briefed three friends to testify that they had been at the skating rink with me that night, and that one of them had even got onto the same bus as me and the girl. They did me proud in court the next week, as I explained that I could not find the girl. I was nearly home and dry. There were four of them and five of us and three suspicious magistrates. One of the latter was a woman, and she was not so easy to convince. She decided that I should be given another week to find the girl. I didn't even bother to try. But the police did, and God knows how, but they found her. They were determined to sort me out well and truly. She appeared the following week very properly briefed. It was obvious that whatever impression I might have made on her that night she had not burned a candle in her window for me since . . . I got three years in an approved school and looked around to see the horror on my mother's face. I ignored the smiles of the police as I was taken to the van. In the last few minutes I had with my mother I promised her that I would behave myself at the school and sort myself out when I got home. She was in tears. I was turning out just like my dad. I wanted to prove her wrong, but not just yet. As they walked me to the little bus with bars on the windows I flew. I raced past three of the cops who had arrested me and dashed into Woolworths. They all gave chase as I pushed between shoppers and shelves, diving under people, jumping from the sweet counter to the electrical goods almost into the arms of a policeman. I got a few punches in the mouth before they installed me firmly on the bus bound for the Ardale Approved School.

That night as I got into my new bed, it collapsed around me. As I put the irons together and made the sheets up silently, the whole room laughed and I realized that I would have to make my mark. I lay under the crisp white sheets with three thin blue lines down the middle and grey army blankets, and wanted to cry. The room was now full of the smell and sound of many sleeping bodies, none of them known to me. In the reek of polished floors and sweaty feet I got a hold of myself and planned to escape as soon as I could. It would be easy once I had got my bearings.

The next day, I sat in classrooms, workshops and meals, ignoring everybody. The other boys were a cheerful lot at heart, when the perverted screws who dreamed of screwing us were not around. I realized there was a hierarchy as there is everywhere in life. Everybody has a governor and in this place, your immediate governor was the hard case in your room. Like a tribe of baboons, the leader was the hardest and under constant threat for his position. I understood that I could not be a soldier in this shithole of pretend reform. I had at best to establish myself quickly as Room Corporal.

That second night when I got into bed, the other boys were chatting away to each other about the sister of one of the kitchen staff who sometimes came into the school. She was fifteen, and everybody wanted to 'give her one'. I was

just thinking that it might be an improvement on giving each
other 'one', which some of them seemed to be interested in,
when the duty officer's head popped around the door. He
switched off the lights and shouted at us all to 'shut up and
keep your knees down!'. A boy with his knees up in bed was
considered to be making himself blind with self abuse.

Within a few seconds of the officer's metal-tipped footsteps
disappearing down the corridor, there was a sudden loud
whispered 'Now!', and I was attacked from all sides by pillows.
In *Boy's Own*, pillow fights are fun and 'gung-ho' but this was
vicious and very, very unfriendly. I leapt out of bed and hit
whoever I could. It surprised them when I did not hold
back. If I saw a face I punched it. If there was a chance I
crushed a set of genitals with my bare fist. I fought my way
through the soldiers making for the boy I had identified as
room governor. The other baboons recognized my challenge
and stopped hitting me. They all stood waiting as Mick the
governor dropped his pillow and clenched his fist ready for
the obvious fight that was to follow. I held up my hand
and smiled as I spoke.

'Look, Mick, I know you're the governor. But I've had
enough of this fucking lark – so just leave it out and we can
get on with things.'

He relaxed a little, his authority unchallenged. 'If you can't
fucking take it, you shouldn't be here, mate. We do this to
all the new boys. It's our initiation.'

'Right . . . can't we just say I've been initiated now, and
be friends? Come on, shake . . . I know you're the fucking
governor.'

I held out my hand. He had puffed up with importance at
my homage to his authority. He felt he was doing me a favour.
Like any great leader he was capable of being generous with his
minions. He held out his hand, and as I shook it I pulled him
towards me and punched him in the face with my left. Both
his hands went to his face to cover it and I punched him in
the balls. His breath left him, he gasped and fell forward. On
the way down I grabbed his hair and pulled his face to my
knee which was on its way up . . . I turned and pulled the

57

end of a bed off and held the metal bar in both hands above my head like a baseball bat. Mick had managed to suck in a desperate mouthful of air. He lay on the floor clutching his balls while blood poured out of his nose and lay in a pool by the side of his face. I leaned over him and prodded him with the bed-end. 'Want any more, you Irish bastard?'

He said nothing. He could not speak, he was winded. I laid the cold metal of the bed-end next to his face and repeated, 'Want any more?' He shook his head. As I turned to the silent gang they started moving back towards their beds. From now on I was the room governor. I put the bed-end back just as the door opened. The duty officer walked in. He took a few seconds to realize what had happened. The officers knew better than to interfere with a dormitory power struggle. He spoke to the gasping boy on the floor. 'Right, Docherty, into bed and clean up this mess in the morning. Richardson, get into bed.'

And with that he left. The next day I was a corporal among privates and Mick was my best friend.

Somebody I had thought of as a friend was now in the witness box giving evidence against me. Alfred Abraham Berman was a businessman who had invested in my perlite mine in South Africa. I had bought a huge plot of land and to everyone's surprise, I had discovered rich deposits of a rare mineral. I then had to run around cap-in-hand finding investors to make it all work. Berman was an investor who had become involved with the project. I called round one day to his warehouse to ask him if he wanted to come to the airport that night to meet my brother Eddie off the plane from South Africa. He agreed, and it was arranged that I would give him a call later to meet up. Now he was in the dock giving an interesting new version of a harmless incident. He was asked if he eventually received a call. He carefully avoided my gaze.

'Yes, sir.'

'Who was it from?'

'From Mr Charles Richardson.' And now the business associate with whom I had been on holiday to South Africa, to Hungary on business, and to countless boxing matches followed by late nights in London clubs, could not look me in the face. The questions continued and I wanted to see just how far down the river I had been sold.

'What did he say?'

'He asked me if I could get him something to eat.'

'Yes?'

'Well, there is a nice restaurant next to my warehouse.'

'Did Charles Richardson know that?'

'Yes, sir.'

'Did he mention it?'

'He mentioned fish and chips and I knew what he meant when he said that; it is a very good shop.'

'So he asked you to get some fish and chips, and what else?'

'Some beer.'

'And do what with it?'

'He said he could not get a beer as he was working late at his office and would I bring him round some food? I said I would and that I would bring some for myself and eat it round at his place.'

'Was anything said on the telephone at that time about the airport?'

'Yes, when I got round to the office he should have knowledge of when the plane was coming in.'

'Did you go to the fish and chip restaurant?'

'Yes, sir.'

'Did you take your fish and chips and go into his office?'

'Yes, sir.'

'As you walked in, who did you see there?'

'Mr Clark, Mr Fraser and Mr Richardson.'

'What did you do with your fish and chips?'

'I put them on the desk.'

'And as you did what happened?'

'To my amazement I saw a man sitting on a chair, naked, with a rope around him.'

'Had the man got any clothes on him?'

'Absolutely naked, sir.'

59

'What did you notice about him? What was his head like?'

'When I first looked at him he looked ghastly, and I had another look and realized that the man was James Taggart, who I knew. I had to look twice.'

'What was ghastly about him?'

'His head was swollen, his ears were swollen and his eyes were swollen. He had marks all over his body and he was sitting on a chair; there was blood in front of him on the floor and blood on the walls behind him.'

'How did you feel when you saw this?'

'I nearly fainted.'

The bastard! I could imagine the story being constructed. You walk into a room – you see this astonishing scene, and how do you feel? You feel disgusted? Frightened? Upset? Worried, angry? No. You faint. That's it, you feel faint. So we will make sure we ask you how you felt and you say you feel faint. What could be a more powerful statement from a big, adult, middle-aged businessman of the world who liked going to the boxing, and had seen some brutality in his life. You felt faint. You bastard! Like Hitler said, if you're going to tell a lie, you might as well make it a big one. Another little tip for story-creating is to position your pack of lies in the middle of a web of truth. I *did* call on Berman to go to the airport, he did bring round fish and chips and we did pick up my brother. And here was another thing. Taggart had been quite adamant that we ate sandwiches and yet Berman was positive that he brought fish and chips. Personally I thought fish and chips gave a more solid south-east London atmosphere to the scene. You could easily imagine us sitting on the edge of the desks with open newspaper packages of steaming chips; imagine us dipping our hands into the greasy fat chips and licking the vinegar off our fingers. Meanwhile, a man naked, naked, NAKED without any clothes on, not a stitch apart from a few ropes, stood or crouched in front of us. But even if he had been beaten to a pulp he seemed to have remembered events and conversations quite clearly; yet he had not been able to distinguish between a pack of sandwiches and a very smelly hot bag of fish and chips. Somebody had slipped up somewhere. Berman of course told the court that he begged for Taggart to be released and was too frightened to leave. A thousand excuses could have got him out of that room and the police there in minutes, but he stayed.

'What happened to the food you had brought?'

'Mr Fraser, Mr Clark and Mr Richardson ate the food and they asked me to have some too but my appetite had left me.'

'What happened after the fish and chips were eaten?'

'Mr Clark untied Taggart and Mr Richardson told Mr Clark to throw Taggart his undervest to make him wipe the blood off the floor and the walls.'

Now, Taggart had told us a number of times that he had wiped the blood up with his underpants. This was a much more interesting piece of cloth for the newspapers than a mere vest. Maybe he wore matching undies, and had such a fat arse that there was little difference between a vest and underpants but it was a detail my memory notes and our robed public schoolboy was happy to miss. If I had said anything they would probably have sent me below to the cells. It was agony having to sit there and listen helplessly to this crap. I desperately wanted to walk out of the room and let them get on with their drama without me.

After the fight with Mick, I sort of settled down in the remand home and seriously got down to my education as a villain. I am not the first person to say it, and will certainly not be the last, but the most ridiculous aspect of our penal system is that it breeds itself faster than rabbits do. If you want to turn a perfectly balanced and sane young man into a raving madman send him to a mental institution. If you want to be sure that a young boy who likes a bit of mischief turns into a fully-fledged adult villain, send him to a remand home or a borstal.

I was used to daily excitement and was filled with the energy of enterprise on the streets of south-east London. Each day outside offered new prospects for adventure and profit. In the remand centre each day offered a dull routine of discipline and short trousers, and the smells of communal life. I had decided that I was going to escape. I waited a few weeks, planned a route, developed a simple plan and at exactly four o'clock one morning, I woke Mick up with a whisper. We giggled and promised to keep in touch as we tied his two sheets and mine together. We hung our makeshift rope out of the window and discovered it was way off the ground. In my careful planning, I had not allowed for the amount of sheet used up to make the knots. We needed more sheets and the only way to get them was to wake somebody up. It was a difficult choice; did we wake up a boy who would be too frightened of us to mention it but just might break under the strain of interrogation, or did we dare risk waking a stronger boy who might well blow the whistle in order to keep his nose clean? We opted for 'Monkee Allan'. He was called Monkee because he was always scratching at real or imaginary fleas. He kept himself to himself, which we appreciated given his condition. I had a little second thought about handling his sheets but we woke him and after a good scratch he smiled and helped us to make our rope. It was still dark as I lowered myself into the grounds of the school. A short hop over the wall and I ran through fields to hide in a bush and wait. And wait! I was still wearing the school pyjamas. My accomplice was supposed to meet me with some clothes. This was escape from Colditz and he was the French Resistance waiting with clothes and documents to get me home. He was supposed to flash a torch three times like a good commando. There was no torchlight to be seen. I got a headache concentrating in the darkness looking for his light and cursing him for being so late. Breaking back into the school was not going to be as easy as getting out, and I was not going to get far in my pyjamas. I was starting to shiver with the cold when I saw a tiny glimmer of light across the field. There were no flashes but it was still worth a look. I crawled and dived into ditches as I made my way across to the source of the light. As I got close I lay and watched. A few seconds later the light appeared again, then once again, and I saw him, my comrade-in-arms, my one-man rescue team lighting a match.

I could see his face in the glow for a second or two. I stood up and walked towards him. When I was very close I whispered: 'What happened to the torch?'

'Jesus Christ, Charlie boy, you gave me the shock of me life! Where the hell have you bin? I've been lighting bleedin' matches for hours!'

'It was supposed to be three flashes of a torch, Dad.'

He smiled, and it was good to see the twinkle in his eye. 'Forgot, didn't I? Anyway, you're here now, lad. Come on, put these on quick and let's get going.'

I started to get changed into the clothes he had brought me while he told me of the trouble it had been to get out to me. I was pleased to see him, but angry at his lack of organization. I stopped dressing for a moment when I realized he had hitched his way and there was no car . . .

'So how the fuck are we going to get home, Dad? Jesus fucking Ada!'

'Watch your bleedin' tongue, boy. You're not big enough yet to talk to me like that! Where'd you get that filthy mouth on you? If your mother could hear you talk she'd spare a tear or two.'

It was fun to be sharing this adventure with my father. I was not worried about how we would get home. He'd work something out. Then an even greater problem presented itself – I was dressed and ready to go with bare feet. He had forgotten to bring shoes and socks. We fell about with whispered laughter until the tears ran out of our eyes. He took off his shoes and gave me his socks.

He lit a cigarette and hid it in his cupped hands. I was dying for a smoke but I did not dare ask him. Helping his son break out of a juvenile prison was one thing, but encouraging him to smoke was quite another – and out of the question. As we huddled in a bush he explained to me that it would be stupid to walk down the street at this time of night. The first copper that saw us would instantly be suspicious.

So we waited till first light and walked to Upminster tube station. On the tube we sat together, a tall dignified man with no socks, and a fourteen-year-old boy with no shoes. A

63

schoolboy in uniform, about the same age as me, asked me what had happened to my shoes. I asked him if he wanted a smack in the mouth. My father turned to me and winked.

I could not go home with him for obvious reasons so I hid out with some friends in Stockwell. The deal was that I would go to sea with my father and get away from it all. I was not pleased at this arrangement but it seemed adventurous and much more exciting than reform school. I had to remain in hiding until he could find a ship for us. While I was waiting I had a great time with the two lads in Stockwell. They had been on the run for months and were living off burglaries of camera shops and jewellery stores. It was easy in those days to throw a brick through a window or force a door and make off in a stolen car. We made hundreds of pounds a week but I could hardly spend it. I bought a pair of shades to disguise myself but I stopped wearing them hastily when a friend remarked that I was the only person in the whole of the Walworth Road wearing dark glasses in December, and that I stood out as if I had been wearing an overcoat, gloves and scarf on a hot summer day.

Eventually I got word that my dad had got us aboard a ship in Liverpool. We were set to sail after the New Year. On Christmas Eve I sneaked home and it was so good to see my mother and two brothers. Eddie was turning into a bit of a local boxer as I had done, and our younger brother Alan was doing well at school. After a good dinner, we all went to bed to wait for Santa to slide down the chimney. It was snowing outside and we were together as a family, a rare event. At five in the morning I heard a bang downstairs. I looked out of the window but instead of a reindeer and sleigh I saw a dirty great police car. There was a commotion downstairs with my dad shouting and fighting, and a few seconds later a copper had me by the hair and was dragging me down the stairs. I ran away in pyjamas and was now being captured in my bloody pyjamas. The Christmas dinner I had in the local nick was quite good considering . . . If you could ignore the strong smell of piss in a cell that had housed a thousand winos it was not such a bad Christmas.

They took me to Wormword Scrubs for a few weeks while they sorted out what they were going to do with me. I was fourteen then so they put me in a cell of my own to avoid embarrassing stories of rape of small boys in grown-up prisons in the newspaper. It struck me as incredible how you can be bumbling along nicking cameras and lead off a roof, and then suddenly out of the blue you find your career takes a leap forward. I had been happily serving my apprenticeship on the streets and in the approved school surrounded by other apprentices. Now, as luck would have it, I found myself out of school and attending one of the great British universities of crime. And I thought America was the land of opportunity!

The screws at the Scrubs were very helpful and even a little kind at times. The other prisoners took me under their wing and as I smoked away they taught me about the grown-up world of crime. It gave me a lot to look forward to. Smashing windows was a desperate and childish act. You could learn a lot more by being just a little bit more clever. Having missed all those days at school I would spend many more years without the benefit of Chaucer or Dickens or Newton, but I was hungry for information about what appeared to be a rosy, exciting and adventurous future. A few weeks later, I was back in another reform school but I had tasted the forbidden fruit. Robbery and violence were the acts of desperate men. Fraud and deception and almost-honest business practices were cleaner, nearly respectable and very profitable. Prison achieved what reform school could never do; it reformed me. I vowed I would never smash another window or steal another car. The big wide world of business offered scope for limitless development.

CHAPTER THREE
Big Deals and Dirty Tricks

In the summer of 1963 the British government decided to burn millions of used banknotes. Some friends of mine believed very strongly that this money should be reintroduced into the British economy and administered by them personally. So they stopped the train carrying the notes and were sentenced to thirty years of imprisonment. The crime became known as the Great Train Robbery. What was 'great' about it was the size of the sentences they received. The police who finally arrested them became celebrities and the Establishment danced around the court at the announcement of these severe sentences that were meant to 'teach the men a lesson'. They were celebrating a huge and disastrous own goal. In order to gain possession of these dirty used banknotes, the Great Train Robbers had used sticks to arm themselves with. Villains up and down the country reasoned that if you were going to get thirty years for carrying a stick, you might as well get thirty years for carrying sawn-off shotguns, and so they did. This increased their chances of getting away without really increasing their likely sentence if they still got caught.

Before and during their trial we tried to help them, as friends do. We had a bit of success; just when the Old Bill thought they were home and dry we cast suspicion on a key witness. The police did not forget our involvement in that caper and neither did they forget the delights of their own notoriety. They had tasted the brief joys of being in all the papers and sitting with their kids in front of the telly watching themselves being interviewed. Just as their fame was fading a new chance to be 'the untouchables' came their way. Two groups of people with very different business practices, but operating on the wrong side of the law were becoming prominent in London. To a frustrated superhero with a wild imagination, these two groups could, if you half-closed your eyes and suspended all your common sense, be considered the embryo of organized crime. To keen careerist coppers hungry for stardom, the Richardsons in south-east London and the Krays in east London could be seen to be the start of the London 'families'. To a budding Elliot Ness the Richardsons had to be 'the Richardson Gang'. The word gang was so loaded with meaning and promise. Anybody could put away a businessman who had been 'creative' in his numerous dealings, but to be responsible for jailing a 'gang' was definitely very impressive. But why stop there; a gang is just a gang, after all. Why not call it a 'torture gang', and then the boss would be 'the torture gang boss'. Me. Charlie Richardson.

It is the public that make people really famous. It is important to be respected within one's own profession but to be recognized on the street you need public acclaim. And the public was screaming out for a capital city with its own gangs that terrorized their 'manor'. We did not terrorize our neighbourhood. We did a better job of protecting it than the police, but Robin Hood was out of fashion then and the Mafia was in. Why should Chicago and New York have all the best stories? Britain was just as capable of producing organized crime as America was. It never really happened, but that was a minor problem. The limelight-hungry police and the excitement-starved British public had created us, and like all good stories we were recorded for posterity. Here the press was happy to play its part in the conspiracy to offer serious competition against America's lurid tales of rival gangs. So the police went for us, happy to have the approval of their paymasters, the public. The press printed anything that was fed to them and with artistic licence invented a few stories of their own.

The judges had tasted blood with the Great Train Robbers and had licked their lips when they realized that they could get away with double the sentences for single figure crimes. Perhaps they thought that if they put everybody away for thirty years, they could take longer holidays as their workload now resided at Her Majesty's Pleasure and ate cold, lumpy porridge in damp, filthy cells. They were happy to play their part in the conspiracy to nip 'organized crime' in the bud once and for all. With them and the police (not to mention the press and the public), our chances were looking pretty dismal. We had to get all the help from our friends that we could muster.

After I was arrested, we had a few friends there looking into the jury situation. It would not have been the first time we had approached members of the jury and made their day with an offer of a bundle of cash that would make their greedy eyes pop. We were experienced nobblers with professional standards to maintain. We never threatened violence against jurors because it was too risky. If a juror had tried to argue our innocence sporting a shiner and a broken arm, I think the other members might have been a bit sceptical. Jury nobbling was practised by both sides. We knew our jury had been vetted by Special Branch so they were not easy for us to approach anyway. Frank Fraser warned us that somebody else just might get to the jury before us.

As we were preparing for another day of *Listen With Mother* to tales of the brothers Very Grim, a screw showed me a newspaper which took the breath right out of me. The mother of one of the jury had been apprehended at a bus-stop and physically threatened. This was unnecessary. They were already winning the case hands down. I knew that nobody friendly to me would have been so stupid as to have tried such a desperate move. It was a dirty trick and the initial shudder of despair I had when I read the story turned to rage. I had had enough of this fiasco. Having to sit for day after endless day listening to a series of horror stories which turn you into a monster is hard enough to take. Now I was being accused of threatening an old woman, when my only social contact with old ladies for years before the trial was to help them across the road and finance trips to the seaside for the old folks in Camberwell. I was disgusted with this little twist in the plot and decided I was not going to go on with this showtrial.

I told my brief that I refused to attend the court that day. If they insisted, they would have to carry me in chains up to the dock. When the word was passed around the others, my brother Eddie, Frank Fraser and Roy Hall also all refused to take part in the nonsense upstairs. We sat below as the case continued in our absence. In the end I found it more frustrating not to know what was going on than listening to them. I also reasoned that if they could create such rubbish about me while I stood and watched then their stories might even grow in my absence. We decided to attend again. It was a gesture that made us feel better but they had scored all the points. It may not have been the authorities that approached the old lady at the bus-stop. It could have been somebody from a newspaper – whoever it was had banged another nail into our collective coffin.

But all was not yet lost, as the questioning of Taggart continued we had our own card to play. The father of the judge was the governor of Wandsworth Prison, and to us and our friends he was not a very pleasant man. He had risen from the ranks and was nobody's fool. Most prison governors are harmless, distant characters who have no idea of what is actually happening in their prisons. As long as they are left alone to read the papers, drink tea and attend conferences they are usually perfectly happy and content. They leave the real running of the prison to the screws. Very often screws are screwed up. Prison officers, so the saying goes, got their nickname from the time when prisoners, alone in their cells, would turn a big wheel with a handle all day. It was part of the 'work is good for the soul' mentality. The wheels did not do anything constructive at all. Every now and again a screw which was forced against the wheel to make it hard to turn would wear down and the prison officers would enter the cell to tighten it.

Whereas some men would run away to the Foreign Legion to recover from a disastrous love affair, others ran to the Prison Service to forget that they were members of the human race. They often escaped ordinary life one step ahead of an overwhelming sense of their own inadequacy. Surrounded in the prison by people they considered even more inadequate than themselves, they achieved a state of relative mental stability. The ones who join for the safe navy-blue security of the job soon develop a deep sense of superiority over the prisoners. How could you kick a man in the balls or spit in his food if you respected him? You would think that under these circumstances, a strong governor who controlled his prison and his screws would be a good thing for prisoners. Lawton's father was a very strong governor who took an intimate interest in the running of Wandsworth, which was the flagship of the prison service – but he was no figurehead. He enjoyed his work and probably saw himself as the public's agent, making sure we all got our just reward for crime which he was going to ensure did not pay. He was hated so thoroughly by the inmates that one of them, so the story goes, hanged Lawton's dog from a tree on the common just to teach him a lesson.

Frank Fraser was one of the defendants in the 'Torture Gang' showtrial. He had a deep-rooted hatred of the judge's father, having spent some time himself in Wandsworth. A couple of years before the trial, Frank and I found ourselves on Victoria station standing next to a man who was a dead ringer for the judge, Justice Lawton. Frank and I had just seen a show in the West End, had a few drinks and I was seeing him off onto the Brighton train before going home myself. We were enthusiastic about a new venture and laughing as we stood on the platform. Suddenly his expression changed from laughter to intense uncontrolled rage. He stepped closer and said through his teeth, 'That bastard behind me is Lawton's son.'

I did not need to be told who Lawton was. Frank is one of the most polite, mild-mannered men I've ever met, but he has a bad temper on him sometimes. I tried to calm him down even though I could see the man's resemblance to the governor.

'Are you sure, Frank . . . he just looks like him, that's all.'

'It's him. It's that bastard. I am sure it is.'

Then, taking a deep breath in order to try and control himself, Frank turned to the man and spoke slowly and deliberately, choosing his words carefully.

'Judge Frederick Lawton, your father is one of the worst men God ever put breath into. He has destroyed more men and driven more people to suicide than any other governor before or since.'

Frank got a short reply. 'Who do you think you are to talk to me like this? . . . Go on . . . get off with you.' As he spoke he took a step back, his voice filled with distaste and arrogance. He waved his hand as he spoke as if he were trying to shake off a smelly dog that was just about to piss on his leg.

Frank made a dive for this snotty gent, but luckily I was a split second quicker than he was and had my arms around him vice-like. The last thing we needed was G.B.H. on a judge. I managed to control Frank with the help of his wife as the very irate travelling snot-rag cursed his way across the platform away from the likes of us.

Now we found ourselves in front of Justice Lawton. Frank thought it was a little unfair that he should be judged by a man he believed he had personally abused a couple of years before. We managed to communicate on the subject. Frank felt the case might go better for him if he was tried separately and so we put the proposal to our briefs. They were shocked at the very idea of challenging Lawton in court. He was a powerful figure in the tight-arsed little world of the Bench. Our briefs were career boys with both feet firmly on the ladder, but we insisted that they make the challenge. During a quiet moment in the cross-examination of Taggart, Frank's brief stood up, very embarrassed, and stumbling over his words. He stood apologizing with a look on his face that plainly said, 'Look, Your Honour, don't blame me, I have to do this, I'm sure it's all nonsense.' Then he coughed and blushed and spoke.

'My Lord, I have received instructions that in the latter part of 1964 or the beginning of 1965, my client spoke to your Lordship at Victoria railway station. I do not know whether your Lordship will desire me to recall the details of the discussion.'

Lawton looked a bit puzzled. 'You certainly may because I have no recollection of ever seeing your client before in my life.'

71

Then Frank's brief gave him the story of the meeting at Victoria. He obviously did not believe it himself and did his best to transmit his doubts and show his loyalty towards the judge.

Now Lawton was interested. He immediately replied, stern Head Boy to Junior Prefect: 'There is not a word of truth in this, not a word, and I want to say that at the earliest possible opportunity. I would undoubtedly have remembered such an event and I have no recollection whatsoever of anything of that kind happening.'

The atmosphere could have been sliced as the court continued its business. Back to Taggart and 'Once upon a time, there was a Big Bad Torture Gang Boss.' After an hour or so a break came in the proceedings as Lawton returned to the former subject. I had watched him and noticed how distracted and concerned he was during that hour. He spoke to Frank's barrister with unfailing authority.

'There is a matter which I want to place on record with regard to your application. You did not do me the courtesy of giving me any warning of the application you were going to make.'

He continued to slap the pink boiled wrist of Frank's squirming brief and told us all that after a lot of thought he had something of a recollection to share with us.

'During the last hour or so which has transpired since you spoke to me, I have been running through my mind the occasions in my life when strangers have spoken to me and I can just, but only just, recollect one occasion on a London station when somebody spoke to me and was abusive. I have no recollection of any mention of my father. I feel that if there had been, I should have remembered it. I have no recollection of who was abusive. I thought that the man was drunk anyway. I am certain it was not in 1964 and I am certain that I have no recollection whatsoever that it was your client, none whatsoever, and I am quite certain that if it had been your client I would have remembered. In the circumstances there would be no grounds at all for my not going on with this trial.'

So that was it! There had been rumours that Lawton had personally asked for this case. Well, he got it, and now he had us by the balls. They all had a grip of our balls and were enjoying the sensation. Berman who had entered the scene to back up Taggart's evidence was somehow more depressing than the rest of them. He was one of us, though you would never think so to listen to his testimony. He was a friend and colleague who benefited from his association with us. And he was actually in the dock, arrested and charged with us. But now he sat in the witness box, a respectable businessman who could not believe his innocent brown eyes when he walked into a room where a man stood or sat in a cocoon of ropes wiping up his own spilt blood with either his underpants or his vest . . . or, or, or. They really should have got their stories straight. As I listened to Alfred Abraham Berman sell us right down the river, I felt great disappointment for such a weak soul. The police had bought that whingeing soul despite his inaccurate recall, his inability to remember his lines properly. Old Alfie Berman sold his soul for a slightly better prison during the trial, the dropping of all charges on this case and of a G.B.H. on another. Nobody in that court could have imagined that Alfred Berman, businessman and pillar of the community, even possibly a Freemason, could have kicked the shit out of a man who was knocking off his wife and beaten the poor Casanova to a pulp. Now even that G.B.H. had been dropped. They dropped the charges and he dropped us in it. Right in it. He turned Queen's Evidence which is posh language for 'grass'. The court sat spellbound and open-mouthed, tears welling up as they heard of how this noble man tried to stop us beating up poor Taggart.

Alfred Berman, or Alfie as he was known to the erstwhile pals he was now betraying, probably thought that he would get out and from now on, go straight. No more dodgy deals, no more creative little projects ducking and diving the Inland. He had had a little frightener and that was enough. From now on he would be content with the reduced income of an honest life. Or so he thought. Cobblers! Within a few weeks he would be at it again, new resolutions all forgotten.

A lifetime of pursuing large rewards for small investment and effort could not be discarded so easily. But I could understand the temptation just to sit by the fire with the telly and watch the world go by without you, without the constant fear of being reprimanded sharply by a society that punishes naughty boys and girls if they try to enjoy themselves too much. I understood the temptation of safety, security and going straight. I'd even tried it once myself.

When I had walked out of the gates of the remand home at sixteen I had every intention of going straight . . . straight into building a scrap business with my own yard. It would mean stealing lead and keeping one step ahead of the law, but when I got my own yard I could afford to keep the local coppers sweet. But when I got home I realized that I had responsibilities. Things had changed a bit and even settled down in my absence. Eddie was still Jack the Lad, especially with the girls, dressed in immaculate Teddy Boy costumes and hanging around the dance halls. I envied his apparent ease in chatting up the girls. He was smooth and charming and had a big dose of that powerful aphrodisiac – confidence. He had a line for every occasion; the girls didn't stand a chance. Whatever villainy he had in him from his father and influential elder brother, he channelled into boxing. I envied him even more for this because at that time I was a better boxer than him but I did not give any time to developing the skills. Our younger brother, Alan, was ten and at school. He was nobody's fool, streetwise and nimble, but he seemed to be avoiding the apprenticeship I had come near to completing. He kept his nose clean which made our mother happy.

So, then, the prodigal son came home from a far distant land, namely the Lincolnshire reform school. They were all very glad to see me and they certainly did kill the fatted calf, so I looked around at this harmony and thought, I should at least *try* not to be prodigal all my life. My grandparents were old but happy, my mother fairly content with the present lack of drama in her life. To her, excitement inevitably meant somebody she loved being dragged off by the police. So I thought I would have a serious go at leading a normal life and stay on the proper side of the law. Maybe I would even grow to like it . . .

We all knew that factories and their like were out of the question. Wandering around with ten boxes of oranges on my head at Covent Garden might have looked picturesque to American tourists, but for thirty bob a week they could stuff it! In the end my mum came up with a great scheme. She made delicious ice-cream which she sold in my grandparents' shop. It was clearly very popular, with people travelling from far and wide to buy it. Our plan was that I would take the mountain to Mohammed and sell mum's ice-cream in parks and suchlike from a bike. It was 1950 and a good summer. The ice-cream sold well. I did give it a bit of help especially in the parks where I would lure kids over to the bike and give them a free taste on a wafer. They could not resist the free sample. I would then suggest to them that all they had to do for a generous helping was ask their parents. I got a few disgruntled parents who were unable to resist the persistence of their whining kids. A few got a slap for this persistence but in the end I sold a lot of ice-cream. I sold *Sporting Life*, and toffee-apples and worked from dawn till dusk, especially at the weekends. I paid my mum for the cost of making the ice-cream and made a small fortune for myself. It was very lucrative but hardly a career for a bright young lad so I kept my end up on the scrap front.

Now that I was older, I could sell direct to the yards and cut out the middlemen, the Fagins. I got to know a lot of the dealers and realized that the average level of intelligence of scrap merchants was not what it seemed to be at first. Under that front of streetwise, seat-of-their-pants expertise there lurked a chasm of ignorance about the value of the metals they dealt in. Sometimes I would buy from one dealer and sell to another less than a mile away. Usually I would find the scrap myself or buy it from local lads knowing where I could get a good price. There was so much of it around and so much money to be made in wheeling and dealing that I sometimes cursed my age which limited my enterprise. I was always excited about the prospect of making money out of what was considered rubbish. In all those post-war bombsites and rebuilding programmes there was a fortune to be made.

I needed a yard of my own and that long hot summer while other teenagers did apprenticeships and were happy to go out on a Saturday night with a few shillings, I sold ice-cream and saved every penny. While they chatted up local girls, I tore the lead off roofs. By the time winter arrived and there was nobody left to buy cornets on Clapham Common, I had saved enough to buy an old furniture van and a second-hand driving licence. I still had a bit of a problem with my age so I approached my Uncle Jim who ducked and dived around but was making a respectable enough living buying used sacks from farmers in the countryside surrounding London. He worked from an old cart pulled along by an even older horse and so each trip took him weeks. I approached him as the new post-war face of capitalism and enterprise. I suggested that we use my truck, work together and spread the collection further afield. We formed a handshake partnership and set out on the road.

When we arrived at each farm and Jim spent half an hour sharing a moan with the farmer about the state of the country, I would start gathering up the sacks from barns and outhouses. I quickly realized that the farmers did not have a clue how many sacks they actually had and was horrified to learn that Uncle Jim had been telling the farmers exactly how many sacks he was taking. This was not because he was a fundamentally honest man, far from it. He was just scared of getting caught and he also lacked the basic skill of being able to distinguish between the odd mean old farmer who counted the squares of toilet paper in the bog and the rest of them, who were too busy with cows and chickens to give a damn about how many sacks they had sitting rotting in the barn. We did well, and I enjoyed our country trips. On top of these outings I was also making a mint out of scrap and old fireplaces. People had no idea that their old fireplace could be worth a fortune. They were just happy to get rid of them and I was more than happy to take them away. All in all it was a prosperous period, almost legal and it used up all the energy I had. Like the ice-cream selling, I saw it as an interim measure before I really got going. It killed time until I was old enough to really go into business. I saved every penny I could and even managed to get myself a legal bank account and cheque book. I was fascinated by the magic of being able to write on a piece of paper and sign it – and hey presto! I had generated my own currency. Of course I realized that the value of the currency was limited by the amount of money in the bank. I also realized that if a country wrote out too many cheques, for more than the value of the money, then you got inflation. If I did the same I was in big trouble. But if people believed that you had more money than you really did then it was days before they found out that you didn't . . . All you had to do was to stop them being suspicious and there was a lot you could do meanwhile in those few days. I got a chance to put the theory to the test a few months after I started collecting used sacks.

We were returning home one day from one of our trips with a truckload of smelly empty sacks when I noticed a massive aircraft hangar in the middle of a deserted airfield. In spite of Uncle Jim's objections I managed to take off the lock on the gate and drove in. I thought there might be some good scrap iron lying around somewhere, but the place was empty.

I picked the lock to a small door at the edge of the hangar and gasped as I opened it. There was no light, but I could see enough from the daylight that shone through the windows and cracks in the ceiling. In the biggest building I had ever seen in my life was a scrap merchant's dream. Rusting away and full of cobwebs was an Aladdin's Cave full of broken-down warplanes and machinery. Nobody had been here for years. I could hardly contain myself as I ran around and fell over rotting metal and aircraft parts. I knew that at the end of the war the government had a lot to sort out. There was no further need for all the aircraft, tanks and trucks but it had not dawned on me until then that they might have them stored somewhere. Some bureaucrat in Whitehall was obviously responsible for this, and like somebody with an old fireplace, he probably just wanted to get rid of it. At least that is what I hoped as I ran out to tell my Uncle Jim about it. He had one look and was immediately defeated by the size of the operation. If he had not been family, I would have kicked his lazy arse in frustration at his lack of ambition. So often when you are young and full of ideas, older people seem to take pleasure in hitting you in the face with a bit of reality. They put up problems to douse the fire of your inspired ideas in order to excuse their own lack of balls. Uncle Jim pontificated that the War Ministry would not sell it to the likes of us, and even if they did we couldn't afford it, and if by some miracle we could, we couldn't store it or sell it. He was happy to spend his time searching barns for old sacks among the chicken shit. I was not. I wanted to get on with things, and this was a big break. At least I was going to give it a try.

When we got home I borrowed Jim's phone and started a bit of research. After dealing with a hundred bureaucrats at the Ministry pretending I was an aircraft enthusiast, I found out that they had already sold the contents of the hangar as a job lot to a large London company that they usually dealt with. Some of it was to be sold abroad as second-hand parts, and the rest to be sold off as scrap. When I put the phone down I had to put up with a smug Uncle Jim saying hadn't he told me so, but I was not going to be put off that easily. I got the phone number of the company and only then paused to think. What the hell did I know about aircraft parts? I thought at least I could buy the scrap from them. What I knew for sure was that they would not have bought it all unless there was a market for it somewhere. I decided to live by my own rules and bite off more than I could chew – then chew it. I told Uncle Jim that I intended to buy the whole hangarful of parts and then sell it. He laughed until he realized that I was serious. I pretended to be confident and calm but inside I was full of doubts. I had worries about it all backfiring but I realized that it was time to make a move.

With a lot of persuasion Uncle Jim eventually agreed to front it all for me and take part, providing he was kept out of the deal as much as possible. He contacted the company who owned the aircraft junk and as I suspected they wanted to sell it in parts. But underneath their sales patter I could detect they were keen to get rid of it all to one buyer who would then transport it all. They would have made a fortune for doing nothing. Jim asked if we could inspect it and the very next day we were at the hangar. Jim was in his best suit looking like he was on his way to a wedding and I was in my working gear looking like his young apprentice. We were taken round by a bored office worker who had no idea of the value of the scrap but was very informative on the usable aircraft parts. Jim, using my name, asked this Mr Dunn how much he wanted. Mr Dunn gave the expected, 'Well, it's worth a lot more but frankly we have so much war surplus it might be convenient to sell it as a job lot and have done with it.' I could have mimed his next words. 'Mind you, there are some very valuable aircraft parts in amongst this lot. I couldn't let it go for under 6000 guineas.'

Arseholes, I thought, and whispered '5000 pounds' to my poor dumbstruck uncle who was visibly sweating. It was a fortune in those days. After all my slogging and saving and ice-cream selling I had only amassed about £500. He offered Mr Dunn £5000 as an absolute final offer and the haggling started. Uncle Jim, bless his sweaty cotton socks, stuck to his offer and Mr Dunn, the swindler, who had probably paid less than £2000, reluctantly accepted the offer. Uncle Jim promised to send the cheque round that afternoon. Later that day, I delivered the cheque drawn from my account for £5000 and held my breath while they opened the envelope. I returned with the keys.

Of course, the cheque was worth much less, but I gambled on a few days before anybody found out. I could not afford an Aladdin's Cave, but I could afford a fleet of eleven trucks, cash paid, to moonlighting drivers who then loaded all the junk up by moonlight and stored it in a decrepit warehouse in Rotherhithe during the early hours. What an adventure! I loved it. As I helped load the trucks I was thrilled with the idea that I was seventeen and employing all these truck drivers and renting a warehouse. As the dust settled around bits of Spitfires or whatever they were, I put phase two of my plan into action. Even after a few whiskies, Uncle Jim refused to phone the company, so I did it myself. I told him that due to unforeseen circumstances our company had gone into liquidation. Athough he was on the other end of a phone I could tell that Mr Dunn was a deep shade of purple. He screamed at me. It was not his money, he was just an employee and what a big mistake he had made. He did not actually say that but it was obvious. What he did say was that he would call the police, the fraud squad and everything but a plague of locusts. I let him get it out of his system and then apologized for the inconvenience that the bankruptcy of our company had caused him, but I was sure that when Mr Richardson returned from his trip abroad he would do whatever he could to repay the debt at least in part. If Mr Dunn could only wait a few weeks until the yard had a chance to sell some of the gear then I was sure that everything would work out. If he told the police then everybody would be in trouble (including him). Like a drowning man he started clutching at the straw of hope I offered. I suggested that with his obvious expertise relating to aircraft parts he might like to help sell it in Mr Richardson's absence. He blew up again. But in the next three weeks we sold all the parts and the scrap between us. It was not a happy partnership, but mutually beneficial. Mr Dunn's employers were never to know and I ended up with £9500 of which £4500 was clear profit. Uncle Jim thought he should get a share of the rewards for his part in it all. After a big argument I gave him a cheque for £500.

I had four thousand pounds! I was a very rich man and I was on my way. On my way to hundreds of deals, to lunches in the Savoy, to international travel and in the end to the Old Bailey. I had learned that you could probably make more money with fraud than getting your hands dirty picking up scrap. It was a long way from pennies for ice-cream. I had not learned at that stage that even more money could be made in perfectly legal forms of fraud. But then I would not have had the stomach to defraud the coffee growers of Brazil or the tin miners of Bolivia through the stock exchange.

In all crime, including fraud, there are those you do it to and those you do not. You do not do it to children or old people or family or friends, but businessmen or companies who do not personally suffer are fair game. In the subculture of fraud I had stuck my toe into, it did not occur to me that somebody from my own group would try to defraud me. Some years and many projects later I got involved with a turd that floated down the Thames to my part of London. Jack Duval was known as the Prince of Fraud who had impressed me so much when I first met him. He had made a fortune from a massive import of Italian ladies' stockings which he had sold at a vast profit. He had travel companies which brought thousands of illegal immigrants to Wolverhampton without ever paying their fares to the airlines. He had his own bank and a flamboyant lifestyle. And the bastard swindled me! I could hardly believe it. I became obsessed with finding him to get my money back and teach him a lesson. The wild moron had swindled the American Mafia, tried to swindle the Krays, and had really messed up my operations. He had police and villains from all over Europe and America after him – but I wanted him personally. I questioned anybody who had any connection with him and smacked a few mouths on the way. I 'interviewed', as the police would say, a man called Lucien Harris who was a partner of Duval. He had an accent and manner to go with his shop-window-dummy appearance and his fancy name. Lucien Harris stood in the witness box at the Old Bailey and had everybody hanging on his next words. If Duval was the Prince of Fraud, Lucien was his favourite courtier and he had learned much from his fat master. He could charm the silk knickers off any public schoolboy and the wig off a judge. As soon as he spoke I knew that I was finished. The Tales of Taggart were nothing compared with the flowing fairy story woven by this eloquent and charming gent. He would turn the clumsy account of the police into an elegant horror story. Their clichés and monosyllabic nonsense would be transformed by Harris into a dreadful epic poem of his life in Hell and his meeting with Satan – me. He was going to be their star and I dreaded the story that was going to emerge from his silken tongue. The pretentious bastard spoke their language better than they did and they loved it. Like any good storyteller he welded fiction neatly into actual events. From the moment he started to give evidence the courtroom could sense that this was a sinister tale full of macabre delights. The press had whetted everybody's appetite with hints that today was the day that the secret of the black box would be revealed. He started off with a gentle warm-up giving the history of the event. He told of a true event when we had arranged to meet. I knew that at some stage he would launch into nonsense but for now he was getting everybody comfortable before he really began. He told of a time when he came round to my scrapyard, Peckford Scrap Metal Works, to pick up some money I owed him. I was not there so he waited with his secretary Miss Henman. The prompt this time was Mr Cussen. He kept Lucien to the script.

'When you got to Peckfords, what happened? Did you leave the car?'

'Yes, I parked the car opposite the front entrance of the offices. I went in with Miss Henman, into the office on the right of the door and asked for Charlie.'

'In this place where you made the enquiry for Charles were there any persons?'

It was bloody strange having Lucien who was digging my grave calling me 'Charlie', and Cussen who was holding out the spade calling me 'Charles'. Lucien continued with musical clarity.

'I would think about eight or nine men.'

'Did you know them?'

'I only knew one of them, a Mr Blore.'

'When you asked for Charles Richardson, was he available?'

'No, he was evidently out somewhere.'

'How long did you wait altogether, would you say?'

'For upwards of two hours.'

'And while you were waiting with Miss Henman did any-thing happen?'

'Yes. There were several phone calls after which it was repeated that Mr Richardson was on his way and messages were relayed that he wouldn't be long.'

What on earth did this have to do with any of the crimes I was supposed to have committed? I knew that this trivial detail was only the calm before the storm to generate a sense of anticipation and suspense.

'Did anyone come in in due course?'

'Well, people had been drifting off. I suppose about at 5.30 Johnny Bradbury came in, whom I knew.'

'And what happened next?'

'Johnny said to me that Charlie was waiting in an office with some money for me and that I was to go with Johnny to meet him.'

Like a lamb to the slaughter, was the shared sentiment of a silent court that was starting to dribble with desire for the horror to come as Harris entered the lion's den, an innocent. A soft-spoken handsome English gentleman with a baby face and the eyes of a boy. If he went to prison his arse ran the risk of being frequently abused by the amorous approaches of lusty long-timers blinded by frustration who could not give a damn that Harris did not share their sexual leanings. But he was not going to go to prison, he was sending me there instead. Mr Cussen let the anticipation settle in the murky stagnant waters of the jurors' minds. He coughed and continued.

'And did you get ready to go?'

'I rose to go . . . yes.'

'What did Miss Henman do?'

'She rose to come with me, but Bradbury said, "You wait here, we shan't be long." So she sat down.'

'And what did you and Bradbury do?'

'We went out to his car and got into it and drove away.'

'Who drove?'

'Mr Bradbury drove.'

Of course Mr bloody Bradbury drove, it was Mr Bradbury's car! I wanted to jump up and shout, 'Get on with it, for God's sake, tell your wicked lies and piss off.' Cussen was like a cat playing with a captured mouse, prolonging the agony.

Did they really think that I was so stupid that I would not recognize this tactic? The crowded salivating courtroom was loving the foreplay. Their bodily fluids were starting to flow in anticipation of a huge and delicious orgasm. With no concern for the cost of lengthy court proceedings, Mr Cussen the Cat continued slowly to draw out the pain of his captive mouse. Me! The bastard.

'Where did he drive you to?'

'He drove around the corner to premises in Addington Square.'

'Did you learn whose premises these were?'

'I gathered that they belonged to a company connected in some way with Mr Richardson because they were used as a warehouse on the ground floor.'

'You entered by the ground floor?'

No, he hopped through a window on the first floor like a fucking kangaroo, what do you think?

'And where did you go next?'

'I went upstairs; why I can't remember. Anyway, up to the first floor with Mr Bradbury.'

'To the first floor?'

'Yes.'

For God's sake, get on with it! But the man with the powdered wig was not to be hurried. He wanted a hungry audience before the trumpets heralded the entrance of the feast.

'And what happened there?'

'To my surprise, Mr Richardson, Charles Richardson himself suddenly appeared.'

Enter the bleeding dragon!

'Did he say anything to you?'

'Yes, he greeted me and said, "Oh, let's go into this office where we can have a quiet talk . . ."'

'And then?'

'I went into the office with him, at the end of a passage, and he asked me where Jack Duval was.'

'And what did you say, in answer to his question?'

'I told him that I did not know.'

'And then?'

'He asked me again where Jack Duval was and I could only repeat that I didn't know . . . this went on for a while and then he said something to the effect of, I like you Lucien and I don't want to hurt you, or something like that.'

Some such phrase from an American gangster film. How did I get mixed up with people like this? Fraud was a good little earner for me especially in the early days. I had not realized that there are people who are total frauds, who will con everybody including their so-called friends and even their family. They have no limits, and their brains get pickled in the lies they tell every day to everybody. The line between truth and falsehood erodes with time so that they end up living for the bubble of today in the fiction of yesterday and leave tomorrow to take care of itself. Jack Duval could not have recognized either the truth or a friend in the deep fog of shit he had immersed himself in. The nearest he had to a friend was a fellow traveller in the mists of his invention, Lucien Babyface Harris, who now held the court under his magic spell. Even Justice Lawton, who had heard a few stories in his time, was in the cast of Lucien's spellbound audience. I understood long ago that anybody can be conned if you play your cards in the proper order. The key is to tell them exactly what they want to believe. Old Mr Dunn wanted to believe that he had swung a neat little deal on the aircraft parts. He could transfer the related correspondence from his thick pending tray into a dusty file on the shelf. He ended up sweating on the phone for weeks helping me sell the parts to punters when he had already sold them to me. He hated me for it and wanted a little taste of revenge. A month after the parts were sold there came a knock on the door of our home in Camberwell. My mother answered it and came into the sitting room with a world-weary sigh to tell me that two men wanted to see me.

They were not what I expected. They were policemen, I could tell that by their smell, but they wore bowler hats and carried briefcases. On closer inspection the smart suits did not fit very well over the usual overfed clumsy police bodies.

They tried to look like civil servants but ended up looking like building labourers in fancy dress. They showed me their warrant cards.

'Are you Mr Charles Richardson?'

'Yes – who wants to know?'

'We have received a complaint regarding recent transactions you have made relating to used aircraft parts. We must warn you that from this moment anything you say will be written down and may be used in evidence against you.'

I was worried. On the face of it, I could not think of anything I had done that was blatantly illegal, but I knew by now that they did not let that stop them if they wanted to get you. My defiance was therefore a bit of a front.

'Are you charging me? What are you charging me with?' The bigger of the two men was confident and spoke my name with a sneer. I was half his size and still a boy.

'Mr Richardson, I hope you will co-operate with our enquiries. We will return tomorrow with a warrant to search these premises. You would be helping us if you could make available to us all the documentation regarding the sale of aircraft parts made recently.'

With that, the big fat bastard smiled and turned to go. They walked down the street chatting and laughing. I panicked. As soon as they were out of sight, I tore round to my Uncle Jim. I was sure that he would know what to do. These were no ordinary PC Plods I could run rings around. I suspected these two had been selected for the Fraud Squad because they could do joined-up writing. I was sure that with his lifetime's experience of ducking and diving, Uncle Jim would have a solution.

I found him in his sitting-room eating his tea with his wife. She was not too pleased to see me and after the rows we had had over the split on the parts earnings he was none too happy either. I secretly wished at that moment that I had been a bit more generous with his split, but I had resented giving him a large hand-out when all he had done was front it at the beginning. When his silent, disapproving wife went into the kitchen I told him what had happened, and finished with a plea that was not supposed to sound as desperate as it did.

'. . . so that's it, they say they'll be back in the morning and want to see the papers. What do I do? I haven't done nothing wrong, have I, so what can they get me for?'

His eyes had widened when I mentioned the bowler hats and the briefcases, and before he spoke I knew that he was more frightened than I was. I sort of suspected his answer.

'What do you do? WHAT DO YOU DO? I'll tell you what you bloody well do, son, you keep me out of it, that's what you bloody well do. I warned you it was a dangerous caper. But did you listen? I should have known better than to get mixed up with a bloody teddy boy who thinks he's a bloody big-shot businessman.'

'You helped me, you're involved!'

'I will deny everything, Charlie boy. You name it, I didn't do it. It was all in your name, nothing to do with me.'

'But I didn't do anything illegal, Uncle Jim – they got their money . . .'

'No use telling *them* that, Charlie boy. You're in the shit, mate. Just make sure that you don't drop me in it as well. I'll deny everything. You'd best tell them anything they want to know and hope that they don't hit you too hard. You can't mess with this type of copper. They're right evil bastards.'

He paused, while I sat there hating him.

'I don't know, Charlie . . . your poor bleedin' mother. I don't know . . .'

That was enough of *that*. I ran out and walked home. I lay in bed, desperately trying to think of a way out of this mess. I was filled with an awful dread of what was going to happen next.

At nine o'clock sharp the two men arrived. Their knock on the door was sharp, too. My mother jumped out of her seat in the kitchen, nervous and frightened. I was nothing but trouble to her, yet she seemed to like having me around. Sometimes even I wondered how she could stick by me through all the heartache, which wasn't helped by the gossip of our neighbours who were even now at the windows peeking from the curtains. I suppose if they did not have the Richardsons to talk about, they might have had to talk about something else and they had little else *to* talk about. Their lives were so repetitive and monotonous and yet at that moment I envied them.

In came Bert and Norman. They introduced themselves by their first names, which meant that they really were looking for trouble. As they put down their briefcases my mother offered them tea which they accepted cheerfully. They were shown through to the living room where they asked to see the papers relating to the sale of aircraft parts. They took out some papers from their briefcases, including an inventory of the goods taken from the hangar, obviously supplied by Mr Dunn. The old bastard had done for me. Visions again of the polished floor and red carbolic blocks of soap in borstal turned my stomach. I had to try to think of a way out of this. They could feel me squirm and were loving every minute of it. Of course I didn't have a piece of paper for every transaction. Some of the scrap I had sold for cash and a wink and a nod to friends who owned scrapyards. They looked at each grubby piece of paper I had kept as if it were vital evidence for the prosecution. After a while, Bert looked up and spoke with cruel, false sympathy.

'It doesn't look good, son. What's a boy like you getting mixed up in big business for at your bloody age? You should be out doing an apprenticeship, and going to dance halls with your mates instead of defrauding honest, hard-working men in respectable companies. No, it looks very grim to me . . . what do you think, Norman?'

Norman was a miserable sod. He did not even try to be nice.

'Very grim, I should say. It's worth eighteen months, maybe even two years, and that's if the judge likes you. Got some previous, have you?'

I hated the soft-bellied turd with foul breath and rotting teeth. My fear turned to defiance.

'I ain't done nothing wrong. I bought some goods legally and sold them legally. So I haven't got all the paperwork. People don't go to jail for losing bits of bloody paper.'

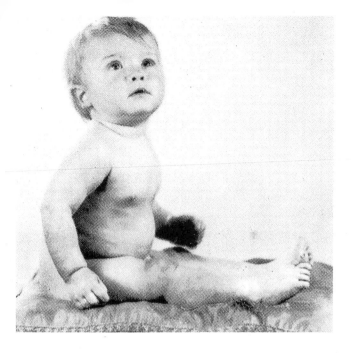

Above: On my first birthday.
Below: With my brothers Alan (left) and Eddie (right). Aged five, nine and eleven, the Richardson gang was already running amok in the bombsites around our home in south-east London.

Right: I always liked to be well turned out. With my mum in 1950.
Below: My grandparents, brothers and other members of our family outside our shop.

Top: Margaret in the family way, in more ways than one, at our wedding on 1st January, 1955.
Middle: The hub of my scrap metal empire at 50 New Church Road, Peckham.
Bottom: The King of the Teds was finally conquered. Eddie and Maureen's marriage.

Opposite page. Top: In my early twenties I could be considered the perfect son-in-law –
clean-cut, well-dressed and with good business prospects.
Middle: On holiday in Dymchurch. My father sits behind me.
Bottom: I wasn't a conventional father, but I was a good one.
This page. Above: A gang boss desperado on a day trip.
Below: On the run in Canada in 1960. It's amazing where dealing with hot bacon can
get you.

osite page. Top: Niagara.

dle and bottom right: Lucien Harris and Brian Mottram pop round to the off-licence the day after ris claimed I stuck a knife through his foot. Photo courtesy of HM Customs who were stigating the pair on fraud charges at the time.

om left: The first time I visited Dartmoor was as a tourist in 1963.

page. Above: Fat Jack Duval (right) and friends have a night out.

w: Major L. H. Nicholson (right), who helped me set up my South African business, had ential friends. Pictured here with Harold Macmillan and Lord Soames.

Above: A far cry from the Old Kent Road. In New Pretoria, 1964.
Below: I made good friends in South Africa where I was treated well and no-one cared about my accent.

Bert made clear his years of experience as a seasoned fraud investigator, with a deep sigh.

'Oh yes they do, son, they most certainly do.' Then he suddenly jumped up and walked over to my mother's display cabinet. His whole manner changed.

'That is an incredible set of medals – who do they belong to?'

I was happy for a break in his questioning. Anything to delay the awful moment.

'They're my dad's. He was in the merchant navy during the war, on fuel and explosives ships. He says he is the most decorated merchant seaman in Britain. It's probably true.'

It probably *was* true. My dad may have been a lifelong villain and local Casanova, but he had nerves of steel and had done his bit for old Blighty during the war years. It was probably the only time in his life that 'proper' behaviour offered the thrill and excitement he needed to feel the blood flowing in his veins. Bert was fascinated by my mother's display cabinet of odds and ends.

'Whose are these?' He pointed to some silver championship cups. I walked over to the cabinet and pointed each one out as I spoke.

'That one's mine, and that one, and the others are my brother Eddie's. We got them for boxing.' He really was interested. Maybe the facts and figures of fraud bored him.

'Very good, very good . . .' he stood up straight and looked at me. 'It's such a shame you had to end up like this.' Before I had a chance to answer, he was down at the level of the cabinet again. 'That is very beautiful, very beautiful.' It was a porcelain figure which belonged to my mum.

'My wife collects porcelain figures, costs me a bloody fortune. We end up eating bread and jam for our dinner because she's bought yet another bloody bit of porcelain. We've got dogs and cats and horses and loving couples and little boys having a pee. She's an obsessive collector. She says they increase in value, that they're an investment. I tell her they are only an investment if she sells them eventually and that always shuts her up . . . Yes, this one is very nice.'

At last I understood what was going on! I could be forgiven for being so slow as I was very young. I left the room and came back a minute later. Bert was still at the display cabinet, while bad-breath Norman was flattening out crumpled papers. I walked up to Bert and whispered, 'I would like to contribute to your wife's collection.' With that I held out my hand with a roll of notes totalling £150. My heart was racing and there might have been beads of sweat on my brow. Everybody knew local bobbies on the beat were on the take, but these were the smart-arsed wizards who investigated fraud and corruption. I had no idea how he would react. He looked at my hand and then with a cold, blank expression he looked right into my eyes. Norman had stopped shuffling papers and was watching intently. At last Bert spoke.

'That's very kind of you, son, I'm sure she will appreciate this little gesture very much . . . yes, she'll be very pleased.' With that he beamed and winked and took the money from me. I should bloody well hope she would be pleased – it must have been at least three months' wages. But Bert had not finished.

'Y'know, Norman's wife has very expensive tastes. Keeps talking about taking the kids on a nice holiday, but you know how it is – on our wages it'll probably be a weekend in Bournemouth.'

I may have been a bit naïve but I was not stupid. I had another bundle of the same amount in my pocket. I walked up to Norman, taking care not to get too near the danger zone of his deadly breath, and handed him the wad. 'I hope you can do better than a weekend, Norman.'

The miserable bastard smiled, showing a full set of rotting teeth. 'Thank you very much, Mr Richardson, greatly appreciated.'

Bert walked over from the cabinet and spoke to his fellow fraud investigator. 'You know, Norman, I don't think we have sufficient evidence to gain a conviction on this. Mr Richardson has given every co-operation in our enquiries and I can see no solid evidence of misconduct of any kind. I believe the transactions relating to the sale of the said aircraft parts were conducted in an unorthodox but certainly not illegal manner.'

Bad Breath gave us the benefit of his rotting dark hole with another smile and agreed. 'Quite right, Bert, quite right. We'd best stop wasting taxpayers' money and put in our reports.'

Evil bastards; who investigates the frauds of the fraud investigators, I thought. As they collected their hats and coats on their way out, I had another inspired thought. I asked them if they would do me a little favour. A look appeared on Bert's face as if to say, oh dear, just when we were getting on so well. He said that they were in a bit of a hurry but that they would do what they could to help a small businessman. I ignored the reference to physical stature and explained that I wanted to play a trick on somebody who had been very unhelpful to me recently. They laughed and entered into the spirit of it all, two ex-servicemen and a Teddy Boy up to a bit of mischief. We walked together for ten minutes acting out our script. When we got to my uncle's house, they gave me a minute to get through the backyard and crouch underneath the kitchen window. They knocked loudly on the door and I heard a nasty exchange between them. My fellow conspirators walked Uncle Jim through to the kitchen so I could hear the conversation. I sneaked slowly up to see through the window. Poor old Uncle Jim was in a right state. He was completely out of his depth. I could hear Bert.

'Are you trying to tell me that your teenage nephew has led you astray? A man of your age? A man of the world . . . I don't think a judge and jury are going to believe that a man like you would be so influenced by such a polite, well-mannered and by all accounts honest young man as Charlie Richardson.'

Uncle Jim was completely flabbergasted. 'Honest? Charlie boy? You've been bloody had, mate! He's a little villain! He's got previous already – I bet he didn't tell you that, the little runt. I had bugger-all to do with this bloody aircraft caper.'

Bert held his ground and kept his face straight. 'Well, he told us that it was all your idea in the first place, that it was you who broke into the aircraft hangar and arranged the transportation of all the parts. I must say it is hard to believe that a boy, even one as resourceful as Charlie, could get hold of a fleet of trucks.'

'Resourceful? Resourceful – he's a little bleedin' villain! I had nothing to do with it. I know sod-all about this, and you've got nothing on me. He wrote out the cheque, he did it all – he's a clever little bastard, you know.'

Bert now took on a stern and authoritative approach. 'Well, I must say I don't know what the world is coming to when a grown man tries to pass the blame off onto a young lad . . . Right! Enough of this. It is my duty to inform you that anything you say may be taken down and used in evidence against you.'

Even though he had not been charged, Uncle Jim sat down at the kitchen table heavily. He slumped and put his hands over his face. It was a pathetic scene. I jumped up and knocked on the window. He was startled and turned to look. I beamed a huge smile, and shouted through the window, 'Be careful what you say, Uncle Jim, sounds like you're in a right spot of bother.'

Bert and Norman burst out laughing. They turned to leave. I was doubled up with tears in my eyes. Uncle Jim suddenly realized he had been the victim of a cruel prank. He went several colours before he settled on purple. As I tried to gasp some breath through my laughter, he ran out to the yard and grabbed a broom. I got a few whacks on the arse as I tried to run away. At the end of the alley, I met up with my accomplices who were re-living the moment and giggling. Bert dried his tears with a filthy handkerchief, and put his hand on my shoulder as we walked down the road. I thanked them for their help.

'Always glad to help the budding businessman,' said Bert. We parted and I sighed with relief. It was months before Uncle Jim spoke to me again though.

That was not the first time I had paid a policeman for my freedom, and it was certainly not the last. Not many years later I was accused, along with my brother and others in my 'gang', of running a protection racket. Even the term 'protection racket' and especially the word 'racket' are imports from

America. Britain wanted so much from America – chewing gum, hamburgers, T-shirts and refrigerators. We even wanted to borrow some of their rich underworld folklore. So just as the British created themselves a home-grown Mafia and stuck the label on us at the Old Bailey some years later, they also created the idea of various 'rackets' including 'protection rackets'. In fact the most lucrative, powerful and extensive protection racket ever to exist was administered by the Metropolitan Police. As I got older and became involved in more and more dealings, legal or otherwise, I made regular payments to the police. It was a sort of taxation on crime. They would turn a blind eye to schemes they knew were illegal for a weekly or monthly pay off. Sometimes I had to pay them for totally legal operations because they could easily find something to charge us with. We would co-operate with them for our mutual benefit. Sometimes we would pay people to be 'found' committing small crimes so that our friendly local protection racketeer in blue could have somebody to arrest and look like he had been busy. As your companies grow and your operations increase, you pay more money to more senior policemen. A very efficient and beneficial system except that they do not in the end honour their part of the bargain. If they feel you are getting out of hand, growing too quickly, they decide it's time you did some bird and so you find yourself being fitted up. Even with a charge against you there is often an opportunity to pay your way out of it. Sometimes, however, the career rewards gained from convicting you outweigh almost any financial reward you can offer and nothing can be done to stop them. You become much more than a sacrificial lamb to convince the tax-paying public that they are getting their money's worth. If the police get massive publicity on a case then everybody can sleep safe in their beds with the knowledge that they are well looked after. The British public desperately wanted a Mafia, but they also wanted an Elliot Ness to catch them and lock them up.

The 'Richardson Gang' stood passively in the Old Bailey courtroom listening to the evidence that created dragons for lots of aspiring little St Georges to slay. The main weapon they had, the lance to slay us, was in the shape of poncy Lucien Harris. To hell with boring old fraud; Lucien could and would deliver the goods – on ritualized torture and the Black Box.

CHAPTER FOUR
Further Education

I felt it was important not to show any fear from my position in the dock. Sometimes panic waves would pass through my body like a slow electric shock. My heart would pump and I would feel drops of sweat run cold in my armpits and down my back as the full depth of the trouble I was in revealed itself in moments of weakness. I would summon forth reserves of internal self-discipline to control my heartbeat. It was very important that I kept face with my friends beside me. Our collective morale was hingeing on our collective strength. One weak link in the chain and we would have been in a mess that the press and general public would have relished. Had we flinched, they would have been quick to crow that here, finally, was proof that a different path inevitably led to a hazardous and thankless end. The only safe life to lead was the straight and narrow route of a slow lingering death. We had to stay strong.

The others in the dock beside me were showing no signs of breaking. Tommy Clark had a fatalistic attitude to life and had always taken things as they came. My brother Eddie was sustained by his rage at the conspiracy against us. Frank Fraser stood as smart, handsome and dignified as ever. Nothing ever got to Frankie. He was a rock. Once when he was in prison, he was in solitary for months – not unusual for Frank. Every day a group of screws would deliver his food but just before the plate was handed to him a screw would spit in it. Frank would throw the plate at him. There would be a fight, Frank would get a terrible beating and the screws would leave him to nurse his bruises for another day. This went on for months. The only food he ate was delivered by a different shift. I asked him why he did not just accept the plate, say 'thank you, sir' and not eat the food or even eat round the part that had been gobbed on. Frank told me that in prison you have fuck-all but your self-respect, and if that goes you are nothing. Then when you come out you have nothing to help you adjust and get through life. He was defending the most important thing anybody has – and in prison, the only important thing. The screws and later the press dubbed him 'Mad Frankie Fraser' or just 'Mad Frankie' because of his behaviour in prison. The thousands of men he met in jail throughout the many years he spent inside had the greatest respect for him. I wondered who was mad, Frank, or a government who enjoyed employing perverted agents to do the job of spitting in somebody's food and then beating him while other men held him down.

The morning that shop-dummy Lucien Harris started to give his evidence, Frank had told me there was a rumour that not only was Lucien going to talk about a 'black box' but that the police were going to produce it. How? The black box didn't exist except in their teeming imaginations, so what were they up to? Mr Cussen turned theatrically to Lucien Pretty Boy Harris.

'And then?'

'Charles Richardson went out of the office and Johnny Bradbury and another man came in. I do not know who the other man was.'

'And after Bradbury and the other man had come in, what took place?'

'The same question was put to me over and over again and I kept protesting that I couldn't answer it.'

'The question being . . .?'

'"Where's Jack Duval? You'd better tell us, you know Charlie wants to know," and so on.'

'Did you make any replies to these repeated questions?'

'I made some sort of remark such as, "Really, you can turn me inside out but I still don't know where Jack Duval is."'

'What happened when you made those answers?'

'Mr Bradbury assured me that they probably would turn me inside out.'

The court collectively shuffled their arses to make sure that they were sitting comfortably for the slow build-up, the hors d'oeuvres, for the scene to follow. Personally, I was getting

fed up with theatrical poses but the audience seemed happy
with them. Cussen, after a dramatic pause, presented a profile
to Lucien.

'And then?'

'He came up to me, I was sitting in the chair in front of
the desk, and he punched me in the midriff somewhere.'

Here we go. The jury and public galleries started to salivate.
The press began to scribble as their gutter pricks started to firm
up. The judge, ever attentive, intervened to clarify details.
'How many punches, if more than one, did you get? Did you
get more than one?'

Lucien turned to the judge as if blowing his arse a kiss of
grovelling respect. A soft-spoken shop-dummy and a man in
a wig.

'Yes, I would think five or six punches, My Lord.'

My Lord. Your Worship. Your very honourable, venerable,
worshipful holiness. They sit in judgement on a world they
cannot possibly understand. Like umpires at a tennis match,
they tell the players if the ball is in or out but just occasionally
they like to get down and have a go themselves. I had met
one or two Honours, Worships and Lords in my time. None
of them had any good news for me.

After my adventure with aircraft parts and the opening of
friendly relations with the Fraud Squad, I wanted to build
up my own scrap business. I rented a yard in Peckford Place,
Brixton and we thrived. It was an activity full of excitement.
I loved the daily hundred and one deals made with people
bringing scrap. I enjoyed the banter and the manipulation that
was a vital part of making money. My mother was overjoyed
that I was more or less keeping out of trouble and she was
keen to encourage me in my business. She told me of a building
with a yard up for sale in Addington Square, just round the
corner from my grandparents in Camberwell. At the tender
age of just turned nineteen, I'd bought the freehold of the
premises. For cash! Peckford Scrap Metal was in business.
Eddie came to work for me full-time. He had been a porter
at Waterloo Station for a while, carrying cases and waiting

for a tip. After a while I persuaded my mother to leave the
tea-shop and come and do the books for me. It was a real
family affair. Everything was in order. I worked like mad –
we all did – and business thrived.

Eddie was a good worker in the scrapyard but he had other
interests in life. While I spent day and night developing the
business and expanding it Eddie spent days in the yard lifting
car engines with his bare hands, expanding his muscles. He
spent nights in clubs and dance halls sporting an immaculate
set of drapes and developing a reputation as a Ted. The
fiercest rows we had at the time were if I borrowed some
of his perfect Teddy Boy gear without asking. Blood would
spill on the bathroom lino in a battle between us because I
had used the last of his Brylcreem. It was a serious problem.
He could not go out with dry hair and he would refuse to
revert to the standby that low life Teds used, a dollop of
margarine.

Always perfectly turned out, extremely strong and a very
hard young man, Eddie became quite well-known. It was only
a matter of time before he would have to challenge Tony
Rolands, the King of the Teds, for the title. It was not that
Eddie was ambitious or was looking for a career as a full-time
Ted, he had other interests. But you could only get so far with
notoriety before you lost any choice and you had to take a go
at the title. To become King of the Teds you did not have a
fashion parade where your expensive drapes and perfect quiff
were judged by a committee of expert Teds. You had to kick
the shit out of whoever was King at the time. Everybody was
keen to see the battle between Eddie and Tony Rolands. These
fights were not arranged by promoters or even scheduled at
all. They just happened as local expectation became so strong
it could no longer be resisted. So at a summer dance in Myatts
Park in Camberwell on a beautiful evening as the band played
on the bandstand and couples jived, Eddie faced Tony Rolands
surrounded by a ring of silent Teds. They paced around a little
looking at each other as they ceremoniously removed their
expensive jackets and passed them to their seconds. Tony
tried to psyche Eddie out.

'You better take your trousers off as well, Richardson, cos you're going to shit in them in a minute.'

Eddie was always a plain talking man who did not go in for all that psychology. He looked at Tony, clenched his fists and without any malice whatsoever he said, 'C'mon, Tony, I've promised the next dance.'

Tony charged and the two of them became a confusion of fists and kicks as the crowd of Teds shouted support and the band played on. They broke apart briefly and stood facing each other gasping for breath. During the pause as they leaned forward and heaved, Eddie landed a punch on Tony's face just below his dishevelled quiff. It was a hard punch with all the power those engine-lifting muscles could muster. Tony stood dazed and Eddie landed another power drive on the nose. Tony staggered back with a puzzled look as if he was trying to concentrate and work something out in his dim brain. He collapsed to his knees and stared ahead trying to focus. It was a very tempting position for Eddie.

Everybody had gone quiet and then somebody shouted, 'Go on, Eddie, kick his fucking face in.'

Then they were all screaming for Eddie to finish him off, like the spectators at the Roman games. He looked around at them all for a second or two, took out his comb and sorted his quiff and said, 'Fuck it, he's beaten, I only have to beat him once, don't I?'

With that Tony's balance gave up and he fell forward flat on his face.

A spotty undersized Ted in a set of drapes he hoped to grow into ran forward, grabbed Eddie's right hand, thrust it in the air and shouted, 'Ladies and Gentlemen . . . Eddie Richardson . . . The King of the Teds . . . do we have any challengers?'

Eddie looked around, his friends cheered and the others avoided the challenge in his eyes. As we walked back to the dance I slapped his back and joked.

'You might be King of the Teds, big head, but you're still my little brother.'

He smiled and with a mouth that dribbled blood he spoke with brotherly affection.

'Fuck off, bastard.'

Eddie never had to defend his title, there were no challengers and anyway he was too busy helping me in the yard. Meanwhile I had to learn quickly how to run a business. Sometimes I was not too sure of the origin of some of the metal, but no scrap dealer could be in those days. The only problem I did have was with insects. I had several six foot bluebottles hanging around the yard gates all the time. It would annoy me if they were there because some of the suppliers were put off by them on their way into the yard. I would go and ask them what the fuck they were doing hanging around my yard when some poor old dear was probably being robbed around the corner. They would give me all sorts of shit about being in a very good vantage point to keep an eye on possible illegal goings-on. I told them to piss off, but I knew what they were after. I had got out of one fix by paying off the Fraud Squad but I was buggered if I was going to pay these uniformed plods when as far as I was concerned I was legitimate. Most other yards paid them and at five pounds a visit it was not extortionate even if it *was* extortion. But why should I? They showed me why a few months later, when I was arrested for handling five pounds' worth of stolen scaffolding. The bastards probably arranged it themselves. At the Magistrates Court it was a small offence, but I was more worried about something else. My fears came true. They noticed in their wisdom that I was nineteen, and wanted to know why I was not in khaki like other nineteen-year-olds. It was no use trying to tell them that I was on my way to becoming a successful businessman and a pillar of the community. They wanted to make a man of me. Conscription did not make a man of anybody, it just reduced everyone to a snivelling toad through a lengthy process of humiliation. If somebody tells you that you are scum and kicks you in the arse for two years, the chances are that you will eventually believe him and go back into society a 'man' who does what he's told and recognizes and respects his betters. Some men look back with fondness at their army days as 'character building' and are grateful for the discipline it imposed on them. But to me the army demolishes character and imposes its own discipline so that there is no self-discipline left. I can honestly say that were it not for the interruption that conscription made to my career development, I would have probably been so squeaky clean that the Freemasons would have put me in one of their funny aprons and a garter. The smart-arse magistrates noted that I had slipped through the conscription net so I was sent to Aldershot in a fresh intake of skinny teenagers to be trained to defend the realm.

Our introduction was a well-practised routine as we were lectured, kitted out and generally abused by bored N.C.O.s all day long. The corporal who was assigned to our intake had watched too many low quality American films. He strutted in front of us purposefully and gave us the usual crap about how he hated us and by God was he going to knock us into shape.

A spotty adolescent with dry dough skin and rotting teeth had latched onto me in a patronizing way. I had hardly spoken since I had arrived and he must have thought I needed looking after. It was clear straight from the start that this amiable moron would become the intake idiot, a receptacle for abuse from both instructors and fellow conscripts. During the first attempt to teach us some drill the corporal had already singled him out as a likely target. With noses almost touching he had screamed at the poor kid that he was a 'fucking abortion' and after a rehearsed pause he added, 'The best part of you ran down your mother's leg.' The boy's eyes widened in disbelief and shock at the crudeness and depth of the insult, but I was almost impressed by its wit – until I saw the vacant cavity behind the dull, dead eyes of the corporal. He had heard it years before when he was being trained himself and had simply passed it on and tried to take the credit. In the army, abuse is passed on from generation to generation of raw recruits like athlete's foot. The corporal had given up thinking for himself years ago. He was going through the normal introductory motions of making us frightened of him. I was terrified that he might stand very close and open his mouth and scream at me. Not that I was concerned with what insults he might sling at me but as he had shouted before I had caught a whiff of his breath. It was a mixture of last night's beer and vomit with this morning's breakfast sausages. Something had crawled into his mouth and died there a long time ago. A blast of that would have buckled my knees, already weak with the nausea this reminder of remand home was giving me.

In the early evening we tripped over each other as the corporal tried to scream us into marching. I had gone along with it all so far. I needed time to think up a plan a little. The night before had exhausted me as I lay with acid in my brain considering with bitterness the bad turn my luck had so sharply taken. When I had first walked into the camp I was overwhelmed by the bland, sweet smell of polish, the emptiness of the walls and the huts full of beds in rows. It was so much like any other prison or remand centre that I wanted to cry out with frustration at the totality of the conspiracy. It seemed a whole system had developed to destroy whatever hope or pleasure in life I could grab for myself.

Having gone more or less straight for so long and managed by my own wits to become a legit, successful businessman I had imagined I was immune. I was keeping my head above water and swimming like an Olympic champion but the bastards had grabbed me by the balls and dragged me under again. I have met some of the greatest conmen in the world, but none of them came anywhere near the massive con played on people by their own governments. It was a more sophisticated system than slavery because the slave-drivers had actually convinced the slaves that they were free men. They conned a whole society not only into being shat on, but also enjoying it.

Conscription was more than a national defence programme, it was a sledgehammer on the head to kill any spark of imagination or originality. It was a crash course on the British class system and your place in it. It had a clear message at the end which declared, 'Go forth and multiply, work hard, don't think or question anything and never forget to grovel at the first sign of authority and shed a tear when the Union Jack is raised.' I was not going to take part in their silly game. I wanted much more than they would allow me to have and I had seen through their conspiracy when I was a little boy. The system which everybody says you can't beat is almost total, almost omnipotent, but it has one skilfully concealed flaw. I had realized many years before a simple truth; authority has no power unless you give it recognition. That realization was more powerful than any pips on the shoulder of an officer, than the wig on the head of a judge, than the truncheon of a policeman or the vicious contempt of a screw. It was a basic mental exercise, like staring fearlessly at a growling dog until it crept away.

We were herded into a huge room in a brick building to join other intakes on rows of wooden benches. An old army Captain sat behind a field table with a Sergeant Major standing bolt upright to one side and slightly behind him like a guard dog. He had a folded drill stick coming out from under his arm like a hard-on. Names were called and new conscripts awkwardly crossed the polished space towards the desk to talk to the officer.

Two years of this! I had expected to be surrounded by young men as eager as myself to get on with life's adventures. Good movers as frustrated as I was by the call-up. It was such a disappointment to see a bunch of frightened boys, pretending to be men, weeping inside for the cosy home they had left the day before. In one day they had accepted it and begun to enjoy complaining about it. Two years! They had already settled down and were so glad to be told what to do every minute. After years of the security of childhood with their parents the absolute authority in their lives, they had tiptoed wide-eyed like Bambi into the uncertainties of adolescence. Now they were relieved to be back in the womb of absolute authority, to be suckled on the enormous tits of the khaki mother. They were glad to swap one parent for another.

Two years! But not for me! Where they had tiptoed I had galloped like a young horse in a field, trying desperately to learn everything and do as much as possible. Even the times I had spent inside were used to make contacts and invest in my future.

Two years! In the *last* two years I had moved from hiring an old horse and cart to collect rusty metal and old fireplaces from bombsites, to owning my own yard. Now I owned a couple of vans and had a few thousand quid in the bank. My mother and brother worked with me to build what was becoming a very successful family business. I was hated by the other dealers in the area, tolerated at a price by the local police and respected by a growing group of friends. I was nineteen and only just starting. Two years!

'Jesus fucking Ada, I don't fancy the chances of this lot defending the realm!'

It was the village idiot again, sitting next to me and repeating a stupid statement he had heard somewhere before. It was like complaining about the weather or the food. I was not expected to challenge it, just wink and say, 'I know what you mean, mate.' *I* didn't.

'What fucking realm . . . what is a realm, you fucking idiot?'

He was shocked. I had hardly spoken before, and now he had to defend himself.

'You know, the country . . . defend the country from the enemy . . . from attack. This lot couldn't punch their way out of a paper bag.'

I wasn't in the mood for this. 'And you could, you spotty prick? What country? What attack? What fucking ENEMY?'

He was puzzled and frightened and most disappointed that I was not the poor, lost friend he could help. He tried to disguise it but his lips were dry and his voice trembled slightly as he attempted to cling onto some dignity in a situation that was beyond his expectations. 'The Russians . . . you know, the Reds.'

I could have screamed at him but his tone had begged for a truce. The poor simple bugger meant no harm. I relaxed and smiled at him and spoke calmly. 'Look, Pete . . . the Russians lost twenty million people only a few years ago. They have entire cities in ruins and people starving in the streets. They're trying desperately to cling on to the half of Europe they won in the War. Why the fuck would they want to take *us* over? If they did, the powdered egg and the rissoles would fucking poison them anyway!'

This offered him a way out and he smiled tentatively. The Sergeant Major behind the officer shouted, 'Richardson, C.W.!'

I was caught unawares and had to prepare myself for my next move on the way to the desk. I sat down opposite the Captain. 'Stand up!' screamed the Sergeant Major and the room froze as a hundred men were quietly glad it was me and not them – but then jumped up sharply without thinking.

'Never sit in the presence of an officer unless you're told to!' shouted the robot with a moustache. It was pathetic that he had so obviously tried to model himself on the 'Your country needs you' poster, but fell short of the image.

'Sit down, Richardson,' barked the old Captain in a monotonous tone. He passed over a sheet of paper with some printing and a space for my signature. It was an excerpt from the Official Secrets Act which promised I, the undersigned, understood the Act and would not divulge any drawing, document, photograph etc. etc. to the enemy. As I stared at the document, stunned by its irrelevance to a nineteen-year-old conscript my mind returned to images of smooth, shiny walls and polished floors. They represented years of some poor bastard's forced labour. Again I nearly retched at the thought of the two years before me and I might have spewed over the Official Secrets Act if I had not been overcome and saved by a sudden wave of bitter and inspiring hatred. I also saw a clear escape route before me.

'Sign there.' The Captain was looking at the list for the next conscript's name and the Sergeant Major was drawing breath to shout his name.

'Robertson, D.S.' he bellowed.

'No,' I said.

The Captain turned and believing he must be mistaken he asked pleasantly, 'Sorry . . . what did you say?'

'I said . . . no.'

The room was deadly still. Out of the corner of my eye I saw the Sergeant Major flick his head and give the corporals a look as if to say, 'Get ready, we've got a right conchy bastard here.'

He pounced into action and shouted in my ear, 'Stand up you horrible little spastic.'

He was trying to frighten me into obedience and I knew it. Because I knew it, I was in control and I felt a shiver of excitement surge through my body.

'Fuck off . . . you fat cunt!'

I wanted to dance around the room giggling with joy when I saw his jaw droop loose and his face burn purple with rage. There was no point in backing down now. I had gone too far.

I realized that I was in for a vicious beating in a cold cell but that was the worst they could do and it was nothing new to me. The Sergeant Major slowly bent down to my face. The discipline of a hundred recruits and his respect in the entire regiment were at stake.

'What-did-you-say?'

He whispered loud enough to terrorize a recruit at a hundred yards. I desperately wanted to laugh and had to grip the chair to stop myself. His face was an inch from mine and he glared directly into my eyes. I glared back and spoke.

'You heard – or are you deaf as well as fucking ignorant?'

He jumped up and screamed, 'Corporal Davidson, Corporal Barnes, arrest this man . . . on the double . . . take him to the guardroom . . . put him in leg irons.'

The two N.C.O.s had me on my feet in seconds but the Captain intervened. 'Wait . . . wait . . . wait. This has gone too far. Sergeant Major, please bear with me. You can deal with this man in a moment but let me just sort out this signature business. Sit down, Richardson.'

I was released.

'Will you sign the Official Secrets Act?'

'No, sir.'

'Why not?'

'Because I don't intend to keep any secrets if I ever get my hands on any.'

'Are you working your ticket?'

'What does that mean?' I knew exactly what it meant.

'Trying to be discharged to avoid National Service.'

'I shouldn't be here anyway . . . I told the Medical Officer, I had a bad car accident a few years ago and I suffer from dizzy spells.'

He sighed tiredly, a man long overdue for his pension and a bit of peace.

'Would you knowingly give secrets to the enemy?'

'Yes . . . whoever the enemy is.'

'The Soviet Union, for example?'

'Yes, especially Russia or anyone else who wanted to fuck up capitalism in this fucking shit-hole of a country.'

'Are you a Communist, Richardson?'

'Fucking right I am!'

This was a good one. I nearly thanked him for it, and just for good measure, added, 'The working class will one day realize its historical destiny and overthrow the landowners and industrialist exploiters of wage labour.'

This last was straight from a poor old bugger who ranted and raved from a soap box in the East Street market until we kids chased him away with a shower of stones. But the Captain gave a weary little smile. He was not convinced. I had gone too far.

'Look, Richardson . . . it isn't as easy as you think. Stick to this and you will spend months being beaten into shape until you see sense and accept our discipline. If *we* can't break you then the least we will do is put you inside a military prison for six months and throw you out on your ear with a dishonourable discharge. Nobody will employ you with that. The military glasshouse makes any civilian prison look like a holiday camp. Believe me, it's much simpler to do two years of this than six months of that . . .'

I looked down, a little subdued by his apparent concern. He misunderstood it for a sign of regret. He spoke in an almost friendly tone believing his reasonable approach had won the day.

'Look . . . you'll have to answer for your stupid outburst to the Sergeant Major. You'll get a few weeks in the guardroom, but it will pass quickly, and you can pass the rest of your two years quietly and get back to civvy street.'

I said nothing. There was a long pause.

'Look . . . I'll tell you what. Go across to the NAAFI, get yourself a cup of tea. Think over what has happened for ten minutes or so and let me know what you've decided.'

The Sergeant Major wasn't having any of it. 'But, sir, this man has . . .'

'I know, Sergeant Major, but please bear with me. Let's get this bit of paper out of the way and then he's all yours.'

He turned to me and smiled.

'Thank you, sir.'

I rose and walked towards the door. The other recruits stared at me in frightened disbelief, but when I tried to catch their eyes they looked away quickly as if an exchanged glance would amount to a complicity noted by the Sergeant Major. They rejected me and I am sure consoled themselves with the idea that in a few weeks I would be well and truly sorted out. Nobody beats the system.

The NAAFI canteen was another large brick building. It struck me as a little strange that all the bland painted and polished rooms were so big except for the little crowded wooden huts we all had to live in. I bought a cup of tea and sat apart from a large group of conscripts who joked about the day's events on the parade square and shooting range. They talked as if it was all such a waste of time and they were above it all. They relished complaining about everything. The food in the cookhouse was disgusting and if *their* wives had served up shit like that they would have had it thrown back in their faces. If their wives had served up so much meat they would have wondered where they had got the money from!

I considered my position and was relieved to realize that I had made a start and burnt my boats. It was no longer a question of whether I should work my ticket or not; it was simply a matter of *how*. There were a few options open to me and I had to decide which would give me the least trouble. The kind of belligerence I had shown to the Sergeant Major was not too clever. That particular path would lead to daily beatings for months. My reasons had got to be medical, but even that had its problems. I had already established the story about the car crash which had left me with serious head injuries that brought on frequent dizzy spells. However, they were quite used to stories like that and it would be difficult to prove. I could pretend to be mad, but how could I expect them to recognize insanity when their idea of normality was so crazy. The N.C.O.s were people who enjoyed screaming at recruits all day, spending hours 'bulling' boots and crawling to anybody with a little strip of cloth more than they had. How were they to know if somebody was mad? I decided to stick to the dizzy spells and perhaps involve some madness for my own entertainment.

The group next to me had reduced the level of their conversation to a whisper. At the counter a woman in uniform was collecting a cup of tea. The men stared and nudged each other as she walked to a table. Her uniform was tight and clearly displayed the individual rolls of fat around her waist. She was grotesque and desperately in need of a shave. I was astonished at the reaction of the conscripts. Their eyes were glazed with a lust that was horrifying in its intensity. I thought of the night before and the stifled little sighs after lights out as the conscripts had dreamed their dreams and beat their meat to spray their spunk into sheets they would have to sleep in for weeks.

I could take no more of it. I walked out of the NAAFI and gave a friendly smile to the soldier on duty as I passed the guardroom. I had only to wait a few minutes outside the barracks before the warm lights of a bus appeared on a distant hill.

Fuck it! I was going home! A tremor of elation passed through my veins as I thought of the scrapyard and getting on with the business. As the bus approached I realized suddenly that I had absolutely no money for the fare. I stood alone in that beautiful time between sunset and darkness and I laughed out loud. I would think of something.

I did think of something. I went home to see my mother

who was devastated that I had run away. She cooked me a lovely meal and I slept like a baby. In the morning there was a knock on the door that could only mean one thing. Two coppers had come to arrest me. I offered them a cup of tea and a fiver each but it was not enough. They took me back and I ended up in a cell in Aldershot.

I had decided that six months or even one year of shit was better than two years of shit so I was going to work my ticket well and truly. I also realized that there was no easy option. You only have one face they can kick, you cannot get more solitary than solitary, and bread and water was just as good (or bad) as the slop they gave you anyway. I had nothing to lose and when you finally realize that it is a great release. All through life even the worst villains are kept in line by what they can lose. Being free from all incentives is a great liberty. So I went completely ape. I ripped up all my clothing, threw food at the spotty squaddies, screamed at everybody who came near me. I put in complaints against every bastard that managed to give me a kicking and then when they beat me again for that I put in another complaint, time and time again.

I drove them mad. When the Duty Officer visited I would be completely normal and sane, then spit on the face of the Provost Sergeant the minute the officer left. I would shout out from between my bars at the marching soldiers, yelling out orders to confuse them. 'Right, left, left, left, left, right, left, right, right, about turn! Squad halt, you bunch of fucking toerags!' So they would avoid going near the guardroom. I would sing at the top of my voice in the middle of the night when the off-duty guards were trying to sleep. Sometimes I was chained and gagged. Almost every day I would pretend to faint and the Medical Officer would be sent for. They all feared and hated me but I was not exactly looking for friends. I loved it. Sometimes my mad, hysterical laughter was genuine as I let go and really let the bastards have it.

Sometimes other men came into the cells who were obviously working their tickets. They were amateurs, some of them, and after a few cold nights and a few broken teeth from regular kickings they soon gave up. One man, Johnny Roach, shared a cell with me. I acted a bit mad but Johnny *was* bloody mad. He was convinced that attempted suicide was the best way to get out. He was a very seasoned trier in all the methods but he had not yet had a go at suicide. One night he pulled out his pyjama cord and tied it to the light-fitting. He made sure it was switched off first (he did not want to electrocute himself). He stood on my shoulders and told me than when he had been hanging for a while and had become unconscious I was to shout for the guard. He said it as if we were both tightening up either end of a bolt together. Without any warning, he jumped off my shoulders and swung into the centre of the room. I switched on the light to watch. He was gasping and gagging and trying to peel the cord off his throat. His eyes popped with the strain and the panic. He tried to look at me and I thought he was begging me not to let him down, but then again maybe he was begging me to let him down. I was fascinated. The power and responsibility of it all was invigorating. I could slip in between the white sheets and tell them I had slept through the whole thing. The power of life and death lay in my hands. From sucking his mother's tits to stealing lead from church roofs, all would be ended; all these hopes, dreams and crazy schemes would be switched off with the light if I chose. He clung onto life and consciousness for quite a while. I tried holding my breath in sympathy but I gave up and still he spluttered. His face went a strange colour and then finally it was obvious he was unconscious. I ran the few paces to the door and shouted for help. I shouted that Roach was hanging himself but the Duty Corporal shouted back, 'Fuck off, Richardson. I'm not that fucking stupid, you know.' I said, 'Honest, corporal, you stupid cunt, he's fucking dying!' He screamed at me to fuck off and go to sleep. I said, 'All right, you ugly twat, you'll have to answer for this.'

I turned round and took Roach's weight on my shoulders and tried to release the cord. Finally the Duty Officer peeked through the door and threw a fit. They got him down and called a medic. Johnny slept a lot after that and when he eventually came round, he lay looking at the ceiling. I spoke to him quietly.

'Johnny?'

'Hello, Charlie – thanks for your help, mate.'

'That's all right, Johnny,. any time.'

There was a long pause and then I spoke to him again.

'Johnny?'

'Yes, Charlie.'

'I don't think I'm going to try suicide, mate.'

Another pause

'Quite right, Charlie.'

And that was that, but I did have a go a few weeks later. I wanted to appear to try to kill myself without such a close shave as Johnny had had. I set light to all that I could find in my cell. I knew it would be ages before the bastards would notice the smoke so I kept near the window sucking in fresh air. Soon the whole room was thick with smoke and I was gasping for breath. Eventually things went very wrong. I was ready to pretend to be unconscious but when nobody arrived for ages I stopped acting and really became unconscious.

I woke up a bit later in the reception office of the squadroom with an anxious circle of faces all around me and the Medical Officer slapping my face and shouting at me, 'Come on, Richardson, wake up – wake up! You're lying there like a pregnant woman!' He gave me another hard slap and within seconds of a return to consciousness I jumped to my feet and looked around defensively like a cornered rat. The M.O. walked towards me. I owed him a slap or two so I gave him one with all my strength on his jaw and knocked him flat. Before the others could respond, I swung round and picked up a small wooden bench ready to swing at them all. So then these trained killers who were so ready to defend Queen and Country and sacrifice their lives for their comrades-in-arms ran into the guardroom dormitory and slammed the door behind them. I stood with a bench in my hands and an army doctor at my feet in an empty room. Outside the guardroom I had another thousand soldiers to get through together with the entire British Establishment. I felt really bloody stupid. I put

the bench down and knocked on the door. I told the guard
I promised not to hit them and tentatively they emerged. I
went back to my cell.

At last they had had enough. They had no choice but to
court-martial me for assault on the Medical Officer. I kept
the mad act up, and my dad turned up at the court to try to
nobble some of the officers to reduce the sentence. I got six
months and a dishonourable discharge. I was sent to serve
my sentence in Shepton Mallet glasshouse where at least I
knew I would be amongst friends.

Shepton Mallet was a finishing school for the future notorious villains of Britain. For months I had acted individually
without fear of the consequences. At Shepton Mallet there was
a whole prison full of soldiers who had worked hard like me to
become so uncontrollable that the authorities gave up on us.
Nearly everybody there was due for discharge. The British
Army were fighting the American war in Korea at the time
and the glasshouses were full of deserters and the like who
had been sentenced to hang. They would be court-martialled
in the field which I supposed was a paddy field. On the boat
on the way back to Britain their sentences were commuted to
life and then to two years and discharge.

Apart from them there were a few murderers who did hang
and regular soldiers who had done something serious. The
rest of us were conscripts working our tickets including an
old friend of mine, Johnny Nash, who already had a name
for himself as a bit of a notorious lad in London. The Kray
twins, Reggie and Ronnie, were there. They were both hard
men, full of ideas and energy and good boxing skills. They
had heard of me and I had heard of them. We all knew
that big futures lay in store for us. We would spend hours
dreaming up schemes for when we got out. I suppose it was
a bit like being young medical students. We talked about the
specialities we wanted to work in and what kind of practices
we would set up.

Ronnie and Reggie were completely identical in looks. Sometimes when one of them got some kind of punishment, the
other might do it for him. They played a lot of tricks on the

khaki screws with their identical looks. As you got to know
them you could just about distinguish them. Their characters
were quite a bit different and I got on better with Reggie than
I did with his brother. We were all friends at the time. Later,
on the outside, we were to become rivals but in the glasshouse
we shared the same manor and the same enemy.

The sergeant screws there were worse than their civilian
buddies in blue. A lot is said by sociologists, criminologists,
psychologists, journalists and politicians about the prisons
being full of inadequate people who are a danger to society.
They are absolutely right. The screws who work in prisons
are usually inadequate and if society didn't keep them in jail
they could be a real danger to the public. In Shepton Mallet,
the psychiatric condition of most of the screws was far worse
than that of the inmates. We had all sorts of perverts and
weirdos locking and unlocking our doors. Inadequate is too
kind a word to describe a psychopath who retires from killing
innocent peasants on their farms in Korea to beating up people
in their cells in Shepton Mallet. The only thing that kept them
under control was the hours every day they spent spitting on
their boots and ironing razor-sharp creases in their trousers.
We enjoyed taking the piss out of them or sometimes literally
throwing it at them.

At the end of each wing was a big galvanized tank with two
handles on it. We had to empty our slop-buckets of turds and
piss into the tank. It lay there until it was full and then two
prisoners would carry it to be emptied into an even bigger
tank outside. Reggie Kray and myself had a bright idea for
organizing the sewage disposal on our wing. All we had to do
was test it out. Every day the screws would congregate round
a board to read the daily 'orders' that were put up for the next
day. There was only one place they could put these notices
and it was just at the end of the wing with a door of bars
between us and them. As they met one day, chatting round
the board, Reggie led the way as the two of us filled up our
buckets from the reeking tank. We ran towards the bars and
before they realized what we were doing, we emptied our
buckets at them through the bars. They went spare while we

nearly wet ourselves laughing at them. They were soaked in piss and the boots which had shone like mirrors were now covered in shit. This efficient method of waste disposal was soon taken up regularly by other prisoners and since soldiers generally lack consummate wisdom, they did not think to try a new place for the noticeboard. It was a good diversion from what could have been a very boring routine. We got a good kicking for it and all sorts of punishments, but in a place like that the difference between everyday life and being on punishment was negligible.

Those dull thick psychopaths whose mirror-like 'bulled' boots covered sweaty feet and flaking skin were best kept away from the rest of society. One of them was a broken man. That is, most of him had been broken by three prisoners due to hang. They really did have nothing to lose so they had a go at killing him. He never really recovered. He was terrified of us all. Each day at work was an ordeal for him. Sometimes I even felt sorry for him. One day I found him on his own and I thought I would have a little private word with him. I told him that if he did not take me to see the room where they hanged men, I would kick his face in. He was more than happy to oblige hastily. I stood in the empty bare room where men were ritualistically slaughtered. Our own human abattoir. There was a thick beam high across the room and the square crack of a trapdoor in the centre. Here it was, civilization's stunted growth. The bare room which was the last sight for so many men was filled with the stagnant ghosts of choking, pleading, dying men with shit in their trousers. I stood in the middle of the room and wondered at the standards of a society that considers murder a serious crime but feels it has the right to torture men to death slowly. I walked out of the room with the pathetic, broken screw who was grateful to get through a few minutes without attack. When I got back to the wing, the other screws were congregating around their orders at the noticeboard. Reggie Kray ran up with a bucket of shit and covered them. I cracked up as they cursed, and they set about me.

That evening I went to the medical centre to get my wounds

seen to by Derek the medic. He was a very pleasant man who always spoke kindly to the prisoners as he patched them up. That evening he was a bit *too* bloody pleasant. As he felt about my body for broken bones his hand accidentally brushed across my prick. I hoped it was an accident but then it happened again, more deliberately this time. I jumped back and shouted at him, 'Fuck off, you fucking poof! Keep your hands to yourself, you dirty bastard!'

He was disappointed but he disguised it as surprise. 'Don't be silly, Charlie, it was an accident – honestly!'

I grabbed my clothes and started getting dressed as he tried to explain himself. As I was leaving Ronnie Kray popped his head around the door. 'All right, Charlie mate?' Then he looked at Derek. 'Busy, Derek?' Derek smiled at him and said, 'No, Ronnie . . . Charlie's just finished.' Ronnie gave me a strange smile and I told him to watch Derek . . . 'He's got wandering fucking hands, Ronnie.' My warning was wasted. I found out later that Ronnie was a frequent visitor to Derek's little surgery where it was his wandering mouth that was in demand. Derek gave a good blow-job to any prisoner who felt the need and Ronnie's need was becomingly increasingly urgent. The story goes that Ronnie arrived in Shepton Mallet full of macho talk about women and what he'd like to do to them but that Derek made him realize his preferences. Prison's not such a bad place if you happen to be partial to the attentions of fit young men. It turns out that a lot of men who on the outside might fancy a bit of queer bashing find themselves sneaking sly looks at their cellmates when they're undressing.

It was not for me, though. Prison was a place of extreme deprivation where the picture of a girlfriend at the seaside could drive you mad. If you can't get it, you want it so much it becomes a painful, desperate drive. I had always tried not to make it too much of a distraction but sometimes nature is stronger than the best resolve. The woman reporter down at the Old Bailey, scribbling down the sordid details as Lucien told his tale, was aware that the gang boss was sometimes more interested in the very occasional glimpse of a pretty triangle of knickers than the prospect of a black box of torture. She and I played our power game. I felt the ridiculous sense of power men feel when they catch a flash of the hidden delights of forbidden fruit. She was relishing the sensation of power over the lust of a man who was notorious, even famous; who could look but not touch. We played a subtle game of bondage sex while the court listened with even greater but less innocent lust to another story of bondage and power. The judge leaned forward on his grand throne and asked Lucien, 'How many punches, if more than one, did you get? Did you get more than one?' For the court's benefit, he could have added – Oh please say yes, we do hope it was lots.

Lucien obliged.

'Yes – I think I would say it was five or six, M'Lord.'

Thanks for the help. My Lord. The woman on the press bench gave me what I thought was a little cheeky look as she crossed her legs.

CHAPTER FIVE
The Biggest Firm on the Manor

When I walked out of the British Army sponsored university for crime on a grand and organized scale at Shepton Mallet, I was twenty years old and it was 1954. I felt fully fledged and I was desperate to fly. It was a beautiful sunny morning (it really was) and I could hardly contain my excitement. I felt like a kid who has been given a whole pile of sweets all for himself and was trembling at the prospect of starting the feast. It was a great time to be young, especially if you had a sense of invincibility. The snot-noses finally emerging from the buggery of Eton and the intellectual wanking of Oxford had three main areas to choose from to gain a foothold on the ladder of a glittering career – law, business or making up stories in the media. My choice incorporated all three, law, business and a few stories.

A war is a great thing for the budding entrepreneur. The economy is fresh for growth and new ideas. And I had lots of ideas. One thing I had picked up in Shepton Mallet was to start thinking bigtime. Discussions with the Krays and others made me realize that the horizon for adventures in business stretched to infinity. When they talked of their schemes I gained such confidence. Before, some of these men working their tickets made my own rebellion seem weak and half-hearted. They did not just ignore authority, they rubbed the nose of authority in its own shit to teach it to leave them alone. The total anarchy of the glasshouse, which was supposed to be a temple of extreme discipline, put a breeze into my young wings. I wanted to get out there and rub some noses just to show people my new strength.

The scrapyard had been doing well enough without me but nothing was growing. I could have just settled down and run a successful little business, got married, had kids and run off to Butlins for a couple of weeks every year. On Sundays I could have stuffed a roast dinner down and had a few pints with friends round at the local pub with the smelly carpet. No worries, no more jail and a nice little pot belly in my thirties. No chance! Like a rampant tumour nothing could stop my growth. Within weeks of walking out of Shepton Mallet I bought up another scrapyard. I actually bought a car, a Ford Consul, and got married.

I had been taking out a local girl for a little while and she became pregnant, so we got married. No drama, no discussions, no great traumas. Margaret was pregnant so we got married. Everybody got married and I liked the idea of having my own home to go to. It would have been interesting if it had all been a great romance and we had declared pure and undying love for each other but it was not like that. I did not meet very many women and had sex with even less. My thrills were not from slipping a sweaty hand up fat sausage thighs to sticky knickers. I got my pleasures in a clever deal where I sold scrap for a good price.

Before supermarkets were established on the British scene I had developed the practice of buying in bulk with small profit margins. I knew a lot of dealers personally and I knew how they judged the market. If one of them was keen on lead and always knew the best prices I would sell lead at a loss and up the price of copper. They thought they had the good deal, but I knew I had it. I rationalized the yards to work efficiently and paid the workers really well. Their wages were normal but I peeled notes from wads in my pocket at the end of the week to top them up. Loyalty became absolutely essential to me. I was working in a world where theft was part of the game. I bought stolen metal and sold it to people who knew a lot of it was stolen. The police knew it was stolen too, so they got their wages every week like everybody else. When I needed to hire people I did not advertise or interview them, I only employed people I knew personally. Once I hired the milkman who delivered to the yard because over the months we used to chat and I thought I could trust him. I wanted people who were willing to give their undying loyalty to somebody they could look up to. The world is full of people who want to

119

doff their caps to somebody. I hired people who would spit in the face of a copper or screw but still wanted somebody to respect and tell them what to do.

I had read about Freud and other bits of psychology in prison and although I never met any man who wanted to fuck his mother and kill his dad, I met hundreds of grown men who were looking for a dad. A lot of them joined the army or became policemen or screws. Some of them with a bit more taste became the trusted grafters for men like me. Many of my close associates were simply men with whom I shared a mutual respect. We knew our friendship would be useful to both of us in the future. There was no Freudian psychology with them but sometimes with others the father figure bit was very real.

Even though I dealt sometimes in metals whose origin was not exactly certain and I paid the police my regular protection money, I had a serious problem with theft from my yard. Serves you right, I hear you say. Well, arseholes to you. There's a golden rule, you don't shit on your own doorstep so if somebody stole from a building site and delivered to me that was fair game. Stealing from my yard and selling to another was wrong and it got up my nose. I became almost paranoid watching out for people in the yard. Sometimes I caught people at it and they got a smack for their troubles, but one day I caught a boy sneaking out with a few lumps under his jumper. I grabbed him and bits fell out all over the place. After slapping him about a bit I dragged him back to the office by the scruff of his neck. He was kicking and fighting all the way, trying to punch me with tight little fists. He was about thirteen and small but there was strength in the odd kick he landed on my shins. I dragged him along and threw him into a chair and screamed at him. All the frustrations of months of petty thefts were vented on him as I paced up and down. Like an army sergeant major I stooped down and screamed inches from his face, 'You little fucking toerag, you cheeky little cunt, what the fuck do you think you're doing?'

He looked up at me, eyes burning with defiance so that I nearly laughed. There was not the slightest sign of fear in his eyes or his posture. He was smart and clean but his clothes were worn and frayed. With big eyes and a fat cherubic face, he looked like butter wouldn't melt. I was just about to soften and let him go when he spoke. 'Fuck off, you old cunt.'

I burst out laughing. I was amazed that anybody could think of me as old. He was confused when I laughed. 'You can't use language like that. I've got a nice lump of red carbolic soap to wash out the foul mouths of little boys. Wait till I tell your dad you've been caught nicking and using language like that – he'll belt your arse black and blue, you cheeky little pup.'

'Fucking fuck fuck cunting fuck I'm not a fucking pup, and I haven't got a dad and stop talking to me like I was a little boy.'

I was really enjoying this conversation. I liked him. 'So where's your old man – run off, has he, and left you with your mum?'

Without any attempt to gain any sympathy he looked at me and in a high voice that was not yet broken he almost spat, 'No he did not – he died working on the railways and I'm the man in the house now. I've got to take care of things.'

'If he died on the railways, he must have got a pension. You don't need to go nicking stuff from me.'

He looked down because I had softened my tone. 'He didn't get a pension and I don't usually nick stuff. I find it and sell it to dealers. It's the only money we get in our house.'

He was a hard little bugger but he had life and energy in him. I offered him a job after school working in the yard. Two years later in 1959 when he was fifteen, I gave him his own yard to manage. He was bossing around men three times his age. Ten years after our first meeting, Roy Hall stood beside me in the Old Bailey charged with all sorts of nonsense, listening to Lucien Harris tell his tall tales of horror.

How did it come to this? Those were the days when we worked and lived hard and the future was an eternal rainbow with a big pot of gold at the end of every week. I could have settled for the life of a scrap dealer extraordinaire, lived in a big house, sent my kids to private school where they would have told their friends their dad was a metal recycling engineer and would have been embarrassed to bring other kids home at half term. I could have had lobster thermidor in any restaurant in the world and ironed my Freemason's garter in front of the telly. I could have raised money for charity in the local Rotary Club where the members would think I was the salt of the earth. I could have been a 'real character'. I could have died and gone to rest with a padded mahogany coffin with a wreath of flowers saying 'Charlie Boy'.

But none of it was possible. I had to move. I had to swim hard upstream and feel the current on my gills. Like any good entrepreneur I had to feel I was growing and diversifying all the time. I opened up yards and drinking clubs all over the place. The breweries had the pubs sewn up so I started clubs where drinking was twenty-four hours. They were a bit illegal, given the licensing laws, but the police were on the payroll. When a big raid was planned they gave us the nod and the target club would be closed when the vice squad turned up.

All these places needed running by trusted colleagues. The payroll stayed modest but the bonuses were big and we became one big happy family that grew in power and influence. The police were paid to protect us from the police but we had to look after ourselves as far as anybody else was concerned. If a rival group tried to muscle in on our clubs and businesses, we had to show them who was running things. I did not try to make us the biggest firm on the manor but there was a stage in our development when we had to let people know it was not worth messing around with us. I realized that the most effective way of doing this was to hit somebody hard and the somebody had to be a *real* somebody. There was no point in running around chasing our tails and giving the occasional smack to somebody cheeky enough to challenge our position. We needed to hit big people in a big way and the rest would leave us alone. Word would get around. We needed our own version of the kind of P.R. a West End company would use complete with plummy tight mini-skirted consultants and boring cocktail parties. We could have distributed 'Charlie

Richardson is Hard' T-shirts, but a better opportunity came along.

As we sat drinking on a Friday night after a good week's work, a man burst in with a swollen and bruised face. It was Reggie Jones. He did not work for me but he was a friend and, what was more important, he was known to everybody as a loyal friend of our firm. He had been in a fight trying to protect another friend of ours, Jimmy Brindle, from a vicious attack by a group of men led by the notorious evil monster called 'Rosa'. He was well-known around the Elephant and Castle and infamous among men who had done some time. When he was in Broadmoor he had savaged the Governor in his own office. Rosa was a big brainless legend who left a trail of blood in his wake. But he was an isolated psychopath without a following that would be upset by any misfortune he might encounter. At school he was a big bully and he never grew out of it.

Jimmy Brindle, the man Rosa had left gargling in his own blood, was not only a friend of ours but was married to Eva, the sister of Frank Fraser. Frank was somebody we wanted to do business with since he had knocked out the notorious villain Jack Spot from his domination of the West End. Frank was doing seven years for his attack on Jack Spot so we had to take care of Rosa in his absence. All these advantages to sorting out Rosa were considered later. Our immediate reaction was to go for him anyway.

While Reggie told his story and the others gasped indignantly, 'Fucking bastards,' and 'We'll sort the cunt out,' I moved over to the side of the bar and picked up the phone. After a few calls I discovered Rosa was drinking in a club at the Elephant called the Reform. I suggested we could participate in his reformation. I set off with Eddie and Roy and a couple of other friends and we drove in a convoy to the Reform. We walked in like a bunch of men on a night out. I stood near Rosa. After I had ordered a drink I turned and smiled and said, 'Hello, Rosa – how's it going?' He looked at me cautiously. He was much taller than me so I got good momentum when I leaned up and nutted him on the bridge of his nose which

I felt crumble under my head. As his hands went to his face and blood splattered between his fingers I punched his gut and waited for him to draw breath. Meanwhile Eddie and Roy and the others jumped on Rosa's friends. We worked together like a well-practised team until they lay unconscious at our feet in pools of blood and broken teeth. We sat and had a drink. Everybody else in the bar watched as we calmly stepped on the broken bodies on the way out. The deed was registered and guaranteed for entry in local folklore. It was not the first time we had sorted somebody out but Rosa was big P.R. and our soaring reputation would protect us from challenges from ambitious competitors.

I found out later that in the world of international big business they do a lot worse to people to establish a reputation. We only broke a few bones. But all the time big corporations destroy the very lives of people in other big corporations in their struggle for market superiority. And like any big, growing business, we also learned to keep a respectful distance from firms of equal strength when a war would only damage both sides.

Ken Docherty was not on our team but he was mixed up with us. He was a friend and one evening while we were having a drink up in the East End a man walked up to me looking liked a bouncer but he was just a drunk looking for trouble. He stood like a cowboy ready to draw on his clenched fist wearing a forced John Wayne smile that was supposed to intimidate me. He loosened up ready to pounce, stared me straight in the eye and almost mimicked the John Wayne drawl.

'Richardson, get the fuck out of our turf. Get back over the river with your bog wog friend where you belong.' He was obviously not looking for a discussion so I thought I would satisfy his desperation for some form of physical contact with another human being. I smiled because I wanted to laugh and carefully put my glass down on the bar. But before I could land him a smack, Ken, who did not like being called a bog wog and took any wicked reference to his Irish heritage very personally, punched our local cowboy on the jaw. The jaw cracked and cowboy Joe fell back, slipped on his own spilt drink and cracked his head on a table on the way down. As he lay unconscious we finished our drinks puzzled by the interruption to our quiet evening. We left to find a friendly club.

The next day our cowboy came onto our territory looking for revenge. This time he was taking no chances. He was leading his own posse of about twenty men carrying guns and sticks, bold as brass down the High Street. In the middle of the group were two old friends, fellow graduates of Shepton Mallet, Ronnie and Reggie Kray. Obviously our cowboy was a Kray man and we had upset him on their manor. Now the Krays had a perfect excuse to invade enemy territory and had moved over the river to annex the south-east. Then with Frank Fraser inside they could move in on the West End and London would be all theirs. There was a lot at stake. What was I supposed to do? Even if we pulled out some iron bars what chance did we have against guns? Even if we crawled out of the blood bath victorious we could never have controlled the East End and the guerrilla warfare led by Kray men. If they won the battle I would have to move away from all I had worked so hard to build. The only answer was a summit conference. I walked up to the group of men on my own. They stopped to wait for orders from the two generals in the middle. Before they gave the order to fire I spoke directly at the twins. 'Reggie, Ronnie, can I have a word?'

Ronnie jumped in before Reggie could begin to negotiate. 'Fuck off, Charlie, you come round to our manor and fuck with one of our boys in our pub, then we'll teach you a fucking lesson you'll never forget.'

Ronnie was looking for a bit of trouble. He enjoyed it. He had been looking forward to it since the night before when the cowboy had run around to tell his miserable tale. I had to think of something that would work on him. Reggie was easier to reason with but Ronnie had his staff drawn and he needed to taste blood. I shrugged, spoke to Ronnie and pointed at the cowboy.

'That's the cunt who wants a lesson, Ronnie. Somebody

should teach him some manners and somebody should teach him some gratitude for the people who look after him.'

Ronnie was confused. 'What do you mean fucking gratitude?'

I had him now, I had them all, especially the cowboy who was totally confused. 'He said you were a poof, Ronnie.' Now there was a silence that would have been shattered if a passing mosquito had farted.

Poor John Wayne was baffled. He turned to Ronnie. 'No I didn't, Ronnie, honest, I don't know what the fuck he's talking about, I never said that, I'd never say that to anybody.' Ronnie was almost foaming at the mouth but confused as to who he should believe. I went in for the kill and addressed the condemned man directly with a line that had the right taste of truth.

'You said you'd rather work for an East End poof than fuck Irish bog wogs south of the river – who did you mean, cunt?' That was enough. Ronnie whipped around with his lump of hard wood and smashed it into the cowboy's face. He screamed at him, 'Nobody calls me that, NOBODY! You cunt!' and hit him again.

Everybody knew that Ronnie had a weakness for playing with healthy young pricks but Ronnie sometimes liked to think that nobody knew. So everybody around him pretended it was not happening and it took a brave man even to mention it. A few years later a brave man, a friend and colleague of mine called George Cornell, called him a 'fat poof' to his face and Ronnie shot his head off the next day.

I apologized to the twins for all the aggro but we were only having a quiet drink until his man interrupted. There was a truce, not too friendly, but they retreated back north of the river. So by accident I found myself heading the biggest firm on the manor and my manor was south-east London. To outsiders it might have looked like a gang, but gangs are what kids have – or big kids on American films. I was a businessman who had to protect his interests. There was no point in turning to so-called legitimate methods of protection. I had the wrong accent and could never get the hang of a funny handshake.

But I took my responsibilities seriously. I bought the local Battersea Boys Club and turned their football team into first division Sunday league. At Christmas I paid for and organized turkeys for all the old people near the scrapyards and we set up parties and coach trips to the seaside in summer for them. We reduced local crime to a dribble. I was pissed off with all the thefts from my yard and I would be enraged when local people would come to tell me of burglaries to their houses. While the police filed incident reports and complaints in their dusty drawers we would know within hours who had done the job, give them a smack and tell them to fuck off to the West End to steal from rich people who could afford an insurance policy. The sad little battered radios and half crowns from the tin in the kitchen would be returned to the victim with our compliments. It might be a bit strong to say we were loved and respected but we were certainly respected.

Throughout all this I worked day and night to expand our business operations. My wife had three more kids and lived outside of town while I pressed on at a rate that exhausted everybody around me. In the little free time I took off I became a pioneer in all forms of self-abuse with the help of the fringes of the pharmaceutical industry. Uppers and downers, coke and dope were the privilege of the privileged, bored at tea parties, Wimbledon, Cowes, Henley and Ascot. The rich have all the fun. Smoking a joint with my accent was breaking exciting new ground in class mobility. I had more hyperactivity than a kid reared in the lead fumes of the M1. I needed a joint to calm me down.

The other pleasure the snot-arses of British Society kept to themselves was boating. My lot were happy with their sixpence an hour on three feet of muddy smelly water in the Serpentine, rowing around in circles and wondering what to do next. I had a smart car, I had a big house in Footscray, Kent, I had a successful business. My suits were the best, made to measure by a tailor who asked me which way my dick liked to hang. I was even screwing the secretary on the desk after work. The one thing I didn't have as a symbol of my wealth and status was a boat. I decided to buy one that I could enjoy and use locally but despite my pleasure in spending large sums of money without flinching, I was stunned at how much they cost. But I bought a beautiful, sleek and expensive speed-boat and tied her up on the Thames near the docks. I loved the thrill of careering down the river and impressing the new contacts I was making. I would arrange meetings at pubs near the river and offer lifts to other businessmen to score or thrill the shit out of them. Women loved it and I loved them loving it, and after a ride at thirty knots they rode me even faster.

I was having a regular affair with a woman called Jean Goodman who worked for me. Sometimes we would take a few hours off in the afternoon to take a spin on the speed-boat to clear the office cobwebs and get the hormones flowing. My youngest brother Alan, who was eighteen and running his own business, was also in the office so I asked him along. He was reluctant because I think he thought Jean and I wanted to be on our own. Alan was a bit like that. He was different from me and Eddie maybe because he was the youngest and our mother tried extra hard with him to keep him from the trouble we were always getting into. He was nobody's fool, though, and he could hold his own. But since I did not see as much of him as I wanted to I was keen to give him a good time on the speed-boat. After a bit of a discussion I talked him into it and the three of us set off.

I stood at the wheel with the others holding on behind me as we eased out of the docks and slowly cruised into the river. Then came the bit I loved. I banged the throttle lever forward and the front of the boat pointed skyward, hesitated and smacked down onto the water. We flew over the river bumping on the small waves with the engine screaming and the wind forcing the skin back on our faces. I shot under the bridges and tightly spun round outside the Houses of Parliament. As we raced by the home of the honourable and dishonourable members I stuck up two fingers and looked around for approval. Jean and Alan threw their heads back and laughed. I aimed straight for the central pillar and just before we hit the black bricks I spun the wheel and the boat heeled to an angle that had us all hanging on for our lives. We all laughed, kids again at the best ride in the fairground. But as I looked straight ahead my face dropped. About fifty yards in front was the wake of a pleasure steamer. It was probably only three or four feet high but nevertheless my big roaring sleek pride and joy shrunk to the scale of a toy. I had no time to slow down and nowhere to go. We hit the first wave and flew through the air. When the boat hit the second wave it spun over on its side and we were thrown out with force into the river. The water hit me like concrete as I skimmed across it like a flat stone and sank underneath, drawn by the undercurrent of the pleasure-boat. I was not a good swimmer but instinct took over as I kicked and spluttered my way to the surface. When my head popped up and I sucked at the air I could see the speed-boat, a little white and red lump on the river, upside down. I swam for it and called for the others. Jean was calling for me and Alan shouted something. I shouted to get back to the speed-boat. Just as I grabbed the smooth hull of my expensive toy a large fat barge – heavy and low in the water – slid past us and missed us by a few yards. I took a quick glance and was relieved to see there was only a small wake from the barge. If I had known more about boats and water I might have realized that its real wake was below the surface as it dragged the water along in a hidden deadly current. The undertow sucked me from my grip on the speed-boat and pulled me under the water, spinning me upside down and dragging me behind the barge. For a few seconds I panicked but then with an unexpected calm I realized I was going to die. The whole of my life did not flash before me but within a few seconds I was almost amused by the irony of the situation. All those years of struggle, worries, pain, hope and pleasure were coming to an end without warning. All those years of planning were to be snuffed out in a few seconds by an accident. In a moment of time whole periods were condensed and experienced as a feeling. As the barge towed me behind underwater as if by an invisible rope, I lost all fear and relaxed. Then, as suddenly as I was grabbed by the undertow, it released me and I was kicking to the top and again I sucked at the air and my lungs filled and my heart pumped madly. A few seconds later Jean Goodman's head popped up like an apple, she sucked and struggled and disappeared underneath the water. She could not swim, she was drowning. I swam over to her as best I could in my clothes and twice again her head popped up and disappeared with a desperate little cry each time. Finally I reached her and as she came up I held her head above the water. She gasped and spluttered and threw herself on top of me in desperation to stay above the surface. She held me under for too long so I struggled with her to get myself to the surface and screamed at her to relax. She obeyed as in a trance and I held her head above the water as best I could with both of us sinking every few seconds.

The pleasure-boat had turned to rescue us and at last I found a round lifebuoy at arms' reach. I pushed it over Jean's head and she automatically put her arms through. I held on to her and together we floated while they hauled on the rope attached to the lifebuoy. And it was only then that I realized. Where was Alan? I looked around with concern expecting to see his head bobbing around and began to panic when all I could see was choppy dirty brown water. I shouted to the pleasure-boat, 'There's somebody else . . . a man – have you got him?' A man on the boat turned to another who ran around looking into the water. For an agonizing minute there was no reply. He came back to the edge of the boat and told me the worst thing I had ever heard in my life. 'There's nobody else . . . I've looked everywhere, there's nobody else . . . and I can't even see your boat.'

I screamed at him, 'What the fuck do you mean there's nobody else. There bloody well is . . . there's another man, he's my brother, for fuck sake . . . he's my brother. Look for him, you bastard, he's got to be there.'

I was hauled on board after Jean and they put a blanket round me. I realized at that moment for the first time that the water was very cold. I was shivering as I ran around the decks among the pensioners and tourists looking embarrassed. I was shouting at everybody. 'There's a man in the river, we've got to find him, he's my brother . . . he's in the fucking river.'

Everybody looked and after a while one of the crew put his arm round me and spoke in a soft voice. 'He's not there, governor, he must have drowned . . . come below and we can get you dry.' I would not, could not believe him but I spoke with resignation. 'He's got to be there, we've got to find him,' and I felt my voice rise in panic. 'We're not going back till we find him, I don't care how long it takes . . . tell your captain I'll fucking kill him if he goes back before we find him.' And so the pleasure-boat and its sad midweek passengers circled in the dirty water with a police launch for hours before I sat on a chair, stared into the murky river and screamed. Then I cried. Nobody came near me as I blubbed like a child.

Alan and my smooth shiny toy boat were found the next day washed up at low tide. For months I was in a numb state of total grief and bitter regret. A hundred times, a thousand times I said 'if only' to myself over and over again. At the Coroner's Court there was a report from witnesses that the pleasure-boat was out of order being where it was and apparently trying to get under the bridge before me. I was paralysed with grief through the whole process and nothing was made of the pleasure-boat's guilt. Even to this day – that experience is the worst of my life and it is painful to recount the events.

I thought of Alan several times during the torture gang trial in the Old Bailey. I thought, no matter what you do to me, you bastards, nothing you do could be as painful as that day on the river. Whatever pain you inflict to satisfy your lust for punishment I've been beyond it before. How could you all create such a monster out of me with your daily rehearsals before the court case? How could such a cold cruel unthinking beast such as the one you have moulded me into have wept at the death of the brother he loved? For a few moments during this show trial I escaped from the Old Bailey Amateur Dramatic Society's rendering of a tatty Perry Mason episode. I put my head on my hand and thought of Alan and relived the grief. When I regained consciousness of my surroundings

My Manor

I looked around with the eyes of an alien dropped unawares into a bizarre and perverse primitive human ritual. The ancient Greeks, Romans or Britons or somebody ancient used to get a goat and in a weird religious ritual they would pass all their collective sins against god onto this poor bloody animal and then kill him, poor fucker. With that they had lost all their sins. The powerful British Establishment and the dull grey British public were loading all their frustrations, anger, impotence and misery onto the small group of men in the dock. The trial was the ritual headed by a high priest in colourful and ancient costume. He was helped by junior priests in less flamboyant costume as they loaded all the shit of their lives on our tired little group. When they were finally finished gorging themselves on tales of blood and gore, they would slaughter us. Our punishment would then absolve them of their own very sordid lusts for violence and the misery of other human beings. Their satisfaction would be short-lived but their agents in blue had a stock of goats waiting at the side of the abattoir.

CHAPTER SIX
The Prince of Fraud

Our jury at the Old Bailey was 'vetted' by Special Branch and lots of people read that in the paper and thought, 'What's "vetted" and who the fuck are "Special Branch?"' and Special Branch thought, 'How do they know we vetted the jury . . . it's supposed to be a secret?' Those were the days before Special Branch or MI5 or MI6 had taps on the phone of so many people they got confused. Nowadays when every old Etonian who prefers boys' bums to girls' tits and socializes with members of the Labour party has his phone tapped it's no big deal. It's almost embarrassing if your phone is not tapped by somebody. It means you're not worth a dog's shit if no other dog wants to sniff your turd. But in the 1960s, surveillance was in its infancy. It had a bright future with a promise of massive growth but it was crude and inefficient. It was so crude, primitive and innocent that international intelligence organizations did not even have a regular tap on British government ministers' phones. The South African secret police were so amazed and frustrated that the British agencies did not have a tap on the Prime Minister's phone (or at least they said they didn't) that they asked me to arrange one for Harold Wilson's private line. They had me over a barrel with my mines in South Africa so I was happy to oblige but was arrested before I could perform that simple task.

So when the British public heard about the vetting of the jury they thought this was serious stuff. Then when the police installed 'hotlines' for each member of the jury so we wouldn't nobble them it only confirmed how serious everything was. 'Hotline' was a new word. The only 'hotline' we knew about was the cold war 'hotline' between America and Russia so the leaders could avert an all-out nuclear destruction of the planet with a chat on the phone. So when the members of the jury got 'hotlines' they became very important people. For added measure we got such a grand motorcade every day to the trial it would have taken a regiment of paratroopers to spring us free. Now try saying you're innocent in the middle of all that. If the jury had been able to see their way through the thick undergrowth of tabloid fiction and found us not guilty they might have been publicly lynched by an angry mob who had sniffed blood and wanted to taste it. The lead dogs in that hungry pack would have been the journalists who, having created a perfect Dracula of uncompromising evil, wanted to report on the ritual when the wooden stake was hammered into our hearts.

For weeks before the trial started the ace in the hand of the prosecution was leaked around for everybody to anticipate. They said they had a 'black box' which was a torture machine that inflicted unimaginable agonies on its naked victims. Day after day the jury, the dull grey perverts who queued for the public gallery, and the rabid pavement, gutter and sewer press listened to all the slow detail of our case waiting for the black box to appear. They relished the slow build-up to the exciting climax. They waited in anticipation like a naked man being gently stroked by a beautiful woman knowing that sometime soon, but not too soon, at last her hand would close gently but firmly round his prick. If the prosecution had gone straight in with their black box it would have been a premature ejaculation and everybody would be left frustrated and even embarrassed. So they merely titillated with minor details knowing full well that Lucien Harris was the teasing hand that would finally go for the black box. I wanted to see it too, not for old times' sake, but because I had never seen it before either. Lucien played their game and enjoyed his part in the tease.

Having apparently given Lucien a few warm-up punches and slaps I'm supposed to have pulled everything out of his pockets and found an address book. I'm then supposed to have leafed through the names and addresses in my relentless search for Jack Duval. Meanwhile my 'gang' pace around poor little innocent wide-eyed Lucien. Mr Cussen of the prosecution, fed a steady diet of American courtroom dramas, wished he could pace around the courtroom for added effect. But he did his best from the bench as he led Lucien by the nose, a flaccid impotent bull. Cussen was not Perry Mason and Lucien was no James Stewart but they did their best. He asked Lucien, 'What was said, if anything?'

'There was some sort of conversation going on, I mean, to the effect that I had been seen with Jack Duval the previous night by somebody.'

'Who said that to you?'

'Charles Richardson.'

Yes, Lucien, I did ask you a thousand times where Jack Duval was. I was desperate to find him. But if I had beaten up and tortured everybody I had questioned as to the whereabouts of Jack Duval I would have rivalled the monsters at the Nuremberg War Crimes trial. Cussen continued to lead Lucien through a conversation that was years old but Lucien was nonetheless lucid in his recall. After the whole court had had a chance to steal a glance at me, Cussen turned back to Lucien Harris.

'What did you say to that?'

'I said whoever told him that must have been mistaken because I certainly hadn't been with Jack Duval the previous evening.'

'What happened next?'

'Charles Richardson got up and came round, playing with a knife which he had been cleaning his fingernails with. He stuck it against the side of my face and, sort of, threatened that, you know, if I didn't tell them where Jack Duval was he would use it.'

Oh come on, Lucien! I nearly screamed from the dock. Whoever wrote this script should be sued by Graham Greene. Now I was cast as tubby little Richard Attenborough playing the cheap little crook in *Brighton Rock*. And cleaning my nails with a knife? What a poor, unimaginative reference to every failed actor playing every one-dimensional petty thug in every American B-film. What an embarrassing and undignified image when my nails were always clean and professionally manicured. What next? Cussen obliged by prompting Lucien in the spotlight.

'And then?'

'Charles' brother Eddie came into the room because at this point Charles Richardson spoke to his brother and they sent someone out to buy some scampi.'

As he said this his voice tailed off, maybe he'd forgotten his lines, but another prat in a wig jumped up to save the day. He didn't want to miss a vital piece of information and the press too were unsure of what had been said. He obliged everybody by addressing the judge.

'My Lord, the witness dropped his voice. He said that at some time Edward Richardson came in and they talked and sent out for some . . .'

Justice Lawton could appreciate the vital importance of this little titbit of evidence. He turned to the learned gentleman and for everybody's benefit he said with the authority of a very high court judge and with an actor's loud delivery, 'Scampi.'

The powdered wig nodded and was very grateful.

'My Lord . . . I am much obliged.'

I wanted to set the record really straight. Was it actually scampi or was it really monkfish that they just said was scampi? If it was important to know what I ordered for my snack it was surely proper to be accurate. What on earth was going on? What was I going to do with the scampi that it mattered so much? But it was not all stupidity. These little details mattered to paint a vivid picture for the courtroom and the public. And it had a ring of truth; it was cleverly scripted by an amateur sociologist who had sat and thought about what I might order from a chip shop. I was working class so my tastes, despite my wealth, might be stuck on fried food and chip shops. On the other hand I was known to be rich so I would order the most expensive item on the chip shop menu. In that area of London you only bought scampi and chips if you were very drunk and had just been paid. It showed what a big gangster I really was when I could order scampi without a second thought. But now that they had laboured the subject I realized I would have murdered a nice plate of scampi after all the lukewarm dog food we had been living on in prison. The other point about the scampi was that according to Taggart and other poor victims of our ritualized tortures, it seemed we had the unusual habit of eating takeaway food in front of our brutalized, naked and bloody victims. With me sending out for food I could sense a collective 'Oh oh – here we go' from the courtroom. They had ridden the slow ride up to the top of the big dipper. They shifted in their seats like hungry dogs licking their lips at the sight of a bone. Cussen asked Lucien what happened next and at last Lucien threw the dogs their bone.

'A man brought in a black box which he put down by the door.'

Cussen allowed the courtroom to chew on this simple but carefully timed line in our mystery thriller. Then, as if watching the masked man in the *Lone Ranger* ride off into the sunset, Cussen turned to Lucien Harris and asked in a tremulous voice, 'Who was that man?'

But the man was not the Lone Ranger, he wasn't masked and Lucien had been briefed to give a satisfactory answer.

'Roy Hall.'

'Can you see him in court?'

He would have had to be blind not to. Roy was standing next to me in the dock.

'Yes. He is in the front row on the right.'

All eyes turned to Roy and then back to Lucien. They listened to Cussen as he was speaking, but all eyes were on Lucien.

'Would you describe, Mr Harris, what it was that Mr Hall brought in?'

'It was a sort of hand generator which is used for testing spark plugs in garages. It takes the form of a wooden box with a handle at one end and two leads which fix onto terminals on the top of it, I think.'

Then, with excellent timing, a bespectacled little man in a suit walked onto centre stage with a big, black and ominous-looking box. The smallness of the man made the box look bigger than it actually was. Justice Lawton was intrigued and asked to have a look. I was flabbergasted. Where the hell had they got this thing? Then Cussen spoke.

'My Lord, may I make it quite clear it has not been suggested that this is the object which was referred to by the witness.'

Our brief jumped up.

'My Lord it is entirely objectionable to take some object almost at random and ask the witness whether he can identify something.'

Lawton was not going to reduce the drama of his courtroom. He answered our brief, Platts-Mills (what a bloody name) as if swatting a bothersome fly.

'He is not being asked to identify something at all, Mr Platts-Mills. If you had heard the question you would not have objected.'

Mr Cussen of the prosecution bathed in the patronage of this kindly judge and continued by asking Lucien, 'Looking at that, what would you say about this box in relation to the one brought into the room by Hall?'

Platts-Mills was on his feet again. He had watched Perry Mason too.

'I object.'

Lawton turned his wig to the wig representing the Crown. 'You object, Mr Platts-Mills?'

'Yes, my Lord. The witness has described something so palpably different from this object that it must be misleading for the jury.'

Of course it was misleading, you naïve idiot. It was intended to mislead. It was all part of the theatrical spectacle to introduce this big black box. They had already admitted it was not the actual box used so why else would they bring it into court? Even now the jury and spectators were beginning to forget the boring detail and accept that this was the black box that was used. I was shocked. All these years of knowing how bent the police and courts could be, how they could manipulate justice to suit themselves, I had never seen anything as outrageous as this. They had introduced an exhibit that was not an exhibit but it had the same effect. Imagine a court case where a man is being tried for attacking another with a knife. The police could not find the knife so they produced a machete as an exhibit and said it was something like the knife used. Platts-Mills and our row of faces in the dock looked to the judge who was the umpire in this tennis match with wide-eyed pleas for a fair judgement. Our eyes said, 'Come on, ref – that ball was out.' The rest of the courtroom looked with begging eyes that said, 'Please don't ruin such a good game please please please your honourable worshipful Lordship say the ball was in . . . don't ruin our fantasy with boring truth and reality and the law.' There was a short pause. Justice Lawton played to the crowd and devastated us. He turned to Platts-Mills and spoke, a stern teacher to an impertinent child.

'Well, I am against you in that.'

The audience in the stalls all but stood and cheered and Lawton could feel it. He turned to Lucien and waved him on with a simple 'yes?'

Lucien picked up the ball and continued the game under the wing of a friendly umpire.

'Thank you, sir . . . I would say that this object is similar in some respects to the machine that was brought in.'

Cussen took control again and prodded Lucien on to the next little sub-plot within the big story.

'You told the court the man went out to get something. Did he return?'

'Yes he did – with a large newspaper parcel of scampi.'

Ah, the scampi. In all the excitement about electric generators for torturing people we had all forgotten about the scampi.

'And upon his return with the scampi what happened next?'

'Everybody present partook of the scampi except me.'

Now who says 'partook' except in the false nonsense of a courtroom? Do people say on the bus when somebody asks them what they had for dinner last night, 'I partook of spam, egg and chips'? And here we were again eating in front of our poor victims without offering them any. But this time the scampi was to take a more significant role in the drama. Cussen asked Lucien like a pre-recorded message, 'And what happened next?'

'Charles Richardson asked again where Jack Duval was and

when I repeated that I did not know he walked up to me
with some scampi in his hands which he thrust at my eyes.
He ground the scampi into my eyes with one thumb to each
eye and then he sort of twisted them.'

What had I done to deserve this? How had I got mixed up
with Billy Liar Lucien Harris and – more the question – how
had I got tangled into his friend Jack Duval's web?

Things had been going well with the scrapyard and it seemed
there was money to be made in all sorts of ways. I dipped my
toe into wholesaling of a kind and it soon got around that I was
ready to consider buying anything in bulk if I thought I could
get rid of it. I even bought six sides of bacon which turned out
to be stolen. I should have been more careful because within
minutes of buying it I was nicked by some Old Bill who I had
stopped paying. As far as I was concerned my operations were
legitimate so why should I pay the police for their 'protection'?
So I was fitted up by petty crooks in blue uniform to teach me
a lesson. I could not face another spell inside so I did a bunk
to Canada where I set up a scrap business. But, in spite of
booming business, I really fancied a good cup of tea so I
moved back to London. That was an expensive cup of tea.
The Canadian business is worth millions today.

When I got back I discovered the scrapyards had been
well-managed by my brother Eddie and Roy Hall. I was bored.
I needed a challenge. Like a mountain climber I had reached
one peak and had my eyes on more rewarding adventures.
The wholesaling business was just like dealing in scrap. You
bought something in bulk for one price, stored it and sold it
to a number of places for a higher price. I had developed a
real taste for metals and minerals but wholesaling all sorts of
imports was an interesting diversion. Also these new areas of
activity led to meeting a new range of people. I always enjoyed
meeting different people and mulling over schemes. I had little
social life that did not involve business partners or possible
new partners. Everybody had plans and ideas, everybody was
in a state of anticipation. They did not seem to do anything
but talk about a big deal coming up. During long restaurant

meetings putting together plans and dreams I met a few people who opened the door to a kind of wholesaling deal that offered more profit than any other. It was simple really. You gathered large quantities of goods from manufacturers and importers or even other wholesalers and you sold them for less than the purchase price you negotiated with the supplier. So if you negotiated a thousand radios at £10 apiece in street markets and shops, the profit was £7 apiece because you did not pay the supplier. I liked the audacious simplicity of it. The key to the formula was getting the suppliers to believe you were going to pay in order to part with the goods. That was easy as I soon learned that people believe what they want to believe and any supplier of goods wants to believe they have found a new lucrative outlet for their goods. So you start off by ordering a fairly small amount of goods and paying cash on the button. These are then sold to retailers for the wholesale price and everybody is happy. This goes on for a few months and they suggest you open an account to be invoiced each month or whatever. If they don't suggest it then you do and in any case references are taken up. You've got a few thousand in your bank account for the company and the referees you give them are other companies you own that have nothing more to their name than headed notepaper. The references come in, you get your account and for a few months you are the best customer they've ever had, always paying within a day of receiving an invoice. Of course he is not the only supplier you are buying from with this bogus company, you have a whole string of happy suppliers. Then one day you run around them all with a good excuse for a really big order. By then you're on first name terms and they are dying to help you. They pull all the stops out to meet your order, excited by their good fortune. It is several weeks before they wonder where their money is. It might be several months before they start chasing you for the cheque and even longer before they realize they are never going to get paid. They run round to your premises to find an empty flea pit which had been rented under a false name. In the meantime you have flooded the market with their goods at less than wholesale and lots of ordinary innocent punters go home delighted at the bargain price they have paid for a radio or toaster. It's sort of Robin Hood; the rich got robbed, the poor got bargain goods and we got rich. That was the basic formula for a long firm fraud. They were called long firms because they took a long time. They took a long time because it takes time to build up people's trust.

Those were the good old days when a fiver fed a family for a fortnight, dog shit stuck to the nails in your boots and fraud was simple. It was not as socially acceptable as it became later. We were pioneers in the art and always on the lookout for possible refinements of our developing skills. Like all good businessmen in the entrepreneurial spirit that put the Great in Great Britain, we sought to minimize our investment and maximize our returns. We did not have the wealth and manpower (or the lack of morality) to travel the world and steal from starving colonials so we confined our efforts to the home front. I enjoyed my work and was happy in the rewards but some friends of mine took the long firm formula a stage further. I devised a plan within which they could diversify and multiply their profits.

They rented a huge warehouse in the City. They then set about filling it with all sorts of goods from a range of long firms operating at the same time. Within a year it was stuffed with very lucrative products which they sold as they could. The advantage of being in the City was that it was virtually empty at weekends. One weekend with a fleet of trucks they emptied the warehouse with the exception of a few bits from each line. They owed a fortune to a range of very angry companies who were getting very worried about their payments. By the time they had emptied it a dozen or so angry suppliers were threatening court proceedings unless they paid soon. As far as the suppliers were concerned the goods they had sold them were in the warehouse. Having emptied it the only thing there remained to do was burn down the warehouse, say all the goods were destroyed and claim the insurance. They would end up with the money from the sale of the goods and the money from the insurance company. Naturally everybody would be suspicious after the fire but there is a big difference between suspicion and proof. Professional villains had always made their living by exploiting that difference. This was their most ambitious project to date, and no-one had the intention of just piling a few newspapers together and spilling a bit of petrol around. Arson is a science in its own right so they looked for reputable specialists. The word on the street was that two characters from up North were the current leaders in their field. Mike Cunningham and Tommy Learmouth were very likeable lads who grew up together and had always played with matches. What they didn't know about starting fires from rubbing sticks together to elaborate incendiary bombs could be written on the back of a boy scout's prick. I met them once in a pub in the West End and noticed them race to light my cigarettes for me. When they were told that a large warehouse had to be destroyed completely so that few traces, if any, of the contents remained, they saw it as a challenge. It was also emphasized to them that the whole thing had to look like an electrical fault.

While my friends were planning the Second Great Fire of London, I was planning a nice weekend away with Margaret and the kids. It was late in the summer season so the waiters and staff at the large seaside hotel spoilt us all. The weather was changeable but I enjoyed the rest from all my work. Things were difficult with Margaret because she suspected that I was having an affair with Jean Goodman, who worked for me, and I hardly got a chance to get home with my family. I always liked kids, especially my own, so I ignored Margaret's constant attempts to discuss our marriage and 'sort this out once and for all'. Instead I made sure the kids had a good time and spent a fortune on fairground rides, toffee-apples and presents for them. I loved the way they enjoyed their pleasures with such relish and found excitements in every moment of the day. We made sand castles and had donkey rides. The miserable old bastard who hired out the tired old donkeys was reluctant to let me jump on one of his sad flea-ridden walking tins of catfood but I slipped him a quid and he waved me on. We had a race and I won because I threatened my nag that if it did not move its arse I would have its balls in batter for breakfast. We fell off our trusty steeds at the end of the ride and I chased my giggling kids into the flat shallows of the muddy beach at low tide. We walked back to the hotel munching sticky sweets to be met by Margaret's sour face. I left the kids with her and went up to my room to read the paper and listen to the radio. The moment the valves in the old radio warmed up I started packing my bags. The six o'clock news on the radio was full of a report that a huge fire was raging in London. A huge warehouse had exploded like a dolls house and the whole street was damaged. Seventeen fire engines were attempting to stop the spread of the blaze. Eye witnesses said it was like the Blitz. A factory opposite the warehouse had collapsed inside. The heavy machinery inside had fallen through the floors. Most windows and doors in the whole street were shattered and lamp posts had buckled. I wasn't sure what I was going to do, but I knew my friends would need help to sort this one out. I did not have to look far. In my office surrounded by worried friends sat Tommy the fucking torch and Mike the fucking match like two naughty terrified boys waiting for the headmaster. And like two naughty little boys I could see they were dreading their punishment. They had come to me because they were terrified of going direct to their employers. They hoped I would plead for them. I might have felt sorry for them but I could see that underneath the false contrition was a total lack of regret. The bastards had enjoyed themselves. I stormed into the room and shouted at them.

'What the hell were you doing, they only asked for the warehouse to be gutted, not the fires of hell and the six o'clock fucking news!'

Tommy was the spokesman (Mike only came to life in the glow of a fire) and I could see he was trying not to laugh.

'Sorry, Charlie . . . I suppose we were a bit over-conscientious.'

'Over-conscientious! Over-conscientious! You nearly started the second Blitz, for God's sake. They must have thought it was a nuclear attack . . . seventeen fire engines!'

I paused for a minute to look at them. Tommy had lost nearly all his hair. His eyebrows hung like a line of little bogies over his eyes and his face was as red as a vintage wino's. Both of them had clothes that were singed and reeking of fire.

'Just look at the bloody state of you. If you're seen like that you might as well sign a confession. They told me you were going to use a remote device to set it off. They said you were bloody experts!'

Tommy took up the story. They had gone to the warehouse early in the day and found the place deserted. There were no passers-by, no shops open and it was a street where nobody lived. They had travelled there in a Mini loaded up to the hilt with petrol in jerry cans covered with a blanket. They thought a small fire that did not spread was the last thing that was needed so they had better make sure. They closed all the windows, stuffed up all the vents and poured the petrol everywhere, especially on the ground floor. Then they closed up the warehouse and went to get some dinner.

'Dinner!' I was amazed.

'But Mike was starving, Charlie.'

Mike the silent one spoke up. 'I was, Charlie – no time for breakfast. I was going to grab some cornflakes but there was no milk and the missus said I could use a tin of milk but I can't bear cornflakes with tinned milk. It's not so bad in tea, I got used to that in the army, but cornflakes, you know, you have to add water . . .'

'Shut up, Mike! Just shut up!' I was going round the bend with these two.

'Couldn't you have just lit the fucking fire and gone for some dinner afterwards?'

Tommy took on the tone of an expert explaining to an interested moron. 'Ah yes, Charlie, but that's it, isn't it? You see if you light petrol it will burn, of course it will, we all know that, petrol burns very nice but if you mix it with air it becomes fumes and it fucking explodes like in a car engine.'

He continued with his story. They had gone to the pub, had some sandwiches and a drink or two to let the petrol spread as 'fumes'. When they went back there was a courting couple in the doorway having a snog. They were there for ages while our intrepid torch experts sat and watched in the car. The couple carried on snogging and the man's hands started to wander all around. I had to stop Tommy going into lavish detail about the very crude technique of the man. Anyway this was only the early sixties so his wandering hands were stopped and the woman pulled away and asked for a cigarette. Tommy paused while we took this in. We all stood round him with our jaws trailing the ground.

'Fuck me, Charlie, I nearly shit myself, he was right in the fucking doorway. If he'd lit a match he'd have been blown to kingdom come. And I know I wasn't supposed to let anybody get hurt. So Mike here had a brainwave. He started shouting at the geezer, stuff like, "Go on, mate. Give her one." And the bloke got pissed off. Called us a couple of perverts and dirty old men and they pissed off. We drove past them as if we were on our way so they wouldn't think we'd done it, then we drove back and did the job.'

Tommy stopped as if that was it. He had explained nothing so I pushed him on.

'How did you light it, Tommy?'

'I used a remote device, Charlie, like I said.'

'What kind of remote device, Tommy?'

'I used a standard remote device, Charlie.'

'What was it?'

'A rocket.'

'A rocket? What do you mean a rocket?'

'You know – a standard sort of rocket, Charlie.'

It took a few seconds but then the penny dropped.

'You used a standard rocket, you mean a Standard Rocket, you mean a fucking Guy Fawkes Standard Fireworks Rocket. You're joking, Tommy. You're pulling my bloody leg!!'

'It's a well-proven method, Charlie.'

'Arseholes, Tommy! What did you get all that money for – to have your own bloody bonfire night? Jesus fucking Christ!'

So Tommy and Mike opened a ground floor window of the warehouse, put a fireworks rocket in a milk bottle and aimed it at the window. The first two missed but the third went straight in, disappeared through the window and within a second, there was a World War Three explosion. Their Mini was thrown across the street and they were thrown with it. They managed to get the Mini going and the rest of it we heard on the news.

I paced around the room cursing while the others watched. I was mad with them but the picture of Tommy and Mike trying to aim this rocket in a milk bottle at the window was too much for me and I exploded in a fit of laughter that had me doubled up with tears streaming down my face. The others joined in and after a change of clothes for Tommy and Mike we all went out to a club.

While all this was going on, Margaret was at the end of her tether. We had been married for seven years and we had five kids. I was nearly thirty and my twenties had slipped by. I had headed more companies than I could remember and I worked day and night. Romance was something in books and magazines. I did not know how couples managed to keep a spark alive in their marriages. To me it was enough that Margaret had a nice house and did not have to worry about money. Our marriage was more to do with conformity and honour than love and romance. I made her pregnant so we got married and we had more kids. In my marriage I began to understand why the church encourages us to walk down its aisles and put on a ring. If anything is going to put a young couple off sex, it's getting married. Seeing each other day after day, seeing each other sick and bad tempered, walking into the toilet when your partner has just dumped last night's pie, chips and beans kills off the urge to jump on them without warning. It had amazed me to discover that sometimes women had smelly feet and I was bowled over by the waft of breath that a night of thriving bacteria can develop to greet you in the morning. I know I had it too but I could not taste my own. And all those beautiful women in magazines (and I had been with a few) yet they still had bacteria busily reproducing while they slept. I got over all of that but lust, love, sex and dreams had never been part of our life together. I needed sex like anybody did. It was a regular hunger that needed satisfying. With Margaret I got egg and chips. It was dependable and took away the hunger, but not a meal that you'd want to remember the next day on your way to the office. With Jean Goodman I got a Sunday roast. Very satisfying, very tiring, too much, sometimes, but a bit of a treat every time. Nobody gave me lobster thermidor but I was not really looking for it. My real buzz was business and learning about the world I lived in. So my egg and chips found out about my Sunday roast and left me, taking the two youngest kids with her. She went to her mother's. When I got home and found the other three kids waiting for their tea I called Jean to ask if she would help. The next day I went round to Margaret's mother's place. The two women sat in the kitchen with mugs of tea. They sat silently and watched as I walked in, picked up my two babies and walked out. I never saw or heard from Margaret again. Jean took over my five kids as well as organising the scrapyards.

The way I lived there was no time for a quiet drink down the pub after a hard day's graft. Life was too short to while it away talking about football and watching telly. I ate out nearly every weekday night in restaurants with colleagues or potential partners. I smoked regular cigarettes and irregular joints. I drank all the time too. It all kept my mouth busy while I listened because I had developed the art of creative listening. Usually we all talk to each other and never listen. When somebody is saying something half our mind is working out what we are going to say next instead of concentrating on what was being said. I wanted to learn and did not want to miss anything so I smoked and drank, listened and learned. Any new deal I heard, any new way of buying and selling, I would try out within days like a mad scientist experimenting. Because I listened carefully I could read between the lines of what somebody was saying and get a fair idea of what was important that they were not saying.

Late one night I was in a West End club. It was the type of club where the famous go to mix with other famous people and the not very famous go so they can enjoy paying a fortune for a drink to rub shoulders with celebrities. Film stars and politicians mingled among businessmen who wore the atmosphere like an expensive suit to impress other businessmen who they had invited. Every time a small group came in through the door, people's eyes would shift around in the middle of conversations to see who was coming in and who was with who. For some reason actors and politicians liked our company. Maybe we were all part of a club whose members' stock-in-trade was pretending to be something or somebody else. We all needed people to believe in us, we were all selling ourselves. When other people invested their belief in us we all made a living.

I was with a couple of friends talking about buying razor blades or soap or car tyres or something. It was a fast conversation full of jargon and big figures. Some of the people I mixed with in those days got a thrill just talking big money. I enjoyed it too and I got an extra thrill keeping up with it all. Each day of my life was filled with a variety of ideas and transactions. I revelled in my ability to switch from selling metals to buying shoe polish to opening a new company. With all my companies I enjoyed working out the transfer of assets and debts from one to the other. I juggled ideas, people, money, businesses and commodities all day and never dropped a skittle as they circled around me, and I had an eye and an ear for them all.

Near us was a large mixed group of backbenchers, aristocracy and starlets of the big and small screens. They laughed loudly every half minute, real belly laughs. Their eyes sparkled wet from their merriment. I was curious of the source of their fun. In the middle of them holding court like a big overweight flamboyant Henry VIII stood a man with a cigar in his grinning teeth. He was expensively but tastefully dressed. On one arm he had a watch that could be exchanged for a new car and on the other arm was a young woman whose lusty beauty was priceless. His features were plain, even podgy, but the woman, despite the excess of handsome young men in the group, only had eyes for fatso with the cigar. The whole crowd was spellbound by his lively banter. They stood with mouths half open waiting for every word, not quite knowing what to expect, but certain it was going to be worth waiting for.

I recognized the man as somebody I had seen at a whole-saler's a week before. He was being treated like royalty by a Uriah Heap executive who was wringing his hands as he brazenly licked arse and kept me waiting. I was pissed off at the time but now I was interested. I asked one of the men with me if they knew who he was.

'Fucking hell, Charlie, I don't believe it. You don't know Jack Duval? He's in your line.'

He leaned towards me. 'Go and ask Jack why you're having trouble selling those nylon stockings.'

I did not need to ask Duval about nylon stockings. I had heard a lot about Jack Duval. Jack Duval, the Prince of Fraud. He had bought a huge consignment of nylon stockings without the money to pay for them. He could not even afford to get them out of customs, but he took samples around London and sold the lot. He got the money up front, released the stockings from Her Majesty's excise men and made a killing. Then he went to Milan and booked into the most expensive hotel in town. He entertained manufacturers and just about anybody who would talk to him for weeks as he set about meeting the stocking factory owners. The industry was not doing so well out there so the businessmen suspended their visits to church to pray for their industry's salvation and lit candles round the feet of Duval instead. They all fell about themselves as Duval wrote big post-dated cheques that were a waste of the paper he wrote them on. He flooded the British market and thousands of English factory girls were delighted to wear Duval stockings on a Saturday night. They were so cheap they could afford to wear them at work. Duval was selling them for less than he paid for them, less in fact than they cost to make. In Italy the manufacturers desperately wanted to believe in Duval and waited with great patience for their money. The smaller companies went to the wall and just as the big companies were about to stop production in despair Duval would send a real cheque. He kept just ahead of the game for month after month. When he got money from very happy wholesalers in England he spent it. He had the appetite of a bored pig for expensive food. I have no idea what he did with women. After all that rich food and wine all he could do in bed was fart. He bought women to be seen with publicly. He also bought his own bank, The Bank Of Valletta, which was a very useful reference when he made deals. His victims of course had no idea that Duval's bank which gave him such glowing references and promised a massive credit balance was owned by Duval. At the same time he was running a massive fraud with airline tickets selling the same seats ten or more times through his own travel agency. Somehow he managed to keep just one step ahead of the enraged businessmen, the Fraud Squad, customs, the banks, the police and his growing posse of ex-wives. Duval was the king of the jugglers who liked to juggle on a dangerous high wire without a safety net. I wanted to meet him.

I excused myself from my friends and joined the circle of people around Duval. They had just finished laughing at one of his stories and my interruption caused them to finish off their titters. I smiled at Duval and put a hand forward. 'Hello, Jack. I'm Charles Richardson.' Duval beamed at me, grabbed my hand, gave it a hard squeeze and put his other hand on my shoulder. 'Charlie! Charlie Richardson – I've wanted to meet you for a long time.' He then spoke to his courtiers. 'This is Charlie Richardson. If you haven't heard of him yet you soon will do. Charlie is one of London's most exciting entrepreneurs. He's turned the scrap business into a multinational concern and that's only a bit of what he does. Charlie, I'd like you to meet Alison.'

I took the smooth hand of the beautiful woman next to him and she gave a gentle, definitely flirtatious squeeze. 'You tart,' I thought as I was introduced to everybody around him. However flattered I was by this recognition and greeting I soon realized that Duval flattered everybody. Around him was Britain's leading dress designer, London's most notorious barrister and the world's greatest actress etc etc. If a waiter had arrived with drinks, Jack Duval would have introduced him as the West End's most conscientious, attentive and handsome waiter. To Jack Duval every hotel was only a stone's throw from the beach even if getting to the beach entailed a forty minute ride in a smelly bus. But I realized people around him suspended reality in favour of the wonderful and thrilling world he created. He should have been employed by the Samaritans. Any potential suicide case would have spent half an hour with Duval and gone away believing the world was their oyster. I enjoyed watching him perform and was impressed by his skills. He talked very big and people swallowed every line, hungry for his attention and keen to be involved with him. Jack Duval really could have got the Pope to invest in condoms.

As we were leaving he suggested we meet and since I had had a few too many to drink I reasoned, why not be his guest, he only lived round the corner. I was impressed by his large expensive flat in a small expensive part of town. I fell asleep on the big double bed in the tasteful spare bedroom.

Within an hour I was disturbed by the beautiful Alison crawling in next to me and stroking me awake. She was a natural blonde and was naturally blonde everywhere. Her skin was smooth as a Pears soap baby but, despite the pearly, even row of teeth, her breath reeked of red wine and cigarettes. It amazed me that she must have spent hours getting ready to go out but did not take a few minutes to brush her teeth before going to bed. I cannot recall what happened. I have forgotten the memorable night she gave me, but I was not fooled by her attention. Either she was diversifying her investments for the future in case Jack's luck ran out or she was a posh bint who liked the odd bit of rough. It even occurred to me that Jack had sent her in to me as part of his business strategy.

The next morning we talked over breakfast. Jack explained his various investments and dealings. He actually did know who I was so he was able to be honest about the dishonesty of much of his work. I was impressed, not just with the dealings but that he could sleep at all at night. How could somebody really live from day to day like that – borrowing money to pay off serious past debts, always one step away from jail or a bullet in the head. At the end of his impressive presentation he offered me the opportunity to invest in one of his schemes. I wrote out a cheque for a big consignment of stockings from

Jean La Grange.

Above: A beautiful painting of a beautiful woman. Jean.
Below: Best of friends. Gordon Winter with General H. J. Van den Bergh, head of the South African Secret Service, at his Pretoria farm in 1979.

Above: Two generations of Richardsons. From left to right: me with my father and brother.
Below: On top of the world. Table Mountain.

With Roy Hall in 1980 when I was on the run.

Above and below: Still on the run in Belgium in 1982. I came back to Britain because I missed a decent cup of tea.

With my granddaughter.

Left: With Veronica, my wife.
Below: A dinner at the Uppercut Club for boxers, with Joe Ryle and Alex Steine. I was elected President in 1989.

Another little terror in the making. My youngest son, William, who was born in 1985.

Italy. Duval pocketed the cheque with a confident smile. He thought he had me on his firm but I was going to get him on mine.

I recognized Duval's qualities. He was an excellent front man who spoke posh English with a slight foreign accent. He also spoke Italian and French. He could slip the Queen a wink and the Home Secretary a Mason's handshake while outside the police were banging on the door to arrest him. But he was out of control, a wild dog running around wagging his tail at some people and biting others. He needed to be brought to heel and trained to be loyal to one master. As I drove away towards Camberwell I was confident I could control him. I just had to work out how.

Duval was not afraid of authority, that was obvious. He saw the police and customs as occupational hazards that could easily be avoided with skilful navigation. He was not afraid of hurting somebody with his deals. He had absolutely no sense of loyalty and was completely without morality. He would grass on his mother to save his own loose layers of skin. He looked like he had always been fat. Fat boys at school are usually bullies or they are everybody's victims for being bullied and scorned. Jack Duval, I reckoned, had learned to talk his way out of being bullied because he was terrified of physical violence. If his best friend went to jail because of him Jack would sleep like a baby, but tell him you're going to pound his nose in the morning and he would lie awake all night sweating at the thought of it. It was simple to realize that the key to controlling him was to make him frightened of me. I mulled it over for a day or so. Punching him around a bit was clumsy and would not create a sense of real fear. I did not want to hurt him, just frighten him. I came up with a simple but effective idea.

I should have known better than to hire Mike and Tommy, the notorious and useless arsonists, but I did not know anyone else. I was a businessman, unorthodox perhaps, but I did not regularly socialize with pyromaniacs. I briefed them well. I wanted a very small charge of explosives placed at the door to Duval's flat. I wanted them to blow out the door and make a little mess. And I wanted something a bit more professional than Guy Fawkes fireworks.

'No problem, Charlie, we've just taken delivery of some jelly – we'll use that.'

'Jelly?'

'Gelignite, Charlie – we've got five pounds of gelignite. That will make a nice hole in the door. And you just set this stuff off with a long fuse.'

They went off to do their job that night. As I sat in a club to wait for their report I got talking to a punter who had done some work for the coalboard. Without him realizing I fished for information about explosives. It only took half an hour beating around the subject to realize that five pounds of gelignite in the middle of a block of flats would just about reduce half the block to rubble. As I was building up to an enraged panic, my two intrepid explosives experts came into the club. Tommy looked dejected but before I screamed at him I gave him the chance to explain.

'Fucking thing didn't go off, Charlie.' I was relieved to hear it but said nothing and listened to their story. It turned out that they had lit the fuse and left the block. A woman in one of the flats had seen them so they did not dare go back to light it again. I told them in a loud whisper what would have happened if the bomb had gone off. They tried to talk themselves around it but it did not really matter. I knew when Duval found the failed bomb it would put the shits up him. It did. That night he saw the bomb and ran to a hotel for the night. A few phone calls to find out where he was and I turned up in his room, sat on the end of his bed with a cup of tea and asked if he got anything in the post yesterday. He got the message. I wanted the stockings now.

So fat Jack went off to Milan and within a week I got a big consignment of stockings. There was a lot of shit among them but I did expect that, as did the traders I sold to. I ordered more and got a steady supply. I sat back and congratulated myself for harnessing such a good money maker and controlling his excesses. Then the supply dried up and I went from pissed off to bloody spare within a few weeks. I sent my kid brother

Eddie to find out what was going on. Eddie was much more suspicious of Duval than me. In some ways Eddie was more level-headed with his feet on the ground than I was. I always wanted to see the value in things when Eddie was looking for the catch. When it came to socializing and travelling Eddie was more interested in it all than me so the benefits of a visit to Italy were twofold. He could have a good time *and* he could confirm his suspicions of Duval.

When Eddie arrived Duval greeted him like an old pal and showed him a good time. Duval had a permanent suite in the very best hotel. He booked Eddie in and whisked him off his feet with a good time. They went on regular trips to Switzerland to gamble in casinos. It did not take Eddie long to plant his feet back on the ground and notice something irregular about their regular trips across the border. Duval was always met by somebody and an exchange took place. Eddie did a bit of asking around and watching before he realized that Duval was using the trips to smuggle diamonds from a jeweller in Switzerland. One of the Italian organized families dubbed the 'Mafia' by the press had put up the money for the project. Eddie was mad that Duval had put him at risk. He left having given Duval a smack on more than his wrist and warned him to get his act together with the stockings or I would be the next visitor. He did, and for a few weeks I got my deliveries.

Meanwhile the Krays, who always had an eye on what we were up to, got interested in Duval. The twins kept their distance from us but they wanted to build an empire that extended beyond the East End. Since they had a few quid they had started to move in ever-increasing circles. They were favourite guests at parties of film stars and the like who were always on the look out for a bit of drama in real life. Some of them acted as villains in films so it was interesting to meet real ones. Ronnie and Reggie wanted to extend to the West End but Frank Fraser and my brother Eddie had that just about sewn up. Sometimes some of the people they knocked out came to us. George Cornell had tried competing with the Krays on their own manor. He was one of the few local Eastenders who was never afraid of them and would even publicly take the piss out of them. He could not beat them on his own no matter how hard he was, and he was a very hard man, so he came to work for me. Later George took the piss once too often, called Ronnie a 'fat poof' just at the time Ronnie was looking for a human sacrifice for his reputation. Ronnie walked into a pub with a gun, blew off George's head and ordered a drink. No matter how hard and fearless you are, if the other man has got a gun the odds are very uneven.

Long before George made that unkind reference to Ronnie Kray's stature and sexuality, the twins kept an eye on our growth and development. With Duval they could smell money so they decided to look into it. Like any budding business, they wanted to go international, so they flew out to Milan to meet fat Jack. They were not really interested in the wholesale business so they got bored quickly with the ladies' stockings scene. Somewhere they had got a whiff that once upon a time in Italian history there had been a lot of painters around who did a lot of paintings that were now worth a lot of money. They also learned from their intelligence source that lots of the paintings that were not taken up by galleries and millionaire collectors were just lying around in churches. It might have been some of the nobs they were mixing with that gave them the idea of investing in art, but in any case they saw Jack Duval as the possible supplier. When Jack was asked he said he knew all about the paintings that were available and he told them they had come to the right place. Of course he did. Duval would promise a cure for cancer if he could smell money. The next day the Krays were taken to a very secret warehouse where Duval had a display of old canvases he could grab from street artists and junk shops. Although neither of the twins had ever been asked to review an exhibition of contemporary paintings for *The Times* they could certainly smell shit when it was put under their noses. They gave up on Duval and left for London. He was lucky – possibly because they were on foreign turf they left it like that.

Duval had heard of the Krays and he was terrified of physical violence but he did have a very loose screw in the head. Sometimes he could not think beyond the pressing debts he had and the impossible lifestyle he led. He was in the habit of receiving business guests while he lounged in the bath with a bottle of champagne in a hotel suite that was reserved for visiting royalty or at least bent Vatican bankers. The very well-connected and powerful organization that had given him a fortune to develop their interests in smuggled diamonds were not very happy when he spent the money. The Swiss jeweller and the Italian organization were both left empty-handed and Duval had the sense not to hang around. He was pursued by the Swiss police, the Italian police, the 'Mafia' and, should he show his face in England, the English police and me. So fat Jack moved to Belgium where he did not die of boredom since the Italians were still chasing him. After nearly a year of climbing out of hotel bedroom windows he decided to slip back into England. In Brighton he would not keep his big mouth shut and I found out soon enough where he was staying.

I should have taken Eddie's advice and given up on Duval but I still believed he had talents that I could exploit. I told him to come and see me. When he did I knocked him around the room to teach him a lesson about the diamond smuggling and to make me feel a bit better. It was therapy for us both. There was no ritualized torture and no knife. Later at the Old Bailey, Duval said I had cut his stomach with a knife and he had the scar to prove it. Everybody who knew him knew that the scar on Duval's undulating waterbed belly was the Jack Duval patent diet plan. With all the food and wine he stuffed into his face he put on a lot of weight. His idea of weight reduction could never involve eating less or exercise. He went to a little Swiss clinic and had the fat sucked out with a hoover. Those were the early days of plastic surgery so it left a cross shaped scar. It only took a week of pasta to replace the layers of tyres around his gut but he was left with a scar.

So I knocked him around and things were sorted out. We went to work and started a couple of long firms. For some time this worked well. A company called Twelve Estates bought and sold bleach and household detergents while a more upmarket company, Common Markets, dealt in things like radios and shirts. He was an excellent front man who had people falling over themselves to invest or supply goods. For months the loose screw was threaded and he worked well but finally things started going wrong again. He started writing out big cheques from Common Markets and opening new accounts connected to the company. I went totally apeshit and before I could sort him out he was on the run. Even then he was bouncing cheques all over the place. Fat Jack, Jack the Rat, Jack the Chequeman was the wild Prince of Fraud who had conned me. I desperately wanted to find him. He had broken a sacred rule. You don't steal from your own, and I was his own. I spent weeks trying to find him and approached anybody who knew him. Lucien Harris was a personal friend of Jack the Rat Duval so I gave him a rough time looking for him. The next time I saw Duval was when I was in the dock and he was a witness for the prosecution. The police must have had a car load of files on Duval but they did not need them. He would have grassed on me for a tenner, he would have grassed on his mother for less. The only deal the likes of Lucien Harris, Taggart and Duval could accept with the police was one where I was guaranteed a long spell inside. The other part of the deal would be to make sure others who would take immediate revenge for my imprisonment would go in with me. So they created a monster who made Genghis Khan look like a social worker and they invented a vicious gang more frightening than an SS hit squad. Then they developed the awful apparatus for us to use in our ritualized torture and interrogation scenes. Someone had a brainwave. It might have been stretching the intellectual resources of the police to come up with it so it could have been Duval, but somebody could see the horrific sexiness of an ominous black box that discharged agony at the turn of a handle.

CHAPTER SEVEN
A Manor in the Sun

Let me set the scene. In the centre of the court is a large black box with a handle and leads. Lucien Harris, smooth talking friend of Fat Jack the Rat Duval, is in the witness stand. He is impeccably dressed in a dark business suit. Near him on a higher level is the judge, his robes and wigs boasting an authority stained with the misery of thousands over the centuries. Every word he speaks will go on the record thanks to the enthusiastic reporters in the press gallery. They in turn know that they have got a sexy story which might produce a spark in the dull eyes of their commuting readers. The public hang on every word and feel privileged to be present at such an historic case. The jury have risen from the ranks of humble ratepayers who wish the trains would run on time to mini judges. They are proud of their importance, never realizing they are only pawns in a game dominated by players not even present in the court. Everybody is having a fucking good time. Our lives are at stake and it's all a bit of a juicy tale and a laugh for these sensation vultures. Some of the people involved are making a fortune out of it all. The lawyers, the judge and the newspapers. But where's *our* cut? After all, our exploits are the skeleton for the story. The flesh was provided by the butchers in Scotland Yard.

Concentration is high as the roving hand strokes the thigh approaching the centre of maximum sensation. Lucien is soon going to mention bits of his naked body like penis and anus, key words for the middle class contingent in our midst. The story so far is that I told Roy Hall to take Lucien's shoes and socks off.

Cussen asks Lucien, 'And then?'

'Hall brought over the portable hand generator and attached the leads from the generator to the big toes on either foot.'

'Then what?'

'He turned the handle of the generator, sir.'

'When the handle was turned what did you feel?'

'I felt a shock. I felt myself jump and I landed on the floor.'

'What kind of shock did you feel? Describe it fully to the court.'

Cussen was obviously disappointed. This caress lacked eroticism and promise. He gave Lucien another chance to slide a silky hand and Lucien did try.

'Well, it's a bit like trying to describe the taste of an orange, sir, isn't it? I mean an electric shock is an electric shock.'

Justice Lawton realized Lucien was not too promising on this part of the story so he helped him out with a slight change of tack.

'Well, try and describe the intensity of it, because we have all had a bit of an electric shock – perhaps when doing the home wiring which one used to do when one got enough time, as an amateur.'

I made a silent prayer that Lawton would find the time for a bit of amateur home wiring in the next few days. Lucien tried to deliver good copy for the press.

'I can only say it was not a burning sensation but it gave a profound muscular shock, a strong muscular shock. You know, your muscles sort of jump.'

It did not seem too much of an ordeal to me but Cussen had a long way to go on this one.

'When it happened were you silent?'

'No, I yelled very loudly.'

'Then what happened?'

'I was bundled back into the chair, the wires were reconnected to my toes, the handle of the generator was turned and again I jumped, screamed and landed on the floor.'

'What happened next?'

'They did this to me two more times and then Charles Richardson told somebody to take my clothes off. I was then stripped.'

At last the court had got the picture it was waiting for just as the audience were beginning to worry that Lucien was a prick teaser.

'Describe what happened to you from there on.'

'The leads were again connected to my toes, the handle was turned again and I writhed around on the floor.'

'Yes?'

'Charles Richardson said it didn't seem to be working well enough and a bottle of orange squash was poured over my feet.'

This sounded very uncharacteristic, given the already proven fact that we were sticklers for cleanliness when torturing people. Orange squash all over the place would mean we would be walking around for weeks with our shoes sticking to the floor.

'What happened next?'

'Again the terminals were connected and again the handle was turned.'

'When you say, "Again the terminals were connected," where were they connected to?'

'Still the toes, sir.'

But wait for it, everybody. He is naked. It would be a bit of a waste if we had stayed on his toes when there were lots of other possibilities. The courtroom was happy to wait, happy to be teased knowing Lucien was sitting there on his bare bum with his balls hanging free. Everybody was sure we would get round to the bits of Lucien's body with the most nerve endings. With a whole room packed full of people you were bound to get different needs. The public were happy to bathe in the warm tingling expectation of pleasures to come. The judge was a numb old hand, who by the law of diminishing returns was a little bored by this ordinary torture. So he intervened.

'Well . . . what happened after that?'

'I had been yelling somewhat, sir, every time it happened. Charles Richardson said "stop him screaming" and a handkerchief was stuck in my mouth which was bound by a cloth as a gag. At the same time my hands were tied behind my back.'

'Was any other part of your body restricted?'

'No, sir.'

Let's face it, there was not much left to restrict except his legs and that would have restricted our scope on some of the little sensitive bits.

'Just continue, Mr Harris.'

'Then the leads were removed from my feet and at various times attached to different parts of my body and the same treatment was repeated.'

This was it. The whole courtroom held its breath. The press stopped scribbling, the judge put down his pen.

'Just tell the court where the leads were attached and how.'

'The ends of the leads were very stiff bare wire, hooked over. They were about two inches long and then the wire was insulated so somebody could hold the wire by the insulated portion without getting a shock.'

The court was still holding its breath, some of the smokers were going blue. Cussen poised for the final deadly stroke that guaranteed the end of all hope for me and my friends in the dock. A few seconds of breathless posturing and he jabbed.

'To what parts of your body were the terminals administered? Take them one by one.'

After many months of briefing, going over his statement a thousand times in a secret little police office during a long secret investigation Lucien's moment had arrived. It was time to deliver the punch line in his sad tale. With practised deliberation he slowly delivered his sordid list of bits of the body.

'First to the calf of each leg, then to the chest and the nose . . .' (a short pause) 'then to the thighs . . . to the penis . . . and to the anus.'

Everybody let out their breath and as they sucked a lungful of air I could sense the excitement in their loins and almost hear the silent fucking hells and Jesus Christs. And I could visualize the newspaper reports and I could hear the British public on buses and in pubs. 'So they stick one bit of wire on the end of his prick and the other up his fucking arse, fucking Ada!' And all sorts of people, many of them in powerful positions, respectable and honest law-abiding citizens, would very secretly wonder what it felt like. If I achieved nothing else for my country I did give Britain a collective tingle the

A Manor in the Sun

next day as they read the papers. I could have congratulated myself for delivering this mass cheap thrill but I cannot take credit for the story. The thought of going two inches from a man's arsehole sent me into a cold sweat of revulsion. It sounded to me like an experimental cure for a severe case of impotence. But it was a clever invention. Lucien had already carefully established that it did not burn him so there would be no scars to prove his ordeal. Anyway, you could hardly expect him to take out his little torpedo and pass it round the jury with Cussen announcing, 'Your Worship, with respect the Crown presents exhibit B . . . one wrinkled penis charred one side and raw the other like a British Rail sausage.'

Exhibit A remained in the centre of the court. A black box. Everybody looked at the black box and looked at Lucien, put two and two together and got a big thrill.

What had justice got to do with it all? Our defence, our denial of these events was boring compared with their stories. It is so much easier to get people to believe you if they want to believe you. They did not want to believe our innocence. It was much more fun to tell the story as a 'true' one. When other matters were dealt with in the court, like fraud allegations, who would be interested in the long and boring complications? Such down-to-earth inanities seemed insignificant when the minds of the jury were so firmly imprinted with the image of a man with an electric torture box attached to his wedding tackle.

It had taken the prosecution almost two years to prepare this case against us. After my run in with Jack Duval I went about business as usual and was oblivious to the investigations initiated by petty no-hoper small businessmen and villains who had reasons to hate me. It was the most productive period of my life where I came very near to being a respected millionaire with a seat kept warm for me in the House of Lords.

There is one area where fact and fiction about villains comes together. Like in the books and films most real villains dream of doing one big job and getting out of it all. In the films they

are usually caught on that last big job. In real life they often
get away with it but some time later they get bored or greedy
and want to do another last big job which is usually when they
do get caught. The skill is to do the job and get away with it
and straighten up your life. There are a few very respected
businessmen who are regulars in the Royal enclosure at Ascot
who did one big job and managed to bury their past.

Around south-east London in the early sixties we had a
character who kept coming to me with hare-brained schemes.
He was an interesting and creative soul but I usually sent him
away with a chuckle. It took months for us to realize we had
not seen him around and after a bit of an unofficial enquiry
I found out why.

Denis had come up with such a good idea he kept it to
himself. He had come out of a Park Lane casino one Sunday
in the early hours and noticed two security men from the
casino take a big bag full of money and drop it in a night
safe near the casino. Being a curious man he sat at the side
of the road and watched for several hours as people from the
surrounding Mayfair casinos and clubs dropped bags into the
hole in the wall. It dawned on him that what they were doing
was just that – dropping money into a hole in the wall. It
was not any hole, it was a hole belonging to the bank and
because they believed in it, people were happy to drop the
Saturday night takings from drunken millionaires into it. He
was inspired. All he had to do was to have a hole of his own;
then he had to make people believe in it.

Under a false name of a false company he rented a ground
floor office building just round the corner from the bank. He
put a big wooden plaque on the outside of the building
advertising a bogus contractor. Behind the plaque from the
inside he smashed a neat hole in the wall. With some help
and a little investment he had a copy of the bank's sign and
a night safe made up. The night safe was installed behind the
wooden plaque in his building. One Saturday night dressed in
overalls he put the copy of the bank's sign up on his building
and removed the wooden plaque to expose a brand new shiny
night safe. All he had to do then was put a very professional

sign over the real night safe at the real bank apologizing to customers for the inconvenience and could they please use the night safe round the corner in their new branch. The reason was building work which would be complete within a few weeks. Just to add a bit of detail he put the bogus contractor's sign on the bank wall and dumped some bricks, sand and scaffolding poles on the pavement outside the bank.

Alone inside his rented offices, Denis sat in the dark with a flask of tea next to his hole and waited. From 11 o'clock onwards through the night he watched bag after bag of money drop at his feet. In the morning he drove his stolen van to Heathrow and flew away to a sunny place where he is now a very respected businessman and well-connected politician. It is not such an incredible story if you remember that our aristocracy and royalty are direct descendants of murdering land and cattle thieves.

I wanted to do my big job and leave, but I wanted to leave the life I led, not the country, so the big job must have no risk of prison because it was going to be legal. Most of what I did was legal at that time anyway. I had the scrapyards and wholesaling business. Eddie and Frank Fraser were running a very lucrative business with fruit machines that they placed in clubs all over the West End and in the provinces. The Krays looked on enviously at their activities but would not dare move against them. In stories of the 'Mafia' you read about 'gangsters' forcing fruit machines on poor club owners who are bullied into accepting 'protection'. As I said before, the only effective protection racket in existence was operated by the Metropolitan Police but some small-time villains of little imagination had seen too many American films and they tried it on. When Eddie and Frank went to a club to install their machines they had to persuade the club owner to get rid of somebody else's machines. They did not have to use force, they just offered a bigger percentage of the take to the owner. It was as simple and undramatic as that. However, very often the owner knew that if Eddie and Frank's machines were in the club then other aspiring protection gangs would leave that club alone. So although later they were accused of running protection rackets, that is 'the Richardsons' were accused, it was not 'the Richardsons' and it was not a protection racket. It was Eddie and Frank as energetic businessmen who were a protection from the protection gangs. They were doing the police's job for them because the police were too busy running around picking up their takings from the likes of me and Eddie and Frank. In fact I had a row with Eddie because he stopped paying the police. I got a phone call from a senior copper one night to sort my brother out or else. Eddie had refused to pay up because his activities were strictly legal. Quite right too, but I had to impress on him that the law was something the police used to finance foreign holidays for their families. It was not a code they respected. I paid the senior copper myself and had a shouting match with Eddie. Poor Eddie, he was still young enough to believe in a sense of fair play. He thought that it was fair to slip the Met a little bundle if you were breaking the law but if you were legal they should leave you alone. I had to impress on him that once they've got your number they will give you a ring anytime they feel like picking up the phone.

Things were easy. I busied myself around the yards and spent very long lunches with various businessmen and occasionally with heads of large public companies. We would chat about big plans and ideas, eat massive quantities of rich overpriced food and experiment with artificial stimulants. I started to seek out the company of very 'respectable' people who liked to show how modern they were by having me at the dinner table. But I was having them. I would sit and listen to the exaggerated stories of the exclusive club chambermaid with 'legs up to her bottom' and a bottom 'like an apple' who had sat on their face for a fiver. And I would sit and listen and say, 'Very nice, Alistair! Very nice . . . I hope she didn't fart.' And as he guffawed I would repeat to him the idea of becoming involved with a new company I was starting. And he would smile and patronize me, his tame ape from the wrong side of the river and say, 'Love to, Charles, really would love to, but I am rather tied up otherwise . . .' And I would interrupt, 'Oh you wouldn't be an *executive* director, Rodney – I wouldn't expect you to get involved in the everyday running . . .' And they would get the picture. 'You mean, turn up for the Annual General Meeting and . . .' And we were on the same wavelength. I would suggest the whole thing could be done by post with the minimum of effort on their part. Then I would throw in the name of another 'respectable' junior aristocrat or Tory vicar who was on the board and delicately mention the fee. They would do some quick mental arithmetic, work out how many chambermaids' bottoms they could get for two thousand quid and sign up. It was a fair system of exchange and let's face it, if you're born with a title and thousands of years of inbreeding leading to scrambled egg for brains, you had to make a living somehow.

In the end I got fed up with it all. I wanted to do the one big job. I wanted to be completely legal. I wanted to be 'respectable'. It was not that I was fed up with the threat of prison or police harassment because that was just a question of finance. I knew that if I really wanted to make a lot of money I could only do it within their rules. I wanted to take a big step up the ladder without tumbling from the top. I did not have to wait too long for the chance.

I had met a mad little Welshman called Richard Aubrey who ran around as if he only had twenty-four hours to live. He ate as he ran and he ate whatever was available at the time. He was stuffed with peanuts and British Rail ham sandwiches. Whenever he needed a piss he would stop the car and aim it at the wheel still talking about some great plan. He was a total worker. He once nearly fainted from the results of his terrible diet and racing metabolism. His doctor recommended Guinness thinking it was the only way to get Richard to take some kind of nutrition.

In his native Wales he had noticed poor people scrambling among slag heaps for the odd good bit of coal. He thought it might be easier with a bulldozer so he bought a slag heap and made a few grand. He then tried to interest me in the project so we bought a slag heap together, moved into a hotel nearby and started to extract the coal. The price of coal had fallen so

it was not such a good deal. Anyway I did not like to take a
living from the poor buggers who lived off the scratchings on
the slag.

I was always interested in metals and for years had dealt
in their recycling. It was a post-war occupation, there was
a lot of junk metal lying around. It would never completely
dry up but the boom was nearly over. There was a need for
metals fresh from the ground and I was fascinated by the
simple idea of digging up chunks of dirty rubble, melting it
and producing double decker buses, ships, wedding rings,
nuts, bolts, knives, forks and tins for baked beans. Aubrey
had been to South Africa and told me his tale of wonder.
The mention of the country immediately conjured up images
of diamonds and gold, but according to Aubrey that was just
the tip of a money-spinning iceberg of all sorts of metals and
semi-precious stones. 'Listen, Charlie, you don't have to dig
for the fucking stuff. It's not like over here with miners
working a mile underground risking their lives for coal. You
walk along and pick up opals off the fucking ground, you trip
over the bastards.' He fascinated me with more stories about
the size of the country, the opportunities for business, the open-
ings for men like us. 'They're so fucking slow, Charlie . . .
they're sitting on the biggest pot of gold in the world. It's
the end of the rainbow, Charlie, and they're too busy going
to church and torturing coloured people to notice. They're
so busy trying to protect what they've got from the fucking
Zulus that they haven't got time to see the opportunities.' It
was the sort of conversation full of fortunes to be made that
I had heard a thousand times but as usual there was always a
flaw, a catch, a small weakness in the dream. Richard as usual
was ahead of himself already and before I could say 'but . . .'
he said, 'I know it's thousands of miles away and they're all
fucking foreigners but the system's the same, Charlie, because
we gave it to them, the law and business stuff – it's all the
same except they're slow and we're not.' He could see I was
still only being polite so he showed me his full hand to prove
he was not bluffing. 'And I know a bloke who's got four million
acres of land full of minerals in a place called Namaqualand,

it's dripping semi-precious stones and minerals. His name is Thomas Waldeck. He's got some partners but he's the main bloke. He's got hundreds of natives who work for fuck all, he's got all the mineral rights, he's got a government minister in his pocket and he's a member of the Broederbond – if you think the Freemasons have got a monopoly on fun and games for men in little secret meetings you should see the Broederbond, they run the fucking country. The only thing he hasn't got is money.'

I was very interested but worried. 'If he's got all that, Richard, how come he can't find any backers?' He had expected that. 'You know what it's like, Charlie, it's just like out here, everybody wants to make money without taking any risks, without working for it. They're bloody worse out there. I've tried to get people interested but they're frightened off by how big the whole thing is. They want it all spelt out. Like bank managers, you have to persuade them you don't need any money before they will lend you any. This thing needs imagination . . . it needs a real entrepreneur and he's hungry for somebody to come in and save him. He's got this wife who wants a big house . . .' I got the picture and I was interested. I was full of imagination and I was a real entrepreneur. I loved the idea of building something from nothing and I knew unless you were born rich the only way you got rich was to take risks. And anyway I liked risks; the cosy life I was leading was slowing the blood in my veins.

Aubrey was dead right about British investors and he knew it was a sore point with me. It was a crude, old trick. When you are trying to convince somebody of something, throw in a few home truths that hit a soft spot and the whole story rings true. Richard had heard me complain a hundred times about English investors who let the Yanks and other foreigners dance rings around them while the grass and weeds grew under their own feet. They sat carefully on their fat arses and expanded their fortunes slowly with cautious investment in certain bets. I was constantly frustrated trying to raise their interest and finance in exciting but risky ventures. We would sit at lunch in a restaurant where they did not tip because 'it only encouraged them'. After having 'delighted' in my company and being 'intrigued' by my 'ingenious' plan, they would make their excuses and leave.

Richard's challenge was the old 'but can you afford it' trick. He was calling my bluff. He had been around the town trying to sell this South African deal and he had got nowhere. It was not because the deal was bad but because the fat cats lacked adventure, and even the few who were attracted to adventure got bowled over by the massive scale of the operation. It was not like me, but I told Richard I would have to think about it. Usually, I made instant decisions, but this would be by far the biggest deal of my life – in a foreign country, with strangers.

There was no point in company searches or asking anybody I knew about the deal. The whole thing hung on Richard Aubrey. I had to work out if I could trust him and what was in it for him. He had done some pretty good deals in the past, but his business ethics might have made a pornographer blush. Only the year prior to our meeting, Richard Aubrey had set up a film company, called himself a film-maker and set about to shoot an important record of the nobility of labour in a South Wales mining valley. God knows where he raised the money from, but I can imagine the stories he told to get it. The whole of that valley of hard-working, poorly paid miners and their families helped in the making of that salt of the earth production. They started by co-operating and ended up sweating day and night in their belief in Aubrey and his commitment to a shared vision. After many weeks of hard work, all the film was 'lost' and the considerable insurance was claimed. The insurance was supposed to finance a re-shoot, but Aubrey shot off with the loot and left hundreds of miners with a chip on their shoulder about film-makers.

As he moved around with the energy of a soldier ant, he left behind him a trail of broken promises and dreams. I asked him once how he managed to get inside the knickers of so many women and he told me of his simple trick. He would decide what 'type' of woman he was dealing with and promise her marriage or a house or a car or all of them, depending on

their particular characteristics. These promises were made
with diplomacy and charm as he wined and dined them in
the poshest hotels and restaurants. When he got fed up with
them, he just left them, without even a twinge of guilt. They
would be left with nothing but a dose of crabs to remind them
of the lobster he fed them.

Yet, while he danced around and broke hearts and contracts,
he had managed to build up a tidy stash of money. He had a
lavish lifestyle and it was not all bounced cheques. I was faced
with a similar problem to that of Fat Jack Duval. I would have
to use him and his contacts within my own control and then
ditch him before he could do any damage.

I knew that the South African project would take a full-time
commitment and I spent a weekend agonising whether I
should make the necessary radical alterations to my life in
order to pursue it. I was thirty years old with five kids and
God knows how many companies to run. I was a good father,
given my lifestyle. If a member of the Social Services were to
judge then they might have found me wanting, but a degree
in sociology and a corduroy jacket are not the qualifications
you need to judge somebody's life. I loved my kids and I saw as
much of them as I could, not because I felt I had to, but because
I enjoyed their company. Jean Goodman was a good mother to
them; they had a loving grandmother who saw them often.
The time I did spend with them did not fit the usual pattern,
but neither did my life. I spent most Sundays with them and,
although they might not see me for days through the week,
I would sometimes drop by their school, pick them up and
take them to the park for the afternoon. I may not have been
a home-every-evening-for-tea dad, but I was a bloody exciting
dad who they knew cared for his kids.

Business could not have been better. We had expanded
beyond recognition. I had managed to get hold of a whole
load of cranes, tractors and bulldozers from a man who owed
me a favour so we were able to get into jobs that were very
big. We started getting lots of jobs from the Ministry of Public
Works. One day, the whole of Central London traffic came to
a standstill as Roy Hall supervised the removal of a massive

boiler from a government building in Russell Square. It was a good job well done and lots more followed. It was legal and proper and we charged a fair price. So I sat in my office in Camberwell, felt my paunch pressing against my belt, looked at the fat, throbbing order book, noted that our taxes were paid up to date and thought, 'Fuck this, much more of this and they'll be asking me to join the local Rotary Club.' The thought of such an instant death to any remaining hope for swashbuckling adventure made me jump into action. What is the worst that can happen? What can they do to me? I thought. If I was totally wiped out by Tricky Dicky Aubrey and his South African Broederbonders, so fucking what! I was still young. I still woke up with a hard-on every morning. It would only take a few months to climb back up again. Bankruptcy was only an accounting procedure that caused a minor hiccup in the life of a good entrepreneur. It was state of mind that mattered. I picked up the phone, dialled one of Richard's numbers and interrupted him promising the world to some poor debutante with a small brain and big tits. I told him we should meet and arranged for tea in a Park Lane hotel. So we paid three pounds for two dainty cups of weak tea and a tray of cucumber sandwiches made from Mother's Pride with the crusts cut off. I told him I had all the money it would take either from my own little stash or raised elsewhere. He then confessed to me that he had come to London with the main intention of selling this idea to the 'Richardsons' or the 'Krays'. That was the final straw, I thought, as he told me. South Africa may be a country ruled by dull-brained Boers who looked like the oxen that pulled their carts, but nobody deserved the Krays. Also, if the Krays were to visit South Africa, they might come back with a false sense of their own intelligence. They were dangerous enough as it was, without running around and trying to be clever. I took Richard's clammy hand, left a massive tip for the long-legged waitress who was very attentive even when she had heard my south London accent, and I left. As I emerged into the evening drizzle, I realized I had not arranged a date to meet Richard again. I turned to go back, but as I re-entered the hotel lobby I could see him helping himself to the tip off our table, slipping it into his pocket and approaching the waitress with a seductive grin. I turned and left. I would phone him.

So I was going to a new country! I bought myself a very nice passport which was a bit more expensive than applying at the Passport Office, but a lot quicker. I realized I needed more than the protection of Her Majesty's Government for this one so I thought of who I could rope in to help. After a bit of thought, I approached the Major for some help.

Major Nicholson was a lovely man. He was a leading Tory and had lots of friends in Parliament. He liked to help self-made people and liked me because of my drive and enterprise. I wanted him in on the deal, but I think he was worried about the scale of it all at first. He did provide me with some powerful letters of introduction from a few political friends who would be respected in South Africa. So, armed with our letters of introduction and some new lightweight suits I had had specially tailored for the occasion, we packed our bucket and spade along with the HP sauce and flew off to Africa. On 24 August, 1964, my brother Eddie, my 'wife' Jean Goodman, a colleague called Ken and slimy Richard Aubrey accepted duty free drinks from the BOAC stewardess as we flew from Heathrow to Johannesburg. We were booked into the Ambassador Hotel and I was a bit worried because Jean was not really my wife and it would show on the passports. Those were the days when things like that mattered. Richard assured me it would be taken care of.

In Johannesburg, everything was taken care of by somebody. The hotel had staff hiding behind the pillars desperate to help you with anything. In the toilet, I was relieved to find I was allowed to wipe my own arse. But I loved it! Who doesn't like to be treated as special? I loved it when people behaved with respect at the first meeting and it all made me realize what a pathetic little shit-hole England can be. In London, wherever I went, in a shop or restaurant, people had me sized up in seconds. Before I opened my mouth, the cut of my cloth and confidence in my posture had them ready to kiss the edge of my coat in grovelling respect. Then, as soon as I spoke and my south-east London working class birthright came spewing out, they straightened up and secretly regretted their first few seconds of bowing to me. Slimy bastards! In Johannesburg, most people knew the difference between my accent and the lazy-jaw speech impediments suffered by the English middle class. But in Johannesburg, it made no difference. The fact that you were there and not carrying a stack of trays of apples on your head in Covent Garden meant you deserved respect. I loved the place, the climate, the food, the fresh, fresh air. I did think it was a pity the whole thing had to be held together by brutality towards the majority of its population. But nobody in the British press at that time thought of having headlines calling the Prime Minister of South Africa the 'Torture Gang Boss'.

I met Tom Waldeck at the Ambassador and decided within minutes to be his partner. I could sense that he really did have something big to sell and behind the quiet, well-bred reserve of landed gentry I could smell the hunger and greed and, most importantly, the fatigue. This man had managed through a combination of very hard work, bribery and corruption to put together a massive hunk of land filled with minerals, semi-precious and even precious stones. His mining rights only lasted a year and had to be renewed each year. That was assured as long as he greased the very big palm of a Broederbond brother in the government. He had to put the deal together with a group of finance partners who were happy to reap the future rewards with no effort. He was spurred on by a wife who only wanted an even bigger house with even more servants. And he was very tired. I could feel it when I met him. He was hoping to meet somebody who would take his head and rest it against their chest and say, 'There . . . there . . . Tom . . . from now on everything is going to be fine . . . I'm going to take care of everything.' Poor tired Tom was like a little boy who had scraped his knee and wanted his mum to kiss it better. So I decided to be his mum and all he had to do was grant me half of an enormous fortune. I left him feeling hopeful for the first time in years and I arranged to meet him in a few days' time.

Meanwhile, we just ran around the place and enjoyed

ourselves being tourists and being spoiled. In the hotel, I really enjoyed just dropping my towel on the floor after a shower without getting moaned at. I loved going to a massive long breakfast and coming back to a beautiful, clean and tidy room that was a mess only moments before. When we returned at night, happily tired from four enormous meals and the fresh clear air, our bed was turned down. After a day or two, I realized that the whites in South Africa all lived like hotel guests. They had servants who did it all. No wonder all their hands were soft and gentle like Mummy's face – they had never handled a dirty dish in their lives.

We also met some people. Richard Aubrey enjoyed showing us off to his version of Johannesburg society. I was introduced to a range of people, most of them boring but friendly. Then at a lunch I met Gordon Winter. He walked up to our table and chatted to Richard with a twinkle in his eye and a constant smile on his dignified and handsome face. Richard turned and introduced Gordon to me.

'This is Charlie Richardson, from London . . . who I told you about.'

Winter smiled, full of charm, and shook my hand firmly and warmly. He joked, 'Delighted, Charlie . . . delighted! I've heard lots about you. . . .' Then with a pause and a twinkle, '. . . some of it very bad indeed.'

I laughed and we sat down together, chuckling. As I introduced him to Jean Goodman, I looked at him and suddenly an overwhelming sensation came over me. It was a strange tingling feeling that was hard to identify at first, but then as the moments passed I realized I was in the presence of greatness. Despite initial appearances and a light grey suit, there was nothing ordinary about Gordon Winter. He was exceptional. As we chatted and made small talk about the 'beautiful scenery' and 'lovely air', I realized that here before me was the slimiest and most untrustworthy man I had ever met. I felt very lucky. Just when South Africa was getting to be a little bit boring, when the sight of another lobster thermidor would make me spew, along came Gordon to spice things up a bit.

Given my unfavourable first opinion of Gordon Winter I was not surprised to discover a bit later that he was a journalist. He was a reporter on the South African *Sunday Express* which was a liberal paper so he met lots of black activists who trusted him, but at the same time he was a 'Republican Intelligence' agent. Some years later, 'Republican Intelligence' became the notorious 'Boss' gang of murdering bastards who learned all they knew from MI5. Winter was a personal friend of Dr Vorster, future President of South Africa, but tolerated by Winnie Mandela because of the newspaper he came from. Eddie, my kid brother, later told me we should keep away from him. But for the time being I was interested in Gordon Winter. At that first meeting, he told me he was a crime reporter so he knew all about me and my activities in London.

'Cheeky bastard,' I thought and leaned forward. 'What the fuck do you mean by that, Mr Winter?' I asked with a little tinge of threat in my voice.

He realized his mistake and said he was joking. I made some comment about the subtlety of South African humour and the moment passed. He quickly realized that he was not dealing with an East End thug and that unlike many of the English policemen he had met I was capable of joined-up writing. He began to take me seriously and tried to impress me with his knowledge and contacts in South Africa. He took me to see Winnie Mandela. Nelson Mandela had only recently been jailed and it was in the newspapers a lot. Winnie Mandela was very intelligent, very beautiful and very young. She received us graciously because she believed both of us were from the press, but she was not taken in by either of us. Gordon introduced me to anybody he could think of that might impress on me his social importance and skills. I met what counted for film stars and glamour people in South Africa. When I got bored with all that, we went boozing and whoring with bent politicians and senior policemen, but I soon grew tired of that, too. Finally, Gordon was exhausted by my energy and his own attempts to impress me so he played his ace. He introduced me to his wife. Then I was impressed!

Winter had invited myself and Jean Goodman round to a little dinner party for four at his place with his wife. I was interested because usually people like Winter kept their home life very private. All of their socializing was done in posh hotels and brothels where they could play at being men before they went home to a wife who would not let them swear in the house. If they went home drunk, they ended up sleeping on the sofa. So, over the years, I met thousands of men, rich, poor, devious, honest, impressive, hard, frightening, powerful and fascinating, but rarely met their wives and especially not at home. For a man to invite you home was a bit of an honour, but in Winter's case I was not fooled. A journalist will offer the sexual favours of his mother for a good story – and I was potential fodder for lots of his fairy stories.

I got fed up waiting for Jean Goodman to get dressed and made up at our hotel. We had a row about it. She was looking forward to the whole thing as a bit of a change from our usual round of restaurants and hotels. I had started to get a bit irritated by her being around all the time. Jean was good to my kids and an efficient manager of the scrapyard, but she did not send the blood racing through my veins at the stolen glance of her ankle. In fact, in order to get enough blood racing to a particular point to keep her happy now and then I had to think of somebody else. But she was a good solid and loyal companion that I could work with and rely on. So in a bit of a huff, together we got a cab to Winter's big house in the posh swimming pool suburbs of Johannesburg.

Gordon Winter met us at the gate to his large and immaculate garden and as we walked to the door his wife, Jean La Grange, walked towards us from the house. I was chatting to Gordon and was only partly aware of her approaching us. As I looked up, I almost reeled back in a kind of shock. If Henry Cooper had smacked me full on the mouth, I would have been less affected than by the woman standing before me. I heard the words coming out of my mouth as if they were somebody else's. I felt dribbles of sweat inside my shirt and I felt my heart pumping and skin tingle. After thirty years of struggle and of negotiating my way through life's daily hazards, I realized that moment what it was all about. Jean La Grange was the most beautiful woman I had ever met and I was in love. What's more is that I knew that second that she felt it all too. A little glance out of the corner of my eye and I could sense that Jean Goodman and Gordon Winter knew what was going on. Jean bristled like a cat with its hair standing on end down its back. She was very jealous and had eyes alive and dancing with acid.

So this is it, I thought. All that shit in books and films. Dickens with 'it's a greater thing that I do now than I have ever done' or something like that. The very idea of launching a thousand ships and going to war to get inside the knickers of Helen of Troy always made me laugh. And what about old Antony ruining a good career in politics for an Egyptian floozy. Then there was poor little Napoleon who ruled half the world, but would have swapped it all for the occasional decent hard-on to keep Josephine happy. I had never managed to believe it all. I thought it was all a big con, a cleverly devised fantasy that was a carrot on a stick to all the poor mugs who pay their income tax and believe that cornflakes turn them into athletes. What a clever idea, I thought. Create a fantasy that is totally unobtainable, but have everybody believe it is possible and then set them to pursuing it or at least pursuing the products that are sold that help you to pursue it. When I was younger, I also thought here was a clever idea sold to women by men who wanted to slip their dipstick into a wet oval warm sump. But when I cast my eyes on the stunning femininity of Jean La Grange I understood the fantasy could be made real.

When I was a kid and we used to hang around outside dance halls and skating rinks girls were something different and a bit exciting. They were plunder for we pirates to stalk; and once you caught them that was just the start of the art of finger dipping. The idea was that they set up an assault course for you to try to get your finger wet and usually that was as much as you got anyway. But it was exciting stuff. As old men say, Boys were Boys and Girls were Girls. As I got older girls were replaced by women who deliberately traded their little furry mysteries for things like a secure future so all the excitement disappeared. There was no fun in taking part in the story if you knew how it ended. You hop into bed and then you trade a nice house with fitted carpets for regular access to a body and a sense of conformity among your friends. At first when you look at her body you want to eat it. A few years later you wish you had. As time goes on you realize with disappointment that women are just the same as men, really, with one or two little bits that are made different. What a shame! All that excitement when you're fourteen and the glimpse of a flash of a triangle of white panties under a skirt blown by a breath of wind will send blood racing from all directions to one little itchy spot under a row of fly buttons. With grown-up life, that beautiful thrill is exchanged for drunken heaving under the blankets after a big dinner and a hard day at work.

As I sat opposite Jean La Grange all the flushing excitement of adolescence hit me. I was again in the presence of something strange, exotic, exciting and desperately desirable. Her skin glowed, her perfect teeth knocked my eyeballs out with every smile. Her beautifully round and solid little french melons rose and fell under a tight low-cut blouse. I desperately wanted to rest my head between those little footballs and feel the fatigue flow out of my overactive and tired body. As she spoke I was dancing inside my own head and she knew it. Jean Goodman, the other Jean from my past, knew it too, and bristled, trying desperately to score points in a match that had an outright winner from the start. And Jean La Grange was interested. Like a teenager, I showed off with tales of daring. We talked about London and the growing myths of gangsters and 'manors'. After a dinner which nobody tasted because of the sexual electricity in the air we left for our hotel. As I squeezed the hand of Jean La Grange I tried to transmit a message that promised we would meet again soon. She understood and the soft look from her big brown eyes said 'fucking right we will, Charlie Boy' – or words to that effect.

Needless to say, that night Jean Goodman cast a roving

hand under the bedsheets to test me and cause a fight. Set on self destruct, she was anticipating a rejection because my prick was now saving itself for another. But she underestimated the cleverness of all my little bits as I rolled on her and gave her the shagging of a lifetime that left her sore and happy and fooled for the moment.

The next morning I woke up ready to take on the world and change it. We met again with doubting Thomas Waldeck to have a look at the land he owned and had the mining rights to. After a two-day drive we arrived in the middle of nowhere and Thomas announced that as far as the eye could see was his. I looked around me at the dried scrub baking in the midday sun. It did not look like it was worth a fortune and I was a bit disappointed. I asked Waldeck about the village that was on his land and he said that we had stopped at it an hour ago. That sad little hut, with a few people hanging around and a few flies hanging around them, was it. After all that travelling we were a bit despondent as we stood in the middle of the hot wilderness, a pasty couple from south-east London surrounded by a gang of foiled hopefuls. Then Richard Tricky Dicky Aubrey, forever the showman, walked around for a few moments and stopped. He knelt on the dry ground and picked up an interesting-looking stone and turned with a smile to the rest of us.

Thomas Waldeck took the stone from him and rubbed it. He smiled and said, 'It's an opal, Charlie, and a good one.' Then with a grin so unusual on that serious face that he looked mad he said, 'And it's mine, Charlie . . . until of course you become my partner . . .' With that he slipped it in his pocket and I felt cheated. I tried to make light of it but I think he could sense my 'finders, keepers' resentment.

'I think you should put it into a bank, Tom, on deposit, and we can share it when I sign the contract.'

He smiled again. I wanted to warn him that if he smiled too much it might become a habit and they would kick him out of the Broederbond.

'Charlie – it's only worth about forty pounds and there are so many of them round here . . .'

'What!' I thought desperately. 'What the fuck did you say?' raced through my head. Only forty fucking pounds!!! And they're just lying around for anybody to nick them! I wanted to run around grabbing at these semi-precious stones, tigers eye and opals. I wanted to put a big fence round the land with some good home-grown security boys on the perimeter. What I wanted to do was sneak back at night with a fleet of diggers and remove the topsoil for a few hundred acres. But I realized I was thinking like a small time barrow boy or – even worse – like a petty East End criminal. This was no nice little earner – this was big time and I had to think big time. I was sweating with excitement at the prospect of all this land with semi-precious stones waiting to be picked up. But little Tricky Dicky soon put to rest all ideas of opals. He walked up to me carrying a small shovel. Still the magician, he asked me, 'Choose a spot – anywhere.'

It was like 'choose a card' and he swept his hand across the landscape. Just in case it was a trick I pointed to a large bush about fifty yards away and we walked towards it. Richard shovelled for less than a minute, then stopped and dropped to his knees. The shovel had hit something hard and he now brushed the dirt away as if he had found a treasure chest. As it turned out he was doing just that. He revealed a hard black layer of rock and turned round to me with a grin. It was not coal but it looked interesting anyway. His grin was in danger of sticking on his face. So I asked him, 'What is it, Richard?'

His eyes danced with the mischief of a little boy. 'It's perlite, Charlie. P.E.R.L.I.T.E. Perlite.'

'What's perlite, Richard?' I asked because I felt life was too short for pretences at that moment.

'Don't worry about opals, Charlie, we'll throw them away to get at the perlite. It's a beautiful mineral that people are desperate to get hold of, especially the Japs. You can build with it, it's dead strong, it's very light and it's a fantastic insulator – everybody wants it. What's more is that however much you dig up you put in a machine and it expands to ten times its size. There's a mountain of it here, Charlie, under our feet. You don't have to dig mines for it, you just get some diggers here and load it into trucks. You quarry it, mate, and it's worth a bloody fortune. This is the pot of gold at the end of the rainbow, Charlie boy, and it's ours.'

I was trembling with excitement, I wanted to grab Waldeck and sign him up, put him in the firm and take him home with me in case he got somebody else. Two days later I was back in grimy grey Camberwell shouting down the phone to a local council official who had received complaints about the noise the scrapyard made in the residential neighbourhood. Fuck you, I thought, I'm going to live the life of Riley with the sun on my neck and an ice-cold beer in my hand.

Everything back home now seemed small and petty. England was a country that felt it had a real place in world history but had not noticed that somebody had sneaked into the bedroom in the middle of the night and cut its balls off. I just wanted to plan my escape from this big open prison where a man's accent mattered more than his mind. I was so excited, so happy and so much looking forward to the future. I was young and healthy, I was in love, I was on the verge of becoming a millionaire. What could go wrong?

'Shit! Something did!' I thought as we came near the end of Lucien's evidence and the story took an interesting little twist. It seems that after an hour of doing a science experiment on Lucien's body with the generator we ran out of embarrassing little bits to connect the electrodes to. We apparently stopped his ordeal and, heaven forbid, started to call him names. Now I may torture people to an inch of their lives during which I do not offer them any of my scampi, but the idea of calling them names! We all listened in horror as Lucien said, 'Well, Charlie Richardson at various times during this said I was a liar . . . and there were various abusive phrases whose exact tone I can't recollect, sir.'

This was a short intermission. I could feel something was coming. Her Majesty's representative, wearing a powdered wig, took Lucien a stage further. 'What happened then?'

'The gag was removed from my mouth and the cord was untied from my hands. I was given my clothes and told to put them on. This I did. After I had dressed I was sitting on the floor putting my shoes on when Charles Richardson came across and thrust a knife through my left foot pinning it to the floor, sir.'

This was just getting ridiculous. I gasped at the idea along with the rest of the courtroom. Then a wave of relief came over me as I realized he would have to prove this with medical evidence. He would have to show his left foot. Then I panicked because the prosecution were vicious and definitely not stupid. They would not introduce this rubbish unless he had a scar on his foot. The prosecution could read our minds.

'Which part of your foot, Mr Harris?'

'Right through the foot.'

Then Mr Justice Lawton, champion of justice for the common man, stepped in to help. 'Well, just step out of the witness box for a moment, Mr Harris, and demonstrate to the jury which foot it was and how the knife went through it.'

Lucien minced his way out of the box and sat pathetically on the floor in front of the jury. They craned their necks to get a good view. 'I was sitting with my leg like that and the knife was pushed through the foot, here, pinning me to the floor.'

'Through the instep? And how did you feel when that was done?'

'Sudden shock, sir. It was very painful, it gave me a start.'

'And when that was done what was done next with the knife?'

'He pulled it out, sir.'

'Who did?'

'Charles Richardson pulled the knife out.'

You evil little lying bastard, Lucien, I thought. This was serious.

CHAPTER EIGHT
Guns

Mild panic. You know all those films and books and stories where the heroes are onto a really good thing and you're sitting there desperate for them to succeed. They are going to get away with a brilliant bank job or something and one little slip gets them caught. Or you have Humphrey Bogart in that gold rush film where he's out in the middle of nowhere and just when you thought everything had gone wrong they discover gold. They dance all over the place and work day and night building up this nice little stash of gold. They are going to be rich men for the rest of their lives. Then one or two of them start to get greedy and the whole thing collapses and they all end up with nothing. You come away from the story thinking, 'If only they had not slipped or got greedy then they could have all been rich now and lived happily ever after.' Of course I know those films are supposed to teach us that crime does not pay and greedy people get their just desert. And I also know in real life greedy criminals own and rule the world. Even so, when I came back from South Africa I had this little niggling fear that would leave butterflies flying around my guts. I was almost shaking day and night with the excitement of it all. It was so thrilling I nearly wished it had not happened at all because I knew I would now spend years trying to hold it all together. I was in love and I was going to be very rich. I was going to be totally legal and even a little respectable in a country that uses umbrellas to keep out the sun, not the miserable pissing drizzle of England.

So many things could challenge everything. I set about making long term plans to arrange my departure into safe and wealthy business life. A lot had to be done. What I should have done was pack my bags and get on a plane and take it from there. But I had family, and friends and businesses. One day I might want to come back so I wanted to leave a clear path.

While I ran around trying to tie up all sorts of loose ends in London I did not want Tom Waldeck to forget me in South Africa. I decided to send out a couple of men to establish some sort of exploratory base camp in the territory. I sent a friend, Jimmy Collins, and looked for another to join him. I thought of a few people and came up with John Bradbury, decided against it then changed my mind back again. I was not sure I could trust him even though he had given me nothing but loyal support. He was known as 'John West' at the time. I was a little bit worried about anybody who would take an alias from a tin of salmon. But my main concern with John was the location of his brain. From adolescence it had slipped to his prick. John was a hard-on looking for a nest. If his wife went near another man he would froth and dribble at the mouth with a terrible jealous rage. Meanwhile he was busy dipping his wick in any warm wet hole he could find. In the end I gave him the benefit of the doubt and sent him to South Africa with a silent prayer that he would leave all those horny female hippos and wildebeest alone.

The two of them set off and I established links with Waldeck using reel to reel tape recorders. Tom Waldeck really was a fussy old thing. Everything to him was a problem that was not worth solving because the solution would just reveal another problem. If I had not needed him I would have told him to piss off and sort himself out before he inflicted his misery on the world. As it was he kept wingeing about money and his wife wanting a bigger house. At first when he met Jimmy Collins he liked him but he did not like John Bradbury, alias John West is Best. I kept him sweet the whole time and became a revolving tit on a tape recorder as his counsellor, friend, business partner and confessor. I had to keep him juggled in the air with a load of other things while I sorted everything out. Things came to a head when Bradbury's prick took over events.

John Bradbury liked to keep up with current affairs. After the death defying, daring and glamorous escape by Charles Wilson the Great Train Robber, the papers throughout the English speaking world were full of it. The hunt was on for Charles Wilson, the Scarlet Pimpernel who had defied the top level of security at Colditz. We all wished him luck. John Bradbury displayed his support by calling himself Charles Wilson and putting it about the clubs in Johannesburg that despite his innocent fat face he was actually escapologist and train robber extraordinaire Charles Wilson. He did not do this for any reasonable or respectable reason such as to impress an adventurous merchant banker into granting a bridging loan while funds were forthcoming. He said it to impress beautiful young starry-eyed starlets into playing with his prick under the restaurant table while he paid the bill with my money. So while the real Charlie Wilson was holed up with nothing more than a copy of *Parade* for company old John West was slipping his pilchard under the blue sky of Africa using poor old Charlie's name and he ended up with a very beautiful model called Elsa Smith who only liked to sleep with men who had robbed trains for millions of pounds. Things were going great for John Bradbury alias West alias Charlie Wilson. He was jumping into bed every night with an insatiable woman of every man's dreams. She was a living, breathing centrefold with the mark of a thousand staples in her navel. At the same time he was constantly writing home threatening his wife with all sorts of nightmares if she so much as glanced at another man. She knew him well enough and got the strong whiff of a rat and wrote to him saying she was on her way out to see him. Shit! he thought, and got rid of Elsa Smith like somebody whisking away a bothersome bluebottle that had landed on his leg. Elsa was very pissed off to have lost her own pet train robber so she made the best of a bad situation. She went into a national newspaper holding a picture of her and John having a very good time in a club with bleary, drunken and happy red eyes to the camera. She proudly announced that the man in the picture was not only her lover who had feasted on the very full delights of her body but that he was in fact Charles Wilson – Great Train Robber from Great Britain and a great screw. The *South African Sunday Times* proudly printed the exclusive story with photograph that Charles Wilson the Great Train Robber was alive and well in South Africa.

Tom Waldeck nearly choked on his toast and marmalade that Sunday morning and frantically phoned me. He had been seen very often in public places with John West, Bradbury, Wilson. I sweet-talked him and promised to sort it out.

It was a big problem. For months Waldeck and I had been negotiating with The Pretoria Portland Cement Company to come in with us on a deal and this association with a 'train robber' could kill it. I phoned Gordon Winter and asked him to sort it out. As I spoke to him I was conscious that within a few feet of the man I was talking to was his wife, Jean La Grange – unfinished business. He promised he would, and true to his word the next day a story appeared in all the papers about the 'mistaken identity' case where a respectable British businessman had been described as Charlie Wilson. I contacted John West and told him he was not best as far as I was concerned so he could piss off. But I gave him the benefit of the doubt. We all have our passions – it is just a matter of how well we control them. Then a few weeks later it turns out he had an affair with Mrs bloody I-want-a-house-Waldeck. Jesus Christ, next thing he would be slipping old Waldeck himself a length of his overactive gristle. Tom Waldeck was totally livid and nothing short of a public castration of John Bradbury-West-Wilson would do. So that is what I did in effect because I sacked him. He wandered the streets of Jo'burg a broken man, a limp prick, jobless and – after his wife had seen pictures of him with the delicious Elsa Smith – loveless and homeless.

This all reminded me at the time of some more unfinished business. There were some other people to sort out. When our boat came in and Tom Waldeck and myself became filthy rich pillars of society there would be a few hungry vultures waiting for their share. Tricky Dicky Richard Aubrey the Welsh rarebit was prancing around demanding this percentage and that percentage of various profits received for his services as a 'consultant'. It's a lovely word, consultant. It very often describes somebody who actually does bugger all but expects paying off, or somebody who does something so shady you can't say what it really is. Because Richard had introduced

Waldeck and Winter and the whole South African thing he sat and waited for a pension for life. I would not have minded if he approached me and offered to put some work into the whole thing but he expected just to sit there and receive. Arseholes to that! I did not totally piss him off. There's no point in closing all your options, but after months of cold shoulders he got the message. But rather than stalk off and live to duck and dive another day he started stirring some easy-stir watery shit around Tom Waldeck's partners. I nearly said 'sleeping' partners but it might have confused Aubrey with West-Bradbury-Wilson. These were sleeping partners in the proper respectable business sense of the word. At the start of Waldeck's enterprise half a dozen or so respectable businessmen put in a few quid and then sat back and waited for poor old Tom to sweat his bollocks off to make a fortune for them. They would phone him up now and again to see if their future was growing. They could afford to wait, what could they lose? Tom had four million acres and he could not afford to wait. I tried to think of a way to get rid of these sleeping partners and their new very lively partner Richard Aubrey. I had just about settled my mind on a long hard struggle of manoeuvres and outmanoeuvres when Tom provided the answer without realizing it.

On his tapes to me Tom Waldeck told me, his therapist, of all his tales of woe and worry. On one particular tape just after the usual mention for the need of a bigger house he told me about pegging and re-pegging. He explained that every year he had to go through a very complicated process of 're-pegging' his land. If he did not do it then all the rights to the land would lapse and it would be up for grabs for anybody to claim discoverer's rights. He said in his boring monotone Sud Afrikan voice that his sleeping partners were no help in all this because they did not have a clue about re-pegging and had no idea it needed to be done. He then went on to reassure me that I was not to worry because his bent pal in the ministry would make sure that his old mate Tom would get the rights back if they lapsed. It was so bloody obvious I nearly screamed. I loaded up my tape recorder and decided against it. I booked a call to Tom and told him of the simple plan. All he had to do was let the re-pegging lapse without telling anybody, especially his dozing partners. The land then belonged to nobody technically. Then all he had to do was claim discoverer's rights, slip his bent official a few quid and re-peg it under the name of his own company. I would then become a partner while the others were left out in the cold. It took only a few minutes for the penny to drop with a dull thud but he finally got it and jumped around the room with the prospect of pissing on his partners. He did tell me that it would take more than a few quid to grease the palm of the official. In fact it would take a brand new car. 'No problem, consider it done, Thomas,' I said and we both slept with a smile on our faces. A few weeks later I sat in a B.O.A.C. plane being spoiled by a posh tart in uniform while the thought of meeting Jean La Grange again caused a stirring under the contracts on my lap.

No chance of a hard-on in the Old Bailey. Even the press girl in the short skirt was so staggered by the drama in the courtroom she had stopped crossing and uncrossing her legs. I could have tried passing her a note saying in effect 'how about a little occasional thrill for the condemned man' but if I had to ask her it would not be the same. No little white triangles of knickers but lots of blood on the floor in a little office above a scrapyard in Camberwell. Lucien in the witness box looked pathetic. His story was now finished and the audience was breathing normally again. It really was like an orgy had just happened and now, if the rules had permitted, they all wanted to lie back, look at the ceiling and pass around a shared cigarette. Lucien had been walloped and smacked. He had felt an electric current pass from bollock to arsehole and back again. A knife had pinned his foot to the floor. We had neglected to offer him any scampi and chips. After all that we sent him on his way. It was half past twelve at night. He had left Miss Henman in the other office waiting patiently while we tortured her associate to within an inch of his life.

'And then?'

'I drove off, sir.'

'Where did you drive to first of all, Mr Harris?'

'I drove Miss Henman to her home.'

'And then after you had taken her home, where did you go?'

'I drove myself home.'

'Where did you go the following morning?'

'I went to the doctor, sir.'

I bet you bloody did. Jesus! I looked around the court, my mouth wide open, stunned at this revelation. Surely the prosecution had slipped up. Surely this was a big mistake. I looked at Tommy and Frank and my brother Eddie. We had all noticed, but the court stared ahead dumb and stupid at Lucien. I wanted to shout out, 'How did you drive? You had a knife through your foot. Your face must have looked like a red cabbage, how could you see, how come Miss bloody Henman did not say anything? How the fuck could you drive!' Nobody had noticed! I sat back on my bench and tried to block out this bloody nightmare. Outside the Old Bailey at the top of the building is a statue of a woman holding the scales of justice. That day a big fat pigeon, overfed by the shit thrown in the gutter by the gentlemen of the press, landed on one of the scales and tipped it against me. My eyes glazed and my mind wandered to those times of hope.

I had a short stay in Johannesburg sorting out the contracts, setting up the companies and signing the partnership agreements. I was a bit worried that so much of it depended on Tom Waldeck and remained in his control. But then again it was all his to start with and he had struggled for years to hang onto it. All I had done was work my bollocks off for months and arrive with two suitcases filled with money so the whole thing could go ahead. The government official got his smart new car and I told Waldeck to take his wife around looking for a bigger house. He was over the moon.

These were times for high spirits: Tommy Clark and Jimmy Collins were in Johannesburg to meet me. It was Tommy Clark's birthday around then and we had a big party in the

Mikado which was a fancy club in a posh area. As I stood at
the bar of the club with a whisky in one hand and a cigar in the
other I had a look around the room. It was one of those rare
moments in life when nobody had a problem in the world.
We all wanted to be there and we all wanted the others to be
there. A word I had only read in books came to mind . . . 'well
being'. I had a real sense of 'well being' at that moment. It was
a great time to be alive. The world was definitely my oyster and
just as I was thinking that, along came the pearl. Stone me! In
walked Jean La Grange and I nearly dropped my drink. She
walked through the crowd like a film star leaving a trail of
gulping men as she approached me. Her long hair was like
a shampoo advert and the body she offered up in a tight but
tasteful dress had my knees knocking. She ignored everybody
else to come to me. When she was close she smiled, a large
mouth, pearl teeth and enormous eyes sparkling.

'Hello, Charlie boy.'

That was cheeky and affectionate and a little shiver went
through me. I nearly said, 'Hello, Jean, have a seat, would
you like a drink and where is your husband Gordon Winter,
famous international journalist and notorious snake in the
grass?' But I came up with a much better line.

'Of all the gin joints in all the world you had to walk into
mine.' Thank you, Humphrey Bogart. Jean knew the film and
she laughed.

'Aren't you going to offer me a drink, Charlie?'

I nearly said, 'Drink what you like, but what about your
bloody husband?' but I didn't.

'Have some champagne, it's Tommy's birthday.' I poured
a glass for her and she toasted Tommy. I wondered what she
was doing here. How did she know, who invited her? I wanted
to know if she had thought about me as much as I had thought
about her since we last met. But I did not, instead I said:

'So where's Gordon? Is he coming later?' I thought her jaw
might drop but instead she gave me a soft, gentle smile.

'No, he's not coming.'

'So you've come on your own?'

'Yes, Charlie. I've come to see you.'

This was too much to handle. I could hardly believe it. The electricity around that spot we shared was sparking off as we stood with our eyes locked on each other. She had delivered the ace of hearts and now she laid down her hand to show the ten, jack, queen and the king of hearts for a running flush.

'I've left Gordon, Charlie. When I met you and I felt what I did I realized all that Gordon and I never had. There was no magic, Charlie, so I left him. I left him for you.'

Jesus Christ. All this without so much as a snog in the back of the cinema or a sweaty hand on a heaving breast in a car with reclining seats. Not so much as the grope of a knee under a restaurant table. I was knocked out.

'Leave it out, Jean. For me? What if I never came back?'

'But you did.'

'But what if I didn't?'

'Then I would have been right to leave him anyway because there should be more in a marriage than we had.'

I was in total confusion. It was the most exciting moment in my life and for once I had no idea of what to do next. I gulped at my glass of whisky. People around us had kind of sensed the importance of the event and moved away. Tommy Clark was being bumped by four men, one at each limb. I caught a glimpse of his round, country bumpkin, beaming, happy face as everybody shouted out the numbers, 'twenty-four . . . twenty-five . . . twenty-six . . .'

'I love you, Charlie.'

That was it, I then threw down all the cards on the table. The next thing I remember we woke up in a big soft double bed in the Hotel Negressco in Nice in the South of France. The sun played patterns through the cracks in the big heavy curtains on the mile thick carpet. The noise of the sea and the Riviera drifted in from the balcony as we lay in a tight grip like two wrestlers in an impossible entanglement. The breeze from the window cooled the little tributaries of sweat all over our bodies after a night of the stored up lust of decades.

Meanwhile downstairs in the lobby reading a French newspaper was Harry Waterman. He was a friend I had taken along as a translator, but the language Jean and I were using was universal. He had phoned up to our room asking if we were coming down to breakfast. We declined and got room service to send a tight-arsed French waiter with warm croissants and coffee. I had asked them for egg, bacon, sausage, beans and tomatoes with a fried slice and a cup of tea, but they thought croissants were more in keeping with local tradition. As soon as he came in with the tray I sent him away for more. I was ravenous. We had barely finished breakfast when I took a long look at Jean and we were at it again. We were at it for five days and five nights which all goes to prove you don't have to be a member of the Beatles, wear little round spectacles and marry a Japanese arse photographer to spend a whole week in bed. We were doing it for world peace too. It must have been the only time in my life that I let the world go round without attempting to have my own way in its direction. For a whole week I could not have given a sloppy pigeon dropping for business and profit and clever deals. The clever deals I was concerned about were between my sensitive little bits and Jean's very sensitive, very smooth, very delicate little bits. In those very happy few days my mind was a blank, at peace, at rest . . . at last. It was obvious that whatever Jean's husband, old 'Geordie', had been up to for the last few years, it was not his wife. She was as starved as me for the pleasures of the flesh and that was the biggest aphrodisiac in the world.

After a week neither of us was fed up. Our touching and talking and room service meals could have lasted for ever, but poor old Harry Waterman had managed to get a message to me. Tom Waldeck, neurotic as ever, was worried about something or other. It seems that there was a bit of trouble on the land in question. One of my people had caused some sort of bother up in the local village with some local men. This was only the top of a list of 'problems' from Waldeck, including the paranoia about his sleeping partners who could smell a rat or two. Apparently they had been seeing something of Richard Tricky Dicky the Toss Aubrey who was still very pissed off with me for the loss of what he thought would be a nice fat consultant's fee. I took a last look at Jean's long, slim, tender body lying on the ruffled sheets and heaved a huge sigh. The honeymoon was over. We had to return to the land of the rising prospects.

When I got back to Jo'burg everything seemed settled. I had sort of expected some kind of panic and chaos from the moment I stepped on the tarmac. Everything was fine. My brother Eddie was running around with a friend of his, Stanley Baker, the actor. They were making *The Sands of The Kalahari* film and there seemed to be nobody around. I had a last lusty night with Jean and headed for the bush to find out what the problem was. The next day I rolled into the village near our settlement. I say village, but all that was there was a big wooden hut that served as a post office and shop. A load of junk littered the place and a few bushes and small trees surrounded it. As I stepped out of the car onto the dusty, hard ground I was suddenly aware of a ghostly and solid silence. There was not even the noise of wildlife. I could see for hundreds of miles all around me. There was nothing, nobody and no sound at all. I have never been the sort to get spooked by a dark alleyway in a dodgy area of a dodgy country but total silence and absence of all forms of life were beginning to disarm me. I walked into the shop. It was not locked but it was empty. I could have helped myself to the very limited range of goods they had on display. I could have grabbed handfuls of government forms and even postage stamps. There was nobody there, but the place felt sort of warm, as if somebody had been there recently. Jesus Christ, I thought, what is going on? I spoke out.

'Hello . . . anybody there?'

Silence . . . so I walked outside and with a slightly forced confidence I stood on the porch and projecting like an actor I said loudly, 'Hello . . . anybody around? I'm Charles Richardson, can anybody hear me . . .' Then a pause and, 'I'm looking for Tommy Clark and Jimmy Collins.' Then I realized – stupid prat! Maybe if anybody could hear me they didn't speak English so I had another try.

'Hello, me Charlie . . . me look for Tommy . . . you help me.'

Not a sign, not a sound. I sat down on the wooden steps

to the post office and considered my next move. I would have just got into the beaten old car and driven up to the small settlement we were building, but it was strange that there was nobody around this hut. It was the meeting place for miles and there were always people around. Also I had a strange sensation that I was being watched and I wanted to sort this one out. I lit a cigarette and waited. After a few moments a man stepped out from behind a bush directly in front of me. He was almost naked, black, lithe and muscular. His skin was shining with some sort of oil and his body was marked all over with white streaks, like some sort of war paint or something. He carried a long wide machete that looked as if it was used to being used. He walked towards me and I stood up, gave him my best fearless fixed gaze and slowly walked towards him to show I was not frightened. Then I noticed something really strange. I thought I could deal with the muscles and machete, but this geezer had great big swellings in his mouth. His cheeks were swollen, like they were deformed. It was like he was blowing down a blowpipe and they had got stuck. It made his eyes pop out and fixed his mouth in a weird grin. He had the face of a Hammer House of Horror escaped loony. As he got closer and I braced myself to take him on, about eight others just like him stepped out from behind bushes and surrounded me. They all just had little cloths around their balls, shiny skin, war paint, machetes and swollen cheeks with popping eyes. Jesus Christ! I thought, what was going on? What had Jimmy or Tommy got up to that had made these otherwise very reasonable and hospitable people so bloody pissed off? They closed in on me with machetes at the ready as I kept my stare fixed on the first one who had started it all. I clenched my fists, that was all I had, and he raised his weapon just an inch or two. I was ready for him.

Then suddenly he stopped. He spat out two massive gobstoppers, one pink, one blue and said in a pure south east London market trader's accent, 'Hello, Charlie Boy, fuck this for a lark. Hows about a nice cup of tea, gawd bless you, Guv.'

With that he beamed a huge pearly white smile at me and they all spat out multicolour gob-stoppers into their hands and burst out laughing. Tommy Clark came running from behind a bush doubled over and weeping, in agony with laughter.

'You bastard, Tommy!' I shouted, then paused and fell about with them all. It took a few minutes for the lot of us to calm down. Every time we were just about settled Tommy would point at me and say, 'Your face, Charlie. You should have seen your face . . .' Then he would fall about again and it was infectious. Tommy had got them all tooled up with the machetes and gob-stoppers and planned it for weeks. He had taught the man who first approached me the only English he knew. When I got back to the settlement I realized that Jimmy Collins had been busy with English lessons too. A group of men were busy digging a trench. They worked in a steady rhythm of digging with their shovels. The foreman of the gang would suddenly shout or really sing, 'egg and chips' and the rest of the gang responded by singing in deep black old man river voices, 'bangers and mash'. Then he repeated, 'egg and chips' and they responded, 'bangers and mash'.

And with that they worked away happily for hours. Jimmy Collins started to tell me what fantastic workers they were. A few coins, a bag of flour and a tin of jam a week and they would work while the sweat poured off them in the heat of the day. With labour prices based more on the availability of strawberry jam than the price of sterling against other currencies, I thought we were onto a winner. So, I sat down with them and asked what the hell was the problem that I had come all the way back from my lust nest in the Riviera to deal with. Tommy's big round face blushed deep red and there was a silence but after a few seconds he explained that there had been trouble, but it was all sorted out now. After a bit of coaxing he told me what it was all about. It seems that Tommy had begun to miss the regular doses of company of young ladies that he was used to in London. After a few weeks of taking in the sights and absorbing the local language and culture of Namaqualand, Tommy started taking in some of the girls and absorbing them. This had worked out fine for a while. Tommy was a kid in a sweet-shop. He had never had it so good with loads of pretty young girls around him. The girls were curious and delighted to investigate the differences of a little white willie and accept the nice presents Tommy gave them. After a few weeks a deputation of local men reported to Waldeck and then arrived at Tommy Clark's caravan to sort it out with him. 'So we sorted it out, Charlie, and now there's no problem.' After a little silence Jimmy Collins laughed and said, 'Come on, Tommy, tell him the rest of it. Tell him about your techniques.' Tommy was embarrassed but we pushed him to reveal more. It turns out that the local men had not come to see Tommy because he was screwing their girls. That did not seem to bother them so much. Tommy, it seemed, had caused quite a stir with his mouth, so to speak. It seems that for thousands of happy years they had screwed away in their own imaginative ways. In recent history their technique reduced to one position when British and Dutch missionaries told them any other way was dirty. Now to add to the confusion, Tommy was introducing them to the joys of oral sex or 'plating' as he called it. The local men were at first pissed off, then curious, then educated by Tommy Clark. For some of them the first words they learnt in English were 'blow job'.

I stayed for a few days, checked out the site and returned to Johannesburg to be greeted by a very happy Tom Waldeck. Something much more important than the life and loves of a south-east London lad had happened. Somebody was very interested in our project. Very interested!

Which is more than I can say for the Old Bailey once the defence witnesses started getting called. There were no exciting tales of blood on the floor wiped up with used Y-fronts. There were no breathtaking moments as black boxes were brought in and electrifying stories told of the tingling current passing from balls to arsehole and back again. Who wanted to listen as witness after witness was paraded by our desperate defence briefs who proved very often that what the prosecution was saying was a load of nonsense? But who wanted to listen as they droned on? I wanted to scream at our defence, 'Make it fucking interesting, you wally! The jury is dozing off, you prat!!' But I did not and I sat there and listened as Platts-Mills questioned a very learned doctor who was a fellow of the Royal College of Surgeons, a Consultant Orthopaedic Surgeon at Charing Cross Hospital with a posh gaff in Harley Street to boot. They were talking about the scars Lucien Harris had on his foot which were supposed to prove that I had stuck a knife through it and pinned him to the floor. They had both been droning on for ages. Even Platts-Mills who was supposed to be on our side did not sound interested. Jesus Christ! I thought, if you bought a brief with a hyphen in his name you should get your money's worth.

He asked our very learned doctor, 'What view did you form as to whether the scars could be caused by a single knife thrust penetrating the whole wound?'

'I think that unless someone had moved the skin to the outer border up beyond the bone it would have been, well, impossible for the outer scar to have been caused by the same weapon as the inner scar.'

Thank you everybody! I rest my case: the learned doctor has just said that Lucien Harris was a lying bastard. He said that the scar that Lucien had was not consistent with having a knife stuck through his foot. Just to be sure, my boring brief covered himself by making sure there was no possibility of the skin being moved by the force of the impact. And what did the very brainy doctor say, Fellow of the Royal College of Surgeons and Consultant Orthopaedic Surgeon to the rich who visit Harley Street? He said, 'Very, very improbable indeed . . . approaching miraculous.'

I wanted to jump up and down and cheer and dance around the courtroom with the girl from the press who was crossing her legs for me again. Then I looked around. People were virtually leaning on each other's shoulders dozing. Even the judge, who had hung onto every word, looked like he had eaten too much custard with his spotted dick. They were just not interested. The doctor had gone on a bit but the real reason was that they did not want to believe I had not done it. They really did prefer to believe that I had stuck a knife through somebody's foot, but not because they could give a damn about justice. They were not that bothered about 'nipping organized crime in the bud'. They wanted to believe I had pinned this lying toerag's foot to the floor because it was a good story and nobody should ruin it. It was a good story that brought a little spark into their dull lives, and for the sake of a good yarn that they could tell and re-tell in the pub while they scratched their itchy balls they were willing to see me put away for ever. If anybody had asked me to make a contribution to the great wealth of British criminal mythology, I would have been happy to oblige, but not at the cost of my liberty. Bastards!

The prosecution had a hyphen on the team as well. As Mr Sebag-Shaw cleared his throat to make his grand entrance everybody woke up and stone me, they were interested again. He went straight for the jugular of this posh expert foot specialist.

'In your experience as a surgeon have you found that sometimes miracles do happen?'

'Yes.'

Yes what? Yes? Well thank you very much, Mr Kessel, you can piss off back to Harley Street where they found you. I was a doomed man, but despite my impending downfall I got a quick thrill as the smart, aspiring scoop merchant crossed her legs and briefly flashed like a friendly wink, for my benefit. Just a matter of weeks before all of this, I was at the absolute top of my life. Now a stolen glimpse of white cotton was received like a precious gift.

In Johannesburg, Tom Waldeck was dancing around like a kid who had wet his pants. He was so excited and so happy I could hardly wait to find out what the hell was going on. It was simple. An American company that I had approached earlier to raise funding for the perlite mining project was keen to get in touch. I had made contact with them at a time when we needed investment. Since then the Pretoria Cement Company were coming along nicely and thanks to some investment from some friends I did not need the capital. Waldeck was keen as mustard to meet them. He was exhausted with all the years of trying to get this off the ground. He just wanted a big American sugar daddy to take care of things. I told him we did not need them and his jaw dropped and bounced on the carpet. They were a big famous company, how could we reject them when they had granted us an audience? I was curious to see what they were thinking about so to Waldeck's delight I agreed we should meet with them. So we did, several times.

Tom Waldeck and I flew out to Miami where we were treated like film stars. We were wined and dined in restaurants where the menus were as big as the tables and the food looked too good to be digested by a mile of intestines. The waiters' only aim in life was to make you happy and no wonder when I saw the size of the tip they got. The Americans did us proud. The hotel rooms were great caverns, the showers nearly knocked you off your feet. A beautiful chambermaid in a very sexy uniform knocked on my door late each night and asked if she could turn down my bed for me. Nothing new in that except after she turned it down she got in it and smiled. They know how to treat a guest in America.

During the days we went through the papers and finally we flew to Nassau in the Bahamas to meet more executives and discuss it further. And as we sat in a huge boardroom around a beautiful mahogany table at the end of days of heavy discussion, their leading negotiator put his pen down and announced he was going to make an offer. I could feel Tom Waldeck tense next to me. He was under strict instructions to say and do nothing. We waited.

After a few seconds' silence their boss looked at me and said, 'A million for all your mineral interests in Namaqualand.'

I was a little boy again who had been kicked under the table and had to pretend that he had been missed. I wanted to scream but I bit my tongue instead and asked, cool and cheeky, 'Pounds, I take it?'

The big boss smiled and said, 'Pounds, of course.' But I knew he originally meant dollars. I paused a little but had to speak before Waldeck jumped onto that table and did an eightsome reel all on his own.

'We will think about it. Thank you, gentlemen.'

We flew back to London and hardly spoke about the offer. It was bloody tempting. There was something magic about the sound of a million. We could have split it in half and lived happily ever after on the interest. But we both knew that what we had was capable of an annual income of a million once it was in operation. We decided to wait for them to make the next move.

Back in London Waldeck busied himself running around, a happy man, shopping like mad in the West End. Every day he returned to his Mayfair hotel with boxes and bags carried by a line of bell boys. I had some shopping to do too. We needed some heavy plant, some tractors and bulldozers and excavators for shipment to South Africa to dig up the rich earth of Namaqualand. It seemed stupid to go and buy new ones from the bulldozer shop, all smooth, clean and shiny in showroom condition. Once they had been working for a day or two they would be filthy. It seemed stupid to buy them at all when everywhere you travelled people left great big bulldozers lying around at the side of roadworks. The M1 was having a lot of work done to it at the time so we arranged for a convoy of plant that was littering the side of the motorway to make a little journey. As they crawled at five miles per hour along through the night it got a bit embarrassing when the motorway police graciously offered an escort to the very slow moving line of goodies that were bound for the dockyards and South Africa.

With that underway I interrupted Waldeck's wild spending spree as I told him we were called to Rome. He was disappointed when I explained it was not the Pope who wanted to see us but somebody with just as much financial clout. The American company wanted to meet again. This time we sat in historic splendour surrounded by renaissance paintings, as they offered us a million pounds, not dollars, and shares in their banana plantations throughout the world. I have always liked bananas and was tempted by the prospect of a free supply for life, but our minds were made up.

I pushed back the Italian designer chair on the cool marble

floor and, cool as marble, I smiled and said, 'Thank you very much, gentlemen. It has been a real pleasure meeting with you over the last few weeks . . . I am very sorry to disappoint you, but I must decline your very generous offer.'

They were surprised. They really thought the bananas would do it. Tom and I walked to the door and just as we were about to leave the building one of the negotiators ran after me shouting my name. We stopped and turned. He smiled at me and gave me his card and said, 'Turn it over, there's a message.'

On the other side of the card he had written, 'You will never forget the day you were offered a million pounds and turned it down.'

I thanked him, put it in my pocket and we left in a limousine to take us to the airport.

Jesus Christ! I thought, not bad for a boy from Camberwell. Not bad for a boy who spent his childhood bumming around the bombsites of south-east London nicking lead off roofs. Not bad for a streetfighting artful dodger. I was floating on air in more than one sense as Waldeck and I returned to South Africa.

I had never been happier in my life. We busied ourselves in Johannesburg and Namaqualand with contracts and rights and equipment and future customers for our perlite. We arranged to buy the machines from Hungary that would expand the perlite. With a few backhanders we made the impossible possible, arranging for the visit of Hungarian engineers to install it when it arrived. Every day was the first day of spring as I raced from meeting to meeting and built our manor in the sun. It was all legal, I was in great danger of finally becoming a pillar of society. I thought nothing could go wrong, but the bogey man was coming.

In all the fun and excitement I had forgotten John Bradbury, alias West, alias Wilson, but he had not forgotten me. He had become a drunk and a mercenary. He wandered around Africa with alcohol-pickled brain or his dick leading the way. One night his embittered mind led him to ring the doorbell of Tom Waldeck. When Tom opened it John Bradbury/West/Wilson shot him in the stomach and my partner in five thousand square miles of mineral rich Namaqualand bled to death on his own front doorstep.

So John bloody West pissing Bradbury shitting Wilson had taken on a new alias, a new role. Avenging fucking angel. But who was he avenging? Now the shit really hit the fan around me. At first nobody said anything but I felt as if somebody had dropped a silent deadly smell at a party and they were all looking at me, but my arse was innocent. At first nobody knew it was John Bradbury so rumours started to fly around that I had actually done it myself. Then when the real culprit was arrested by an insurance investigator they started to look at me as the paymaster. John Avenging Angel Bradbury started to shoot his mouth off that he was there but he had not done it himself. When that failed he tried another story. He was only the messenger with the bad news. He was told to do it, ordered to do it by none other than Charles Richardson, leader of the notorious Richardson Gang in south-east London. That was a much more stimulating and prick-teasing story than another boring old shooting by a jealous disgruntled lover, and desperate ex-business associate possibly working in cahoots with other business associates.

Then the British Sunday papers started to pick up on it all. They could not believe their luck. For decades crime reporters had sat at their desks twiddling their thumbs waiting for organized crime to come along and make them stars of the chip wrappings. The only reason we were the Richardsons was I had a brother. What would they have done if my old man had discovered condoms on one of his foreign trips and decided he liked the fit? What would they have done if Mrs Kray's little egg had not split into two idiots but remained one? It would have been Charlie Richardson and his gang which is not so sexy as 'the Richardson Gang' which was a 'family' of villains. Just like *The Untouchables* late on a Thursday night. One crime reporter was watching *The Untouchables* with Elliot Ness on a Thursday night and he saw some words he liked. Being a word merchant he liked words so when he saw 'Murder Incorporated' which was shortened to 'Murder Inc' he liked the sound of it. He tried it out a few times in his head and then, when he wrote it down, he liked the look of it. 'What a good headline,' he thought. Then he sat at his desk and waited while stories of middle aged white witches with soft, pasty and fallen bottoms dancing at night around a bonfire landed on his desk. He got stories of vicars and choirboys, vicars and showgirls and co-op shop wage delivery snatches. Then one day a little story arrived from Johannesburg, South Africa. It talked of Tom Waldeck being shot on his doorstep and guess who he was mixed up with. None other than Charlie Richardson . . . but hang on a minute . . . wasn't there another Richardson? . . . doesn't that make them the Richardsons? Now where are they from? . . . south-east London . . . perfect. The Richardson Gang, the notorious south-east London family. Organized crime and wait for it . . . Murder Incorporated. Why not? It was a bit of a stretch of the imagination, but why not? They were hardly racing around the streets hanging on the runnerboard of fast cars and firing machine guns all over the place but would it not be good enough for now? With luck they would develop. So a Sunday toilet paper writer who called himself a journalist at parties jumped up from his desk and danced around the room with glee. He typed 'MURDER INC' at the top of the page and wrote a story. His editor ruined his fun a bit by taking out the names in case he got sued but then they printed a story about Tom Waldeck's murder at the hands of 'Murder Incorporated'.

As if I did not have more important things to do I found myself hiring several lawyers to sue the paper. At the time I was running around trying to sort out the mess. Lots of fingers were pointing at me but they were pointing in the wrong direction. For a start although Tom Waldeck had about as much muscle as a schoolgirl's fart and as much drive and determination as a garden slug I did like the man. Apart from that I had not cast my weary eyes on the sorry walking dildo that called itself Bradbury or West or whatever for many months. He had got the sack for his impersonation of a great British train robber hero. Apart from that he had screwed around with Tom Waldeck's wife while poor old Tom was out trying to build a business to buy her a bigger house. Never mind all that, people still pointed the finger as if I had shot Humphrey Bogart in the Klondike just as we had discovered gold. The point was that all my interests in our venture were totally tied up with Tom Waldeck. Everything was in our joint names but in his control. It was his nationalization as a South African that allowed us so much. He was the one who knew the dodgy government official who at that time was driving around in a new car that I had bought for him. It was Tom who was a member of the secret brotherhood, the Broederbond, the group that launched a thousand handshakes and back scratchings. Without him I was a sharp young scrap merchant from England. With him we were going to build a mining empire to overshadow the biggest in the world. So why should I have him shot? I might as well have shot my own balls off.

Somebody nearly did get his balls shot off. Well, actually it was his arse. Just as I was regaining control of the situation in South Africa. Just as I had managed to get the company going again. Just when the Hungarian engineers had expanded the first bit of perlite from Namaqualand. Just when I had big international companies begging me to meet with them to discuss supplies of perlite. Just when it was all starting to look incredible I got news from London. I got it in the worst possible way. I was sent a letter with a news clipping that had the same ring to it as 'Murder Inc'. It showed more evidence of the American importation of crimespeak. It demonstrated that most of the British press had spent a childhood of sticky Saturday afternoons with a bag of aniseed balls, peeing over the balcony, at the local fleapit cinema. The headline read, SHOOTOUT AT MR SMITH'S. It might as well have said 'Shootout at the O.K. Corral' but it was not a corral, it was a nightclub and it was not O.K. It was a bloody disaster. It was a bloody bloodbath. It was not John Wayne who got shot either. It was my brother Eddie who got shot in the arse. Both him and Frank Fraser were badly beaten up and shot. They were also charged with causing an affray.

Eddie, my kid brother, and Frank Fraser were doing well

in the West End. They had good and powerful friends and everybody kept well clear including the infamous cockney twins who were still watching with jealousy as Eddie and Frank's fruit machine empire grew and grew. Their machines were in great demand because with them you got ten per cent extra for yourself and you got an amazing lack of trouble in your club. Their influence extended beyond the West End so when a new club opened in Catford called Mr Smith and the Witchdoctor the management naturally asked Eddie and Frank to install their machines. The problem was that an ambitious set of would-be gangsters who watched too much TV had muscled in on Mr Smith from the moment it opened. The brothers Hayward, that's Billy Hayward and Flash Harry Hayward, wanted to be a south London family to be reckoned with. They were amateurs, but reckless amateurs, so Frank and Eddie went down with a few friends to sort them out one night. In the early hours when the club had emptied the two groups of men faced each other. Eddie and Frank got themselves ready for a routine tumble where a few glasses would be broken. There would be a lot of noise and a few pools of blood to mop up but in the end Eddie and Frank would be the night cleaners who left the club safe for punters to spike the drinks of their girlfriends for years to come. It was all going reasonably well. Eddie was busy knocking the shit out of one of Hayward's men when Dickie Hart the Catford Fart took a sawn-off shotgun from its holster under his jacket and blasted it off. It was a very sawn-off shotgun with only a few inches of barrel so the pellets went everywhere. When it went off it was like a starter's gun and wild chaos was the result. In the end a man lay dying in a pool of blood, Eddie and Frank ended up in hospital. Frank had a bullet in his leg and Eddie had to suffer the indignity of lying on his belly while the surgeon removed shotgun pellets from his arse. While they lay in hospital several members of the local police who were not on the payroll found it easy to arrest them.

They were in trouble so I had to help. I had to make arrangements to get back to London to find some good character witnesses who would explain that getting into fights and having their arses blown off was not a regular activity of my brother and his business associate. I thought that I could perhaps talk to some members of the jury and offer them a little roll of notes to make sure that British Justice was not only done, but done properly.

Meanwhile back in the East End Ronnie Kray patted the neat round buttock of a good cockney born within the earshot of Bow Bells and well versed in rhyming slang. He thought to himself that it was about time he killed somebody. He thought he imagined that he had detected a faint note of disrespect around him recently. He was sure he had overheard a few little giggles as he walked down the road with his latest boyfriend not on his arm but close enough to cause a few heads to turn. Inside that little head of his, Ronnie's brain must have been in turmoil as he tried to sort it all out. Ronnie was actually frightened by two things. He was worried people might take the piss out of his night-time hobby and he was terrified that people might think he was soft. There were several ways he could deal with his problems. He could establish himself as a dynamic force with the use of a highly developed intellect or he could reduce people to jelly with disarming wit. On the other hand he could blow their heads off with a shotgun or stab them with a big knife or – as he did sometimes – he could do both at the same time, just for luck. While he tortured himself trying to think which hard-case he should brutally murder so that everybody would respect him the answer came to him in a blinding flash.

He got news of my problems in South Africa as well as the recent shooting at Mr Smith's. He realized that with me distracted and with Frank and Eddie in hospital things were wide open for wild expansion. There was only one thing, one person, standing in the way. George Cornell was a very hard man, feared and respected throughout London, and he was a loyal friend and associate of mine and Eddie's. George was frightened of nobody, including the Krays. He was a perfect choice for Ronnie who could kill several birds with one stone, so to speak. Then just to confirm George Cornell was the right choice, Ronnie got a report that George had recently shouted out publicly that Ronnie was indeed, despite appearances, a 'fat poof'. That was it. While George sat with a friend in the Blind Beggar pub in Stepney, Ronnie Kray walked in and pointed a revolver at George's face. George smiled as Ronnie fired. As blood squirted out of his face from bullet after bullet George Cornell walked towards Ronnie Kray with a confident smile on his face until finally he fell at Ronnie's feet and the blood pumped out of his head onto the floor of the pub. Ronnie Kray had his own special way of coming to terms with his sexuality. Everybody was a bit taken aback with what happened in the Blind Beggar. The police ran around chasing their own tails for weeks trying to work out who had done it. Finally they came up with a brilliant and very perceptive solution which they proudly presented to the press. Whoever had done the shooting in the Blind Beggar was the same geezer who had done it at Mr Smith's. Of course everybody else knew who had done it. Roy Hall was very pissed off with George Cornell's murder. He liked George and Roy was loyal to the firm to the last. All those years ago he had been caught nicking from the scrapyard and had worked with us since then. At a time when the whole East End was walking around on tiptoes in fear of the terrible twins, Roy Hall psyched himself to do to Ronnie Kray what Ronnie had done to George. Two nights after the Blind Beggar shooting Roy drove round in the early hours to Vallance Road where the Krays lived with their mum. He stood in the middle of the deserted street lit by the streetlights and shouted for Ronnie Kray to come out and meet his destiny. When nobody came Roy shot the windows of their house out and finally a window opened. Roy got himself ready to become the man who shot Ronnie Kray. But it was Mrs Kray, the twins' mother, who opened the window. She shouted at Roy angrily. Who the hell did he think he was coming round this time of night and making such a racket? He was told that her boys were asleep and if he had any business with them he was to come back at a reasonable and decent time. Roy put the gun in his pocket and walked to his car. Nobody argued with Mrs Kray, especially the Krays. If he was going to kill Ronnie he would have to wait until his mum was not around.

When I came back to London I could hardly understand, never mind control the confusion. Guns, guns, guns – where had all these guns come from? Everything had changed. Any idiot with a few quid could buy a gun and become a local myth overnight. What was the point of eating raw steak and keeping fit when a seven stone weakling who just happened to be a psychopath in his spare time could blow your head off with a gun? What nerve did it take to pull a trigger? I realized that it was an emergency now. I had to help my brother, then get back to South Africa and build a legitimate empire based on mining, not guns. I wanted to compete with men who wore business suits because they were businessmen, not because they liked to look like businessmen. I had spent years fighting with my fists and with my wits. Now that guns were everywhere I wanted all my fights to be in boardrooms. As the actress said to the vicar, I wanted to be respected for my mind not my quick right hand.

CHAPTER NINE
Crime and Punishment

On 30 July 1966 England won the World Cup. It was only a minor event in retrospect. Of all the things I can remember about that day it is at the bottom of the list. When people ask you if you can remember what you were doing when Kennedy was assassinated I cannot tell you but I know every moment of the day that England won the World Cup.

Very early that morning I lay awake in bed waiting for an 'unexpected' caller to arrive. I was at home in London. Even though I was completely exhausted I had not slept very well. A thousand worries had been racing through my brain all night as I lay alone. Jean Goodman had walked out on me a few weeks before because she had found out about Jean La Grange. Fair enough, I had to think about Jean La Grange when I was with Jean Goodman to be of any use to her anyway. Jean La Grange, my exotic beauty from the Southern Hemisphere, had been back in Johannesburg for a week representing my interests and doing her bit to build a life for us out there. In May John Bradbury had been found guilty and sentenced to hang for Tom Waldeck's murder. His final story was that he only acted as a driver and that he did it because he was frightened of me. Nobody believed him so the judge put a little black cloth on his head while he gave John the benefit of his wisdom and told him to get his neck in training for a straining. As it turned out John Bradbury stroke West stroke Wilson lived to tell another lie or three. After a little visit from some English detectives who had it in for me his sentence got reduced to life.

All of that was starting to settle down a bit and we were at the beginning of a new era. I was too bloody busy at home with my brother's case to give the rich minerals of Namaqualand the time and trouble they deserved. A man called Tommy Butler had got himself heavily involved with the whole episode of

Mr Smith's. Tommy Butler was Sherlock Holmes and Tommy Butler was Wyatt Earp and he was also head of the Flying Squad. He had become very famous as the copper who had put away the Great Train Robbers and he was desperate for a few more interviews on telly. Tommy Butler ran around like a dog sniffing randomly at other coppers' arseholes hoping to get the scent of something exciting. Where he sniffed the press followed and a whole series of headlines started to appear. One tabloid journalist was sober just long enough to develop the idea of 'Murder Inc' to 'Crime Inc' and while innocent children were being burned alive in Vietnam the British press had leaders which shouted 'Smash the Gangs' at an innocent public. They demanded a 'Special Commission' to investigate and destroy organized crime. They could not wait for a Bugsy Malone or a Valentine's Day Massacre. They wanted Elliot Ness and the Untouchables now! Tommy Butler was a very poor substitute with his vest tucked into his skiddies but he was all there was on offer. So they took what they could and although they could not mention people by name they came bloody close. They called Tommy Butler the 'thief catcher' – very original! It's like calling a bus conductor the 'ticket collector'.

While Butler was sniffing around I got my own sniff. Rumour had it that he had introduced himself privately and discreetly to a few members of the jury on my brother's trial. There was nothing unusual about coppers having a few words with jury members as a form of insurance. I mean they sometimes spend months fitting somebody up only to be foiled at the last minute by some wally amateur of the public who knows nothing about how hard it is to be a copper. So I had a little tip that it was possible that Butler was up to an old trick that we had pioneered. It was my duty as a ratepayer and a taxpayer to report corruption wherever it came from. There was no point in repeating it to the police since he was the sheriff and all his deputies were frightened of him. So what I did was all that any law-abiding supporter of British justice could do – I went straight to the Houses of Parliament and reported my suspicions to a very prominent MP. Anyway he went straight to the Attorney General who told the 'thief catcher' Tommy Butler.

As I lay thinking about Tommy Elliot Ness Butler that fateful day England won the World Cup I heard a noise downstairs. I did not move because although I was alone in the house and nobody was supposed to be downstairs I knew who it was. There was no doubting that the racket going on in my living room was definitely the noise made by a copper silently slipping in through the french windows and tiptoeing through the house. I heard him open the latch to the front door to let some of his totally silent and undetectable detective friends creep in. I heard one of them whisper and another go 'shshshshsh!' I lay waiting for them to get up to the bedroom. I did notice a big wad of cannabis on the dressing table but I thought even if they did recognize what it was it was only worth a slap on the wrist and a small fine. Certainly not worth getting out of bed for.

They would have woken the dead but in fairness I was expecting them. One of their bent colleagues had given me a whistle the night before. He told me there was a dawn raid. I was too bloody tired to worry about it. It had been so long since I had done anything even a little bit naughty that it was bound to be a fit up. Somebody thought I was overdue and was having a go. Fair enough, it would cost me a few grand to sort out but it would have been pointless to run.

Finally a very embarrassed, scrubbed, round, overfed face poked round the door. Just as it did I closed my eyes and pretended to be asleep. I listened while several more came in behind him. One of them shook me and I opened my eyes. I smiled and asked in a warm and friendly voice:

'And who the fuck are you?'

The boss, the one who could piss the highest up a wall, said, 'We are police officers and we have come to arrest you.'

I sat up in my pyjamas, put my feet in my slippers and asked, 'Time for a wash and shave? I like to look my best when I'm being arrested.' He nodded and I said, 'The kettle's downstairs; mine's with two sugars.'

I had a wash and shave. When I got to the police station I

learned that I had been arrested by an aspiring star of print and small screeen, Gerald McArthur. I also learned that sixteen other new 'associates' of mine had been arrested as well and so had Jean Goodman. Then I realized that this was a very serious fit up. I had upset somebody very big and I was in very deep shit. I sat in that police cell which as usual was fresh with the reek of wino's urine and disinfectant trying to balance each other out. I tried to work out what was going on. I was shocked.

When they started to 'interview' me about all sorts of incidents that meant nothing to me I got curious. When they started to mention names of people like Jimmy Taggart and Lucien Harris I had to think about them. They rang a bell, but I had to dig them up from memory. Even Duval who was the lowest form of crawling life known to man was history to me. What was going on? I kept asking myself. This was all very bloody strange. Those bastards were up to something. They searched all the homes and workplaces of everybody arrested. All they could come up with was the gun that Roy Hall had used when he went for the Krays. They took some papers and some drugs from my place and that was it. Then we started appearing in magistrates' courts with motorcades of armed escorts and helicopters hovering above. The press started doing stories about 'The Torture Gang' and 'The Electric Chair Torture Case' and they talked about us and they said I was the evil boss of this 'Crime Inc'. A hundred times I wanted to cough humbly and say in the court, 'Excuse me guv'nor, but I think you have made a dreadful mistake. You have definitely picked up the wrong geezer here. Yes, I appreciate I am overdue a short stretch, such is the system, but this is way out of my league. This is out of the fucking league of anybody in Britain. This is fantasy stuff, you frigging wanker, so why not just let me walk out of here and I promise we will forget all about the embarrassment and indignity you are causing me and the grief you are causing my family.'

But the bastards had not made a mistake, they really were going for me. I should have been flattered if it were not so ridiculous. I really was shocked by the circus round me. The screws looked at me as if I could cut their balls off with my eyes. Young policemen handled me with the respect reserved for popes and pop stars. Like a throbbing tumour I watched a myth grow out of a little mushroom of a young boy who had wandered the bombsites of Camberwell and wanted one day to own a goldmine. That was all. Was that so wrong? I wanted to say to everybody that I could really sympathize with their need for a bit of colour and excitement. I could understand they wanted a gangster mythology without relying on American imports. But not me, please, go to the Krays, they liked being gangsters. They would have appreciated all the fuss, especially the motorcade and the helicopters. And then 'not me' turned to 'why me?' and I agonized as I paced up and down that stinking cell or as I sat in the dock of the Old Bailey. Why me? I do not know. Maybe because I was nearest? As the case developed and the lies poured forth out of a hundred heads like vomit I switched moods day by day and then hour by hour then minute by minute. One minute I would be seized by a gripping panic that made my limbs go like warm jelly. Then I would switch to resignation as my system collapsed inside its shell. Then I would be defiant and angry and even laugh at it all as I felt strong surges of blood push their way through muscle. On the outside I was always calm and cool. On the way to court we all behaved like naughty schoolboys going to see the headmaster each day. We made faces at people in the street and we sang and shouted. But we knew that we were in for more than a hundred lines and six of the best. Sometimes I looked out at the grey people going to work and just for a second I envied them. I wanted to be a railway porter or a car worker or even a civil servant if they would let me. I was tempted, just for a bit, by the idea of a little council flat near the railway line with carpets and a three piece suite on HP. For the first time in my life I ached to be nobody and nothing, and to spend a regular life like everybody else, waiting to die. I did not want to be the victim of the fostering of a myth. I just wanted to mine minerals. Now I really was Humphrey Bogart at the Klondyke. Just as we were about to be rich and happy, this happened. I wanted to weep when I thought of how close we came to being millionaires, achieving a place in the House of Lords, an obituary in *The Times*. I did not weep, I would not give them the satisfaction. I did think about it once. I thought that if I cried in court the myth of the gangster baron would be shattered and that would teach the bastards for making me one. I did not do it because I had to hang onto my self respect more than anything else.

The worst thing about the trial was the long moments of loneliness. It was worse than the lies and the fear. I had spent most of my life with other people nearly all the time and now I spent so many hours sitting on my own in a dark cell. I was not frightened of the dark but for the first time in my life I felt absolutely alone and it weighed me down with its deadness. I could not enjoy anything at all in those moments. On the outside my mother and five kids were full of support along with lots of faithful friends but if a Wembley Stadium full of people were supporting me I would have still felt alone. The judge summed up and it took him forever. He went through each point with meticulous care which only scantily clad the direction he gave the jury. They did not need his help. They had no choice but to find me guilty. It would have been bloody unpatriotic to do anything else. They would have been traitors to the human race to have let us walk free. After all the publicity and lies it would have been like having Caligula, Genghis Khan, Hitler and Stalin all in one box and taking the lid off to let them scuttle away. So they found me guilty. Lawton had already formulated his punishment but he adjourned the court until the next day to give his sentence. This gave the case the maximum chance of drama. Now everybody had the story. How could they miss the punchline? They would have to wait until tomorrow.

That night before sentencing I could not sleep. Only five of us out of the seven who were finally charged were found guilty. With me at the end were my brother Eddie, Frank Fraser, Roy Hall and Tommy Clark. I tried to work out what our sentences would be. It sparked me up a bit to realize that beneath all the media shit about 'Murder Inc' and 'Crime Inc' and 'Torture Gang Boss' I was actually charged with a bit of long firm fraud and five counts of grievous bodily harm. Nobody was dead, maimed or even bloody scarred. I was not a monster who beat up old ladies or ate children with a fried slice for breakfast. I had just slapped five hooligans around and had defrauded large companies out of money they were able to write off without even noticing the difference. Out there in the big bad world there were murderers and rapists and vicious cruel people who really harmed innocent people so why should I get such a big sentence? Yes, I could see that the press had made a myth of me and my family but surely it is not for a judge to concern himself with gutter press exaggeration. Regardless of his past notoriety for cruelty, surely this pompous Red Robe had to show the legal world that justice will be done. This trial was too public for him to get carried away with his own personal gratification. He was already overfed, overpaid, overrated and over-indulged. Why should he want to be famous too? His name and that of his father were already infamous amongst the thousands of people already in prison and their families. Why should he want to be a household name? I thought all night about the judge and his sentence. While I sat in that lonely cell he was having dinner at home with a glass of wine and thinking, 'Six, no seven, well, they were very naughty so maybe eight, but then again maybe I should set an example . . . nine. But when you think about it ten is such a nice round figure and if I am going to set an example then it's best I go for something that sticks in people's minds . . . yes, ten.' Ten years for five counts of GBH and a few long firm frauds was excessive but I knew I had to prepare myself for the worst. It was sickening that this pumpkin had such power. To him the difference between, say, seven or eight years was a professional decision. It was just a sound. To somebody being sentenced the difference between seven and eight years is eight months at least. Eight months of cold porridge and a bucket of shit in the corner of your room.

I sat in that soulless cell drinking a mug of stewed tea and heard the sound of a lorry engine arrive outside. My heart sunk and moths, not butterflies in that dismal place, started to fly around my stomach. The doors of my cell flew open as if I was a wild bull that would attack any casual enquirer. I picked up my carrier bag of personal effects and walked onto the landing of the prison. Here before me was a mass, a parade of uniforms, of screws. It had been like that every morning but on this special day there must have been twice as many. It was incredible because it was obvious they had taken extra care with their 'kit' the night before as if they were attending an important parade. Most of them were not going to the court so this was their parade. There was an immense sense of occasion in the air. I could imagine the chief screw the night before briefing them with, 'Now, lads, tomorrow morning we are taking the Torture Gang Boss to court along with his adjutant, quartermaster and other officers. I want you to make sure your boots are so shiny that I can see my ugly face in them and I want to have a shave with the creases of your trousers.' And they had all responded, 'Yes, sir!' done a quick about turn and marched off. Poor bastards, they were missing all that mindless discipline they had grown up to cherish before they were kicked out of the army for failing the intelligence test. I suffered the usual indignity of being asked like a child if I wanted to use the toilet. So with a sea of faces waiting to hear my splash I stood and peed. It took a little time. It's not easy to pee when all those people with sharp creases in their trousers and caps with peaks across their faces are waiting. When I had shaken the drips off and rinsed my hands under a tap I turned round with both hands held out together. The chief officer stepped forward but not with a towel. He handcuffed me while Roy Hall and Tommy Clark were being handcuffed and giving the screws the normal and expected complaints about them being too tight. We were led along a corridor of cells and I could feel the hundreds of eyes at the judas holes trying to catch a glimpse of our ridiculous procession. Still shackled, we were locked in a black maria. The maria has twenty-four cells inside. Each cell is so small your knees touch the opposite wall when you sit. In a noisy procession of police sirens and car horns we were driven down Brixton Hill surrounded by several police cars front and back, four motorcycles each side and a helicopter above. All traffic was stopped to let three very ordinary men get to court on time to hear what his lordship, the most worshipful, reverend, venerable and holy Frederick Lawton, had decided to do with us. There were no songs as we raced along Blackfriars Road when on other mornings there was always time to sing 'Doing the Lambeth Walk'. We were silent in our own thoughts of our futures.

After a short while I caught a glimpse of the Thames through the tiny windows in our shared steel hearse. A glance at that muddy brown water brought back memories of my brother Alan as we passed over the exact spot where the speedboat had catapulted and he had drowned. I had never got over it but as we passed by I remembered that in the year after it happened I had sunk to the pit of despair from which I thought I would never recover. It had been the very worst year of my life, and I got a strange comfort from the idea that nothing these bastards could do to me could be as bad as what I had experienced with Alan's death.

We arrived at the Old Bailey and were led down through dark corridors into the bowels of that shithole of human misery. Built on the foundations of Newgate, the Old Bailey had been the site for human suffering at the hands of British justice in all its wigs, robes, shackles and ropes for hundreds of years. Just after we arrived Frank Fraser and my brother Eddie arrived from Wandsworth prison, each handcuffed to two screws, one on each wrist. In a complicated manoeuvre we managed to shake hands taking great care not to shake the clammy hand of a screw by mistake. We were then led to our individual cells where we had the horror of waiting while the public and press above us snuggled in for the final act of this farce. I could imagine the excited chatter between them all. I had heard that our public had not grown in quantity, that was impossible, but it had certainly grown in stature. Large sums of money had probably been paid by Lords and Ladies and bankers, and a sprinkling of film stars. 'Ladies and gentlemen, roll up, come and see the Torture Gang Boss have his balls chewed off in public by that graduate of Battersea grammar school, or was it Battersea dogs' home, the right honourable, the right worshipful, his lordship . . . Judge Frederick Lawton.' This was the day to be in court. It was the end of an exciting adventure story for them, but the start of a nightmare in purgatory for me. How much time I got in purgatory had nothing to do with how many candles I had lit at the feet of the statue of the Virgin Mary. My living hell would be determined by a grammar-school graduate and ex-fascist. What if while he sat there sentencing he had a boil on his bottom and it chose to irritate him at that precise time? Somebody told me once that Karl Marx had boils on his bum as he sat and wrote his words of wisdom in the British Museum. Just look at the social experiments that emerged from that tortured bottom's soul.

So upstairs the judge placed his powdered wig on his head and put those thick, soft red robes on that soft pink body. The air was filled with a sense of carnival. As far as the weasel-faced representatives of the press were concerned if the Russians had bombed New York this trial was still the front page story for today. Tomorrow my face and my life as told through the lying teeth of alcohol-pickled journalists would wrap the cod and chips of a million fish suppers all over Britain. Drunks wandering home from a night of self abuse would see the face of 'the Torture Gang Boss' in front of them as they sprinkled it with salt and vinegar. Beneath all of this merriment I waited alone in a cell. Finally the circus above was hushed ready for the entrance of the stars of the show. My cell door burst open and five embarrassed spotty screws came in. I was led like a condemned man to a small white room with stairs leading in different directions. I was stopped at the bottom of the stairs to Courtroom Number One. I had been unshackled in my cell and now a chief officer approached me with a set of handcuffs. I looked at him and said, 'What do you think you're going to do with those?'

He stopped and a row of dull-eyed screws watched his next move. 'Come on, Charlie – you've got to wear them.'

I was going to say, 'Don't you fucking Charlie me, you cunt,' but he was trying and I was tired of it all. I spoke in a voice that warned of the consequences. 'Forget it . . . put them away.'

He retreated and formed a little huddle with his colleagues where I could overhear him telling them that he was not going to 'delay proceedings' by pushing the point but to 'keep an eye on the bastard, we don't want him trying to do a runner'.

Then the doors at the top of the stairs opened and the silent and pregnant noise of the courtroom glowed before me. I walked up with moths in my gut to take my place centrestage. As I stood in the dock on my own apart from the screws I looked around at the public gallery and caught sight of a bishop and a famous pianist. The crowd were in their Sunday best, young, old, rich and poor. All that was missing were the ugly women knitting at the front row of the guillotine. I stared back at them focusing on them individually and watched them blush and avert their stare as my eyes caught theirs. There was just one exception. The eyes of the beautiful journalist with the winking triangle of white panties met mine and they danced with a smile of mischief as she gave one last sensual leg crossing. This was a true gesture of compassion to a condemned man. I turned round to face the front just as, Blow me down with a feather! in walks Judge Lawton and all his loyal subjects jump to their feet to pay homage to the noble Lord. He raised one hairy eyebrow and Sebag-Shaw got to his feet and asked if Chief Superintendent McArthur would kindly take the stand. McArthur took the Bible in his hand and swore his oath word perfect as any seasoned copper. It was his job to read out my form, so having reminded everybody that he was the Assistant Chief Constable of Hertfordshire he started to tell my life story of crime. I have to say it did not sound like the life of a desperate and dangerous head of a crime syndicate. This man McArthur, it turns out, had spent years running around behind me picking up bits of evidence and taking statements from inadequate petty crooks. While I was running around creating employment and contributing to the wellbeing of my community and the wealth of the country he was using taxpayers' money to put a case together against me. It had to be him because the Met Police were so bent that no Met copper would have worked for a week, never mind years, without tipping me off. McArthur knew that, but I did not hear of any investigations against all the coppers who were supplementing their income at my expense.

So what was the catalogue of evil crimes committed by this 'Torture Gang Boss'? For a start I got two years' probation when I was eleven for stealing a book off a lorry. Before any bleeding heart social worker could interpret that as a desperate quest for education and knowledge from an underprivileged child I went on to three years at an approved school for stealing a car when I was fourteen. Then at the age of nineteen I was conscripted into the army but discharged seven months later. Lawton's ears pricked up and he interrupted, 'Was it stated why he was discharged?' and McArthur replied, 'No, my Lord.' Thank God the army had trouble finding clerks who could write. 'When aged twenty-two Richardson was sentenced to six months for receiving,' and again Lawton asked, 'Does it say what he received?' and McArthur again had to disappoint the judge with 'no, my Lord'. Again, thank God for that. I had been given six months for receiving six sides of stolen bacon, one month for each side. I think in that tense and wound up courtroom they may have pissed themselves laughing at this dangerous villain before them who was a receiver of stolen bacon. So that was it . . . a book, a car and six sides of bacon, not exactly a long and vicious career in crime but the way they said it I might as well have committed regular mass murders since I was at primary school.

With that done my brief rose to give his mitigation speech to the judge. The courtroom waited a second while my barrister, Crispin, who was being paid more for his time than most coalminers earned in a week, cleared his throat. We waited for pearls of wisdom from this educated man of french letters. He turned to the judge.

'My Lord,' he said, then he turned to me and back to the judge and shrugged his shoulders. 'You toerag!' I thought, 'Why should anyone believe me if you make it so clear that you don't?' This licensed bandit of the bar continued, 'My Lord . . . my client Charles Richardson still maintains his innocence of these charges he has been found guilty of. I ask you, my Lord, not to impose a sentence upon him which will destroy him. I ask that you do not sentence him to a world of darkness. Let him have some light at the end of the tunnel.' Was that it? Hardly Perry Mason! Hardly likely material for the *Oxford Dictionary of Great Courtroom Speeches.* All he said really with his gestures and his tone was, 'Please forgive me for being involved with the likes of Richardson but I am only doing my job, guv'nor . . . please don't let this unfortunate incident get in the way of my otherwise very promising career.' The bastard betrayed me.

I was then asked by the clerk of the court if there was anything I would like to say before the sentence of the court was passed upon me. I looked at my barrister, that great orator, and wanted to say, 'My learned friend, I hope your next shit is a hedgehog.' Then I looked at the press and wanted to tell them that at that moment in time I felt morally superior to them. Whoever I was, whatever I had done, I was not happy to watch a man be condemned by an evil mythology just to further a sorry career in Fleet Street. Everybody there knew that the worst I had done was to smack a few low lives around because they had broken the accepted rules of our community. They all knew that but they wanted to believe I was Ivan the fucking Terrible. The golden rule that people believe what they want to believe had done me proud in the past. Now it was working against me. Everybody was impatient for the broken sobs of the condemned gang boss. I looked the judge in the eye and said, 'No.'

It was Judge Lawton's turn now to say what he thought of me and it brought no surprises to anybody to discover he did not really like me very much. Just in case anybody doubted that, he told me just what he thought in front of the whole courtroom, and with the very eager assistance of the press, the whole world. He spoke for some time and concluded:

'On the evidence I have heard I am satisfied that over a period of years you led a large, disciplined and well-organized gang for the purpose of your own material interests and the purpose of your criminal desires. You terrorized those who crossed your path and you terrorized them in a way which was vicious, sadistic and a disgrace to civilization. When we hear what you did to Harris one is ashamed to live in a society with men like you. Your punishment must be severe because it is the only way in which our society can show its repudiation of your criminal activities. Only by a long sentence can you be prevented from doing the same again. I have viewed the prospect of rehabilitation but I have decided there is no known penal system to cure you. You must be kept under lock and key. Your sentence will show clearly to all those who set themselves up as gang leaders that they will be struck down by the law.'

Strong stuff! My heart sank. I realized I was in for a long one here. I was going to be made an example of. I was in for a ten-year stretch, even twelve. Then to prolong the agony Lawton sentenced me for each offence at a time. I got four years for grievous bodily harm to Jack Duval and a further seven years for robbing Duval with violence. Then I got fourteen years for grievous bodily harm on Lucien Harris and so it went on until it totalled ninety-eight years! He said the longer sentences would run concurrently so he sentenced me finally to serve twenty-five years. He also ruled that since my assets were estimated at £250,000, I would pay £20,000 towards the court costs and as a final kick in the ribs he ordered an enquiry into how I had managed to get legal aid.

Twenty-five years! Twenty-five years! Jesus Christ! Twenty-five years. I was winded. All my breath had left my body. I nearly doubled up in shock and horror. What had I done? A book, a car, six sides of bacon and a few bruised villains. Twenty-five years! People kill people and only get life which can turn out to be fifteen years. I was thirty-three – I would miss the rest of my youth and all to create the myth of a gangland London to make England proud. I stood there while the whole courtroom gasped and wet their pants and they could not believe how privileged they were to be so lucky as to see such an extreme example of human cruelty. They revelled in the pornography of my suffering while the blood raced and my heart pumped like the pistons of a traction engine. Finally I managed to draw breath. It was all a circus, a show, a fiasco. The performance was over. I turned to the jury and bowed and said, 'Thank you very much indeed.' I turned and disappeared from the court to the cells below.

My mind was numb and I tried to keep it that way as I was led through the corridors by a gang of nervous screws and we came to the rows of cells with even more officers trying not to catch my eye. I ignored them when I heard a shout and could see one shining eager eye at the small judas hole of a cell. Even though all I could see was an eye I could distinguish who it was behind each door and I could see the hope in each eye. I stood where they could see me and showed two opened hands and then closed them, then opened them again and I could see the surprise in each eye. When I opened one hand yet again I could read shock, disgust and anger all in the flickering of an eye at a small hole. I was led to my own cell which already had my name with twenty-five years underneath chalked on the door.

Lloyd Eley, my junior barrister, came in to apologize for the situation and to talk to me about an appeal and the new parole system coming into force. He desperately wanted me to make him feel better but I thought he should have at least one sleepless night of guilt to make up for the thousands of nights of lonely misery I was to suffer. My lunch came in and while I eyed with horror the rock hard roast potatoes and thin slice of meat lying inches from the spotted dick and custard I asked Lloyd Eley to excuse me while I ate alone. He was grateful for an excuse. He left to have a few brandies with his friends and be the life and soul of the club as he traded his personal insight into the 'Torture Gang Boss'.

After lunch I sat on the table which was cemented to the floor. How can I describe my feelings? I was in my early thirties and I was a whisker away from being a millionaire. Now instead of that I was a turd in a sewage farm to be treated like shit. It's not a good comparison because unlike a sewage farm, the prison system takes in human beings, turns them into shit and discharges them as untreated sewage. I could not take it in. It was too big. I did all the calculations and with all the will and hope in the world I would be at least in my mid-forties before I got out. All that life was to be pissed away as worthless. I started to think of the possibilities of escape, as a gang of screws poured into my room. Like a kid going on a school trip I was told I had better go now since I would not get a chance later. Again I pointed Percy at the porcelain in front of an audience of blue uniforms and my dripping hands were shackled to a screw on each arm. I was led to the yard and we clumsily managed to squeeze into the back of a white Jag. It certainly was a squeeze with a fat screw on each arm. With another Jag in front of us and a Jag behind the yard gates were opened and our little convoy crawled forward through the yabbering throng of press and public. As our car approached them the pitch of their wild pushing and shoving grew in the desperation for a glimpse and a photograph. I grabbed a book and put it over my face. Photographs had been in the papers for days so I was not worried about being recognized. I just hated them so much I could not bear to give them the satisfaction of getting a picture of me. Eventually we sped through the streets of London and onto the A1. Our noisy convoy of police cars had a silent and isolated gang boss squeezed between two uniformed Michelinmen with a shared glandular problem that was obvious even to an insensitive nose.

We sat in silence in our now noiseless convoy as we travelled through the length of England. I was so choked and stunned at the day's events I could not be bothered to ask where I was going. Eventually we arrived in the dark outside the glow of the old and forbidding Durham prison staffed by stocky screws from the mining villages. Living and working in corridors of dark misery was part of their ancestral heritage. In the reception area I was given another VIP treatment in front of a parade of about thirty curious screws. The idea was to intimidate me from the start. I was given the usual reception procedure. They gave me an ill-fitting uniform, a pillowcase, towel, cup, spoon, comb, bar of soap, toothbrush and a blunt tin knife. I was weighed in at twelve stone two pounds, asked if I had ever had VD and told I was going to a special unit for category A prisoners. This unit was famous for its inhumanity. It was built within Durham prison after the escape of the Great Train Robbers, Charlie Wilson and Ronnie Biggs. The other train robbers were in there and I looked forward to meeting old friends again. I was given a meal of three slices of white bread, a tot of margarine and a slice of corned beef which I washed down with a mug of sugarless, stewed tea. I sat in that concrete coffin with not one, not two, but three sets of bars at my bulletproof window. At nine o'clock my door was unbolted and I was given a cardboard box and told to undress and put all my clothes in it. They took the box away and I was left standing naked in my cell. At ten o'clock the light in my cell went out and I sat cold and naked in a room brightly lit from the floodlighting outside. The bars cast a shadow on my wall. 'The journey of a thousand miles begins with a single step' came into my mind. I crawled into the lumpy bed and tried to get warm. I began the very long journey of my prison sentence that night.

My brother Eddie got ten years and so did Roy Hall. Tommy Clark got eight years. Frank's sentence was deferred, but he later got twelve years.

I languished at Her Majesty's Pleasure for a very long time. It would be futile to try to explain the prison system and its injustices within anything shorter than *The Complete Works of Shakespeare*, so I will not even try. What I would just say is that it is not a question of being inhumane or unkind to people who are outcasts from society. Above all the British prison system is stupid. It is expensive and it just does not work. It does not make people 'better' citizens; it makes them worse. It does not cure crime; it creates it. It is a cancerous tumour that feeds upon itself and grows. I languished for years. Durham Maximum Security became the focus of attention for an enquiry headed by Lord Mountbatten. He said in his report that the Maximum Security Wing of Durham had conditions that 'no civilized society could tolerate'. In the middle of a blaze of publicity the Home Office closed the wing down and introduced the dispersal system for Category A prisoners. It was a simple idea. Me and men like me were passed around the prison system like hot potatoes. We were not allowed to stay in one prison long enough to plan and execute an escape. This meant that we were always on the move with no opportunity to make friends or settle in any one place. It also turned out I met a lot of people who were inside. By the way, as soon as they had closed down Durham 'H' wing for men and nobody was watching, the Home Office sneaked women in there to live in conditions as bad as we had suffered. There was only one Category A woman at the time but that did not bother them. They just filled the rest of the wing up with all sorts of women. Women who had nicked a bag of 'pick 'n' mix' from Woolworths found themselves inside a maximum security prison with underfloor monitoring.

As my five children grew up without a father I tried hard to survive the indignities of prison. I realized from the start that when they took my clothes and put them in a cardboard box I did not stand naked in my cell. I had one thing left that they tried hard to remove from all prisoners but I clung onto it desperately. I was hanging off a cliff with the rocks below and the small branch that I grasped to save my life was a sense of my own dignity, my worth as a human being, my self respect. I hung onto that and I kept my brain alive. A lot of prisoners devote their lives inside to trying to save a few of the lost years by physical exercise and obsessive body building. Very often they neglect the very important little muscle that lies gasping for exercise in their skulls. All my life I had desperately pursued knowledge out of a wild curiosity for everything around me. I used my time inside to read and to learn. I joined whatever courses I could get on to: woodwork, English literature, history, and economics. Finally I realized I was severely lacking in languages so I decided I had to learn a foreign language. With that in mind I applied successfully to the Open University to study sociology. It taught me a little bit about the society I lived in. I understood, for example, the difference between Karl Marx and Marks and Spencer's. The ideas of one produced a retail outlet for the best underwear in Britain and the ideas of the other turned half of Europe into an open prison. It certainly taught me a new language with a wide new vocabulary. I got to know and understand that the way people think is an 'ideology' and something going on was a 'phenomenon', while some situations were 'syndromes'. It was exciting stuff. I came across one word that stuck in my brain forever. I read it somewhere and looked it up in my *Concise Oxford Dictionary*. The word was 'atrophy' which was defined as 'wasting away for lack of nourishment'. It was an important word because every time I felt too lazy to pick up a textbook I was haunted by a little ghost that would whisper into my ear, 'Don't let your brain suffer atrophy.'

Sociology also taught me another valuable skill. I learned from it very quickly that you can say or write a lot without actually saying anything at all but sounding like you know what you are up to and that you are pretty damned clever. So this armed me for conversations with prison staff and governors where they caved in under the weight of my argument even when they were right and I was wrong. I also saw straight through a lot of the probation officers and psychologists because they did not realize that I was fluent in sociospeak which was later called bullshit.

I met a lot of people in prison. There is no use in saying what they were like which is just about as clever as saying what Americans are like. There are good and bad, rich and poor, thick and bright, big and small and kind and cruel in most prisons. That went for some of the staff too. Most of the screws had bruised knuckles from walking on all fours but some of them were human beings. Even some of the governors were good people, like the governor of Maidstone who encouraged me to start and edit a prison magazine. Most of the official board of visitors were Rotary Club, freemasons, prats who felt they were doing their bit for Britain by dealing with the arsehole of society. But some were genuine people. Lord Longford started to visit me and my brother. I did not have to wear a rosary and pretend to have received a visitation resulting in our instant conversion to get his genuine help and support. A lot of the 'cons' I met were fascinating people. If they had anything in common it was simply a desire to have an exciting life but this had been engendered without the means to do it. They realized very often that money does not talk, it screams. It screams 'take me, I am yours' so they have a go and very often they fail. As I moved from human warehouse to warehouse I despaired at the total chaos of a prison system that assumes that with so many laws anybody who breaks them has something in common with somebody else who breaks them. What on earth can you do with a system that understands and treats an armed bank robber the same as somebody who knocked off his wife?

The problem is the idea of people 'paying' for their crime: not because it changes them but because it makes the public feel better. If the public could just let go of feeling better and deal with the problem without prejudice and emotion, then maybe we could get somewhere.

When I was in one of these smelly Victorian warehouses of misery I came across a man who, like a lot of other prisoners, interested me a great deal. When he arrived on our wing the story went around that he was in for taking and driving away a car. That was a common enough offence but not for a man of his age which was about forty. It was also unusual to be in a security wing but it turned out that it was his fifty-sixth offence of stealing a car and he had clocked up about fifteen years in small sentences for the same offence from the age of twenty. He must have had the British record for 'recidivism' which was another interesting word I came across for the 'habitual relapse into crime'. One day during 'association' when we had a short opportunity to talk to each other I got chatting with him and I found he was educated, intelligent, articulate and witty. What's more, he didn't seem to be off his rocker. I was fascinated that such a man could nick a car fifty-five times and then go and do it again. I was annoyed that such a man would get caught fifty-six times. How could he be so careless? The more I dug into him the more I got interested. After that I kept trying to speak to him to find out what made him tick, or should I say 'nick'. I avoided asking him straight out because I knew he would put his guard up and the answer he gave would just be to put me off. I really wanted the truth so I persevered and got to know him well.

One day when we had been playing backgammon for the hundredth time I asked him straight out, 'Why did you nick all those cars, Kenny?'

He looked at me and said, 'I never had a car of my own, Charlie.'

'Yeah, but why did you nick them when you could have saved up for a few years and got an old banger?'

He thought for a minute then looked at me and I thought maybe I had gone too far. He gave me the look a woman sometimes gives which says 'not you, too . . . and I thought you wanted something else from me other than a quick fuck'. So many people had tried to find out about Kenny and his cars and like an obstinate virgin with a dynamite body he had refused all their persistent advances. But for some reason he decided to give me the benefit of the doubt.

'Trouble was, Charlie, after the first few times I had a record so I had problems getting a job so I had trouble buying a car so I nicked one so I ended up inside and it went on. It was a vicious circle.'

'But why take a car at all?'

'I needed transport.'

'What, every time?'

'Yes.'

'Couldn't you catch a bus?'

'No.'

'Why did you need transport so bad?'

He looked again and tried to back off.

'I just did, Charlie.'

'What for?'

'I just did.'

'Come on Kenny, what was so important you needed to nick cars all the time?'

'OK, Charlie, I will tell you this much but only because it's you. Promise you won't tell anybody else?'

'On my life, Kenny.'

I waited. He had trouble getting it out but at last he did.

'I had to get to the countryside, Charlie. I just had to get there.'

'What! Is that it? You had to get to the countryside! What does that mean, for God's sake?'

'That's it, Charlie, that's as much as I'm telling you.'

'But why, I mean are you an obsessive rambler or something?'

He would say no more and I was twice as curious. I was so desperate to solve the riddle of Kenny the Car that I slipped a wad of notes to a few key screws and managed a change of cells so that we ended up cellmates. I introduced him to the joys of a joint to relax him and after months of gaining his trust I decided to make my move. After a warm up we got into the discussion and I finally went for the jugular.

'Why did you have to get into the countryside, Kenny, that you would nick a car fifty-six times?'

He took a long draw at a fat joint and sighed, 'It was more than fifty-six times, Charlie. I only got caught fifty-six times.'

'*Only* . . . that's a bleedin' understatement. How many times was it?'

'Hundreds.'

'Jesus Christ, Kenny, I can't stand it any longer. Why did you have to get to the countryside? Are you a mad nature lover or something?'

'Sort of.'

I toned down my voice a bit. I did not want to sound too eager and put him off. I took a draw at the joint and passed it back to him.

'Kenny, why don't you explain to me what the hell you are talking about?'

As he lay in his bunk and I lay back on mine the cell was lit by the glow as he drew on the joint.

'You won't tell anybody, Charlie?'

'On my life, Kenny.'

Now there was a pause that you could slice. I knew he was going to tell me at last and I almost wished I had not asked. He took a deep breath and said it.

My Manor

'I had to get to the countryside, Charlie, because I like to fuck horses.'

You could have knocked me over with a feather. I stared into the darkness and he continued.

'I couldn't get a bus because where they kept horses was never on a bus route. Well, not at night anyway, and I always got frisky at night. So I would nick a car and drive into the countryside.'

Now there was no stopping him – he went on to tell me exactly how he had sex with horses. It turned out they were male horses and he said how important it was to him that the horses enjoyed it too. After all, he said, he had always been an animal lover. 'Me too,' I thought, 'but there are extremes.' I could imagine him when he had finished, lighting a cigarette and turning to this great stallion and saying, 'Was that all right for you?' And this beautiful monster giving him a satisfied snort.

I really did wish I had not gone down this path. After years of making sure I did not share my cell with a gender bender of the Ronnie Kray type who might have a wandering hand in the middle of the night I end up with a man who not only prefers sex with another male but also with a male horse! Anyway, I thought, as long as I never go down on all fours he would never be interested in me.

As I lay in the dark I wondered what the system could do for the likes of Kenny. It costs two or three times the national average wage per week to keep a man in prison. If you include court costs and legal aid and police time Kenny had cost this country a fortune. If it was possible to get to the root of Kenny's problem it was possible to escape from the nonsense of wanting to punish him. If it were possible just to diagnose the situation and without prejudice prescribe the treatment, the prognosis could be very very good for everybody. The answer was very simple. The Home Office should have given Kenny a couple of retired pit ponies and a field and let him get on with it. You would have had a law-abiding citizen, two happy horses and it would be at a fraction of the cost of banging him away like a criminal.

Prison was full of characters, most of them very interesting. The one thing that was in abundance was imagination and a sense of adventure. At first when people told stories about how they got nicked for dangerous armed robbery of a bank and it turned out to be a newsagent I used to get pissed off. Later I learned that the thing to do was just enjoy the stories and to hell with the truth. In a place where men are beaten into submission by subhuman apes or subdued by the drugs prescribed by so-called 'doctors', how can the truth be important? In a place where you can get as many strong tranquillizers as your system can take, but even a governor's application will not get you a vitamin pill, how can truth matter? In a place where some men display their disapproval of other men by raping them while the screws turn a blind eye and where self-appointed 'patriots' beat IRA prisoners to an inch of their lives, you have to consolidate your responsibilities. Your only responsibility is to your friends, your family and yourself. The only weapon you have in prison and the only thing that does you any good when you finally get out is your self respect. As the years rolled by and the people came and went around me I hung onto my self respect and I made sure that the most vital organ I had that lay behind my twinkling eyes did not 'suffer atrophy'.

CHAPTER TEN

A Stone's Throw from the Beach

I lay in bed waiting. I could hear the muffled footsteps of the night screw as he walked along the landing. The footsteps stopped every few paces and paused as he looked into each cell. As he approached mine I jumped out of bed and leaped the few paces to the door and screamed at him.

'Jesus Christ! How the bloody hell am I supposed to get some bloody sleep with you making this bloody racket?'

I almost instantly regretted it. He was not a bad man for a screw and he was shocked by my reaction. His face showed his hurt. His eyes whimpered at me 'but I thought we were friends'. His voice broke a little as he tried to hold his ground and speak through the door.

'I'm only doing my job, Charlie.'

This was cruel but it had to be done. I jumped into the air kicking my feet out like a can-can dancer and did a wild dance in my small cell and mimicked him with a mad chant.

'I'm only doing my job . . . I'm only doing my job . . . I'm only doing my job.'

In for a penny, in for a pound. I continued the chant with, 'More than my job's worth mate! . . . more than my job's worth! I don't know about that, lad, you'd better ask the chief. You'd better ask the chief.'

I did that wild dance and commotion every night for weeks and sure enough it got round the screws. They wanted an easy life. They stopped checking on me at night and every new screw who arrived was told to leave me alone at night. With that little chink in their security well established I moved on to the next part of my plan to escape from Spring Hill open prison.

It was 1980 and I had been eating dog's vomit with three white slices and a tot of margarine for fourteen years. I had been up for parole for the last seven years. Each year I had applied with hope. I had waited for months while a decision was made during which time I would keep telling myself not to get excited. I would tell my kids, who had grown up without me, not to get excited. When we sat together in visits the parole was not to be mentioned. If by accident it was brought up then we would try to prepare ourselves for the worst by assuming it was not going to be granted. But no matter how many times I told myself, 'Don't think about it . . . you won't get it,' I still got excited and my kids also secretly got excited. Then when it was refused we were all devastated. The last four applications were actually endorsed and approved by the prison authorities and turned down by some flabby-arsed bureaucrat in a Burton's suit at the Home Office. Each knockback just about finished me off mentally. Despite all the regular workouts I gave that tough little muscle in my skull, with all the hard personal discipline that involved, it nearly collapsed forever each time. The last year I spent before moving to Spring Hill was in Maidstone which was an old shithole of a place. After my seventh knockback, after watching murderers arrive in prison after me and leave before me, they decided to send me to Spring Hill.

Open prisons are not what they are cracked up to be but they are definitely an improvement on the old Victorian hellholes with the shit of three men in a bucket in the corner of a cell the size of a toilet. As soon as I arrived at Spring Hill I did what any self-respecting 'gang boss' would do when trusted to be moved to an open prison – I planned my escape. People are sent to open prisons for a variety of reasons. A common reason is that they are middle class and the judge and the system instinctively look after their own. They put all the businessmen with university degrees in one place to keep them away from the nightmare of mixing with ruffians. They put people like me in places like Spring Hill as a kind of glimmer of hope. It means you may be going out soon. It helps you prepare for the outside world. It's also a way of compensating you for not getting parole when you should have done.

After fourteen years of being posted around from toilet to

toilet and then being moved to the relative luxury of Spring Hill you would think the sensible response would be to wait just a little bit longer. After fourteen years what's one or two more, after all? It would just mean a couple more prison pantomimes with a fourteen stone rock solid heap of muscle with a hairy chest playing Cinderella. After fourteen years you would think I could manage just a little bit more. But I could not. I just could not do one more pissing year inside prison. It was like doing two hundred and ninety-nine push ups and I just could not do three hundred even if it broke the prison record.

On the last knockback I sat with my mother and five kids on a visit and I watched them all cry together and I realized something had to be done. In all this time I had become a grandfather and my eldest daughter was breastfeeding at that time and she lost her milk. I did not have a choice of just hanging on a few years and then getting out. I was facing total meltdown so something had to be done . . . now!

After a few weeks of screaming at the screws when they came near my door to dissuade them from doing it any more I was running through a muddy field in the middle of the night. I was behind schedule because a few cows had been pissing around earlier. I cursed and swore my way through bramble bushes and undergrowth. I tripped and stumbled and screamed silently inside as every now and again one of my feet would find an unseen rabbit hole. I had arranged for someone to be waiting in the car park of a pub near the nick at 10.45. If I was not there at exactly 10.45 he was to drive away. As I ran across the last field my heart jumped when I saw in the dim glow from the pub a dark figure sitting in a car. I could even see the green glow of the car radio on his face. Then I could see him hold his arm up to look at his watch and twist his arm to get the light and read the time. I found some extra energy from somewhere and broke into a sprint. I almost broke into a helpless panic when I saw him lean forward and start the car and turn on his lights. Another burst of adrenalin found its way into my blood and I ran even faster. I wanted to bellow with frustration as he drove out of the car park. He had to stop to gain access onto the main road and for a second I had a little flicker of hope as I pounded across the last bit of the field and finally threw myself through some bushes. He pulled away and I was in the car park. I could not shout. I stopped and thought my heart was going to burst its way out of my ribcage it was pumping so hard. A man came out of the pub and I caught a few seconds of the laughing chatter of the pub as the door closed behind him. I threw myself in the bush as he staggered towards me. As I lay in the dark he let rip a great torrent of spew into the bushes. He left his steaming deposit of steak and kidney pie and lager with diced carrot and staggered back into the pub to abuse his system some more. I crawled through the bushes around the car park and lay in some long grass and stinging nettles by the side of the road. I made a silent prayer that he would come back even though he was under orders not to come back. He never did what he was bloody told anyway. He always knew better so I lay and hoped that true to form he would do what he pleased, ignore what I had said and come back. After about half an hour as the pub emptied of its happy drunken load of free people I realized the bugger was not coming back. For once in his life he did what he was told to do and it had to be now! It was pointless going on with the escape that night. There was a whole elaborate plan to get me out of the country. It would be stupid to get caught wandering around in the dark. So I had the indignity of breaking back into the prison which was much more difficult than breaking out. It was not the end of the world. I had arranged as an emergency measure for the return of the car exactly twenty-four hours later. That next night I took no chances and arrived early. I lay in the bushes near the car park trying not to listen to two young people with orange and green hair get to know each other better. As I lay there I realized that things had changed a lot. He did not look into her eyes and say passionately, 'The moonlight becomes you.' There was no awkward adolescent, 'Oh, go on, let me, I won't ask for anything if you just let me touch your tits.' It was straight into it and grunting and rutting like animals. She knelt on the ground with her white arse in the air and waited impatiently while he sorted himself out. After a few seconds she turned her mohican orange head around and cursed, 'For fuck's sake . . . get on with it, what's the matter with you?' They continued this tender embrace, this meeting of souls, in silence except for a few slurps from the area where their souls met and a few grunts from the heart. There was a final grunt from him, then he withdrew and put himself away. She realized a little while after the event that he had finished and said, 'God, fucking hell, is that it . . . last of the great fucking lovers.' They both adjusted various designer holes and safety pins that they were dressed in and went inside. Just as I was thinking that these two misunderstood youths of today probably had parents who were proud of them, a car swept with ridiculous speed and drama into the car park. It was him! I stood up, walked to the passenger side, opened the door and sat in the plush comfort of that big car. That was it. I was free. We sped through the night, I smoked cigars and drank brandies and talked and talked and I was a very happy man. As we leapfrogged from traffic jam to traffic light through the streets of London I stared out of the window like a little boy from the outback on his first trip to the big city. We had a quick wander around the steamy sights of Soho where I was ecstatic in the glow of the multicoloured lights and multicoloured people. Fashionable professional people spilled out of the Chinese restaurants and other professional ladies offered a wide range of hidden delights and I loved them all. I was reluctant to leave but I had a daring prison escape plan to complete. I did what most escaping prisoners do when they escape, I went home. I did not hang around but I had to see a few friends and family and I had to see Camberwell. I went on to Jersey to see one of my daughters who was ill in hospital. I stayed for a few days and then caught a ferry to St Malo and then on to Paris. I ate something so delicious I could not pronounce it in Maxim's and moved on to the Negressco in Nice. It still held some magic and a lot of memories of Jean La Grange and our historic five day attempt at the Olympic record for continuous frollicking. With my very new Irish passport I moved on to Majorca where it was nearly the height of the season and I mingled happily in the Spanish sun with thousands of English tourists.

Meanwhile, back at the homestead, where steamy puddings and warm beer had been replaced by black forest gateaux and lager, the gentlemen of the gutter were very busy. As umbrella bumped into umbrella on the drizzled streets of London, newspaper stands were full of mugshots of me at an earlier age. The Torture Gang Boss had escaped and was at large. He was believed to be in Europe. Actually I was in Majorca wearing a silly hat with my trousers rolled up paddling in the sun with a choc-ice. As I approached the parade of shops and restaurants I was stopped in my tracks by my photograph staring back at me from the front page of the *Sunday Times*. I bought every copy the newsagent had but I realized that Majorca would be flooded with them. It was Margate in the sun with more need for English papers than Spanish. I packed my bags and went on to mainland Spain and travelled around. I was eventually drawn by the lure of fish and chips and genuinely missed my own people so I ended up in Benidorm for a while.

The hotel I stayed in was pleasant, if a little bare and spartan. One day I picked up a brochure for the hotel in the lobby and carried it to my room where I sat on the balcony and read it. A phrase they used caught my eye. I had read it a hundred times on my travels. In the first paragraph under an 'artist's impression' of the hotel which employed a lot of creative licence, it said that the hotel was 'a stone's throw from the beach'. I sat there and even though I was just able to see the sea between some other hotels I could not imagine throwing a stone that far. I thought I would give them the benefit of at least trying so I went downstairs and picked up some stones from the street. Back on my balcony I threw a few and tried not to hit innocent tourists. Failing to get anywhere near the beach I went up to the roof of the hotel and using all my strength I could not even get a fraction of the distance to the beach. Did they test this idea with an Olympic discus thrower who for the sake of a few quid threw some stones for them? If they did, it was hardly fair since it should be based on an average stone's throw. Perhaps there could be a British Standard Stone's Throw which defined precisely the necessary distance. I talked to a few English tourists about it showing them the brochure and they all laughed and said, 'They always say that.'

Of course it was all nonsense. It was a lie that people accepted as part of life. To me it was a significant moment. I began to realize that fraud could be developed into an acceptable business practice.

With all the shit in the papers about me and my escape I thought I should intervene. I used my best possible sociospeak and wrote to the papers. The *Sunday Times* published a long letter with a photograph. After a little while another smell came along for the dogs of the media to chase and they left me alone. I slipped back into England unnoticed and started to look around for new ideas. I did not get very far. A few weeks later I was arrested and shoved back into a toilet with two other men for four years.

During those years nothing very much happened other than I met some good honest cons and some bent perverted screws. I also met an interesting accountant who had been very creative in his art. He was doing six years for fraud. He told me a story which fascinated me. It seems he used to be a pay sergeant in Kenya in the British army. This was at the time before independence when Britain was fighting the Mau Mau. Every week he had to do all his accounting on what he called his 'acquittance rolls'. He had to account for all the money he had paid to the soldiers. They did not get paid much but they got several allowances. One allowance the soldiers got he called the right hand allowance and on his acquittance rolls there was a column for R.H. allowance. It was a simple fee that was paid to soldiers for the right hands of Mau Mau 'terrorists'. They went out into the bush looking for Mau Mau and when they caught them they would kill them and cut off their right hands. Those hands would be brought back and the soldier would get a bonus for each one. This pay sergeant would then have to hang on to these hands to have them counted by the paymaster who would then release the money. Fair enough, perhaps, but the problem was that they realized after a while that a lot more hands were coming back than made sense. Some soldiers were just getting hold of any black people they could find and lobbing their hands off for less than a few quid.

When I heard this story I sat there and thought of how, in my court case, we had spent so long talking about whether Lucien Harris actually had a knife through his foot. It went on for days and in the end people did not know what to think. I did not put a knife through Lucien's foot, but just suppose I did. I got a twenty-five year sentence for smacking some hooligans around. If I was in the British army in Kenya they would have paid me to do much worse than I ever did in Camberwell. I could not have done what those young men in Kenya did. I could not bring myself to cut off the hand of an innocent man I had shot, just for a few quid. So I languished in a shithole for half a lifetime for a few smacks in the mouth and yet young soldiers pissed it up in the NAAFI on the proceeds of their own barbarism.

Those last years inside were full of bitterness. Throughout my stint inside I never got over a sense of gross injustice when I thought about my trial. Details would keep taking on a new significance especially when things were found out later. When we were arrested one of the key co-defendants was a character called Brian Mottram who I had worked with. He stood charged as being one of the 'Richardson Gang'. Much of our defence depended on his involvement. But he was excused prosecution on the recommendation of his GP for his heart condition. We thought it was lucky for him and unlucky for us but we should have know there was more to it. It turns out that Mottram was involved with Fat Jack Duval, and they wanted to keep Duval's squeaky clean image squeaky. A couple of years after my trial, despite his weak heart, Brian Mottram was arrested with Jack Duval and charged with a long firm fraud with a company called Fairfax Ltd. They had been running it for years. Jack the Rat the 'chequeman' got ten years and Brian Mottram got twelve.

While I sat in some shitty hole reading yesterday's newspaper I read about Taggart and a couple of his mates being nicked for some fraud with a big glass company. All of these revelations either emerged too late for appeals or they did not constitute 'new evidence'. I did try appealing anyway, but I had no success. As I lived one-day-at-a-time-sweet-Jesus for seventeen years my father had been bringing up another son by his second wife. Of all the names in the *Concise Oxford Dictionary of Names* my father Charlie called his new son Charlie. So now there were three Charlie Richardsons. My dad, Charlie, and his two sons, Charlie and Charlie. So my new step-brother, Charlie, grew up visiting me in prison all over the country. In 1983, my brother Charlie Richardson and my daughter Michelle climbed Big Ben and dropped a huge banner which read 'RICHARDSON – 17 YEARS LONG ENOUGH'. I watched them on the news on telly and I was very proud of them and, call me biased if you like, I thought they were fucking right. Come on, guv, fair's fair – I had done long enough. Finally after eighteen years of my twenty-five I was released into the world, an innocent, but not for the slaughter.

It was 24 August 1984. I had read *1984* by George Orwell years before so when I stepped into the Rolls that was waiting for me outside the nick I asked my friends where Big Brother was. They told me he was a social security investigator who followed people who were claiming unemployment benefit. He also stood outside the council flats of separated couples to see if they were sleeping together. I had no time to bother with that as I was catapulted into a hundred lobster thermidors and a thousand bottles of champagne. It only took me a few days to realize that things had changed since the 1960s. I had left a country where the world was your oyster if you only realized that. I emerged in 1984 into a country where the world was your oyster only if you could offer oysters.

A friend flew me to New York where a stretch limo picked me up from the airport, took me into town for lunch and dropped me back at the airport for a plane to the Dominican Republic where I ate steaks that dribbled fresh blood and I lay on the beach to watch my belly grow. I had a fantastic holiday and returned to a miserable British late summer to try and get something together.

After a few days I sat one evening in a Covent Garden I could not recognize. I was in a wine bar with a friend who was an old lag like me but was not growing old gracefully. We sat drinking cocktails with plastic umbrellas in them and talked of old times. As we talked a phone rang near us. We were at the bar so I was just about to give the barman a wave when my mate from the old days picked up a small phone next to him. He excused himself and turned his back to me and had a heated discussion. I was amazed at the technology that made such communication possible. After a little while he put back the aerial and switched the phone off. I asked him, 'Who was that then, Arthur?' He told me it was his wife Jeanne who told him not to forget to pick up some mangetout from Sainsbury's on the way home. I had never heard of Sainsbury's, never mind mangetout. Over the weeks I noticed lots of people with all sorts of technology falling out of their pockets. Before my sentence in the 'good old days' the only people who had bleepers were doctors. Nowadays everybody wants to feel important and necessary. The jobs have not really changed much, it's just how people think they should be seen. So very ordinary people are running around and being bleeped in the middle of a pint at lunchtime. They have personal phones and personal computers and filofaxes to organize their personal lives. If that's not enough they have electronic organizers to do it for them. If you want to meet an old pal for a night out you have to have a twenty minute conversation while they fit you into their bleedin' diary. Everybody is busy running around chasing their tails and trying to look impressive. They have to try because underneath it all we are just the same old frail, weak, corrupt, smelly armpit of humanity we always were.

I had realized before I got a huge slice of my life taken away from me that there was good money and adventure to be had without breaking the law. You would think that all I had to do was be 'honest' to be straight. Far from it. I soon learned that the real way to make a lot of money without much effort was to take on a level of amorality and dishonesty that was in the end too much for a 'Torture Gang Boss' to stomach. In 1984 the big bubble that the economy was enjoying revolved around the City. I played around in the Stock Exchange and rubbed shoulders with the bright young things from Oxford and Cambridge who had turned their back on a proper, responsible contribution to society in order to play the markets for huge stakes. Fortunes were made as the bubble expanded in a ten year bull market where companies were valued in gross excess of their wealth. When the Big Bang came along and they all got computerized the game simply changed from old fashioned casino roulette to brand new electronic space invaders with flashing lights as they sat at their terminals making a fortune. The bubble kept expanding until its stretched skin was thin and strained and still they kept on gambling. I learned a lot from my experiences in the City. I understood for the first time that the City might determine the fortunes of us all but what they are busy doing is just gambling. The bubble enclosed ordinary people who bought into privatization issues and lived in houses which they viewed as investments rather than homes. And the bubble kept on getting bigger: like blowing up a condom you are amazed at how big that little thing gets. I also realized you do not have to be clever to work in the City. I was disappointed with the people I met. They had no soul and no individuality. They bought Porsches because they were a status symbol, not because they admired the amazing engineering. A lot of them were not very sharp except with their clothes. I realized that a degree from Oxford might mean you can fart in Latin but it does not mean you are clever. They worshipped success and success was viewed by one criterion . . . money, so they worshipped money. They made money out of money. They loved spending money because it showed they had it. They drank more than they could manage and would end up vomiting over their expensive, handmade shoes. They snorted coke because it was expensive and because they hoped it would make them sound confident that they were clever instead of just confident. They were very confident. The bubble kept growing and the world was their oyster. They could afford oysters but their tastebuds were too numbed by excess to enjoy the subtlety of that snot-like creature from the rocks of our polluted shores. I stayed for a while and realized I was in the middle of an orgy where nobody stops to have a bath. I left to look for something real to get involved in. I like taking risks and even taking gambles, but around the development of something that exists. It was a good decision to get out because the thing about bubbles is that they always burst and sure enough this one did. Suddenly the music stopped and they all looked at each other with their flies open and scrabbled for the door.

Then things became even more ridiculous. Everybody had moved into a hotel that was 'a stone's throw from the beach'. Underneath the jamboree the country was decaying like a rotten plum. The difference between the real world and the fantasy the bubble created was bad enough when the bubble was there. When the bubble burst people just carried on as if everything was doing all right. It did not matter how things really were, what mattered was if you could make them look good. This attitude went all through society until plumbers and electricians took no pride in what they did as long as they made a lot of money. Mugging old grannies became normal. You did not have to hit her on the head and nick her purse – you just had to sort out some double glazing for her or cure imaginary woodworm in her attic and run away with her money.

I was genuinely shocked at the growth in crime in London. I was amazed at the level of theft from cars and how common burglaries had become. But what can you expect when many of the top people who are supposed to set some kind of example are employing lawyers to help them break the law and get away with it.

Greed had become a national sport. It is unfair to confine the fun to members of the club only, everybody wanted to play. You have to expect less articulate and less well-connected people to play the game in any way they can. Nothing seemed to matter much any more. In 1966 when I was in court the country appeared to be filled with indignation and moral outrage. If my trial had been in 1986 instead of '66 I would have employed a PR and marketing company to syndicate me. There would have been 'Charlie Richardson is innocent' T shirts and 'Teenage Mutant Charlie Boy the Torture Gang Boss' cuddly toys for kids at Christmas.

I turned my back on all the poor bastards who thought they were good fax salesmen but who actually spent their life paying off their credit cards. I needed something real, something of genuine value to work with so I turned to what I knew best. I started to concentrate my mind on mining projects. A few months later I was sitting in a restaurant having lunch with Lord King, the chairman of British Airways. I remember it well. I was humming quietly to myself 'We'll take good care of you . . . fly the flag' when I heard a little fifteen minute bleeper on somebody's watch on the next table. It was to remind him another fifteen minutes of his life had just passed by and he still had not 'made it'. Lord King knew who I was and my history. It did not put him off. In fact, I realized that with some people being the Torture Gang Boss had a novelty value. We discussed his possible chairmanship of a company I had formed and I thought again, 'Not bad for a boy from Camberwell.' In the end nothing came of it, but I carried on pursuing my interest in and expanding my knowledge of the present minerals scene. During this time I also met with Rupert Dean who was the foreman on the jury that found me guilty all those years ago. I had dinner at his place and after a few more meetings he helped and advised me with what became a very successful project. I met and lived with a woman called Sue and we had another child called William and I have enjoyed watching him grow and I determined I would be there for all his growth.

In 1988 history really started to repeat itself. For a start I fell in love again with a beautiful woman called Veronica. Not only did she revive in me a whole set of feelings I thought were long dead for ever but she helped me with my business. She quickly analysed the situation and realized I had divided my energies among so many projects that none of them were receiving the attention they deserved. With her help I identified a project that deserved total commitment. It was a very big mining deal that could become enormous. Together we worked day and night for two years to turn it into an amazing scheme of massive proportions and huge potential.

The banks and insurance companies would have nothing to do with me but despite them we triumphed and then history repeated itself in another way. My brother Eddie was arrested but this time there really was nothing I could do for him. History repeat number three is that he got sentenced to twenty-five years. Just as this was happening we were approached by a big company who wanted to buy our mining interests from us. It was like Rome all over again. This time they are offering one and a half million for 51% of three of our mines. It is tempting. We would be left with 49% as an income for the future. They would do all the work and all we would have to do is sit back and watch the money come in. On the other hand they are offering one and a half million because they know it is worth a hell of a lot more. It would mean more work and even more struggle for us but the potential rewards are massive. I am not greedy but I do like to work. So what should I do? Do I take the money and buy a nice big house in Kent and settle down to regular meetings at the Rotary Club? We could go skiing every year and buy a second home in Monte Carlo. We could take a cruise on the QE2 and feed smoked salmon to the dog. Or should we take the risk, struggle on in life's great adventure, turn down their offer and reach for the stars? What do you think?

All Pan Books are available at your local bookshop or newsagent, or can be ordered direct from the publisher. Indicate the number of copies required and fill in the form below.

Send to: Macmillan General Books C.S.
              Book Service By Post
              PO Box 29, Douglas I-O-M
              IM99 1BQ

or phone: 01624 675137, quoting title, author and credit card number.

or fax: 01624 670923, quoting title, author, and credit card number.

or Internet: http://www.bookpost.co.uk

Please enclose a remittance* to the value of the cover price plus 75 pence per book for post and packing. Overseas customers please allow £1.00 per copy for post and packing.

*Payment may be made in sterling by UK personal cheque, Eurocheque, postal order, sterling draft or international money order, made payable to Book Service By Post.

Alternatively by Access/Visa/MasterCard

Card No.

Expiry Date

Signature _____

Applicable only in the UK and BFPO addresses.

While every effort is made to keep prices low, it is sometimes necessary to increase prices at short notice. Pan Books reserve the right to show on covers and charge new retail prices which may differ from those advertised in the text or elsewhere.

NAME AND ADDRESS IN BLOCK CAPITAL LETTERS PLEASE

Name _____

Address _____

_____

_____

_____

8/95

Please allow 28 days for delivery.
Please tick box if you do not wish to receive any additional information. ☐